This book is the first full-length analysis of the London working population and the effects of the industrial revolution in London to appear for over sixty years. Prior to the mid nineteenth century London may not have experienced the direct effects of the industrial revolution to any great extent, but the indirect effects were felt strongly. L. D. Schwarz disagrees with the view that 'the industrial revolution was a storm that passed over London and broke elsewhere', and seeks to judge the effect of industrialisation on what was the country's largest manufacturing city. Its size and role as national capital meant that London was in certain important respects unique, but it was nonetheless susceptible to many of the wider economic transformations that occurred during the period 1700–1850, and Dr Schwarz offers a detailed analysis of the changes to the economy and social structure of London that these wrought. He analyses middle-class wealth, the incomes of the working classes, living standards (defined very broadly to include the impact of the seasons and of the trade cycle), the fall in the death rate, the changing nature of the labour force in general and of artisans in particular, money wages and perquisites and the economic role of women. All suggest that beneath a façade of apparent continuity significant disruptions and dislocations were commonplace.

London in the age of industrialisation

Cambridge Studies in Population, Economy and Society in Past Time 19

Series Editors

PETER LASLETT, ROGER SCHOFIELD and E. A. WRIGLEY

ESRC Cambridge Group for the History of Population and Social Structure

and DANIEL SCOTT SMITH

University of Illinois at Chicago

Recent work in social, economic and demographic history has revealed much that was previously obscure about societal stability and change in the past. It has also suggested that crossing the conventional boundaries between these branches of history can be very rewarding.

This series will exemplify the value of interdisciplinary work of this kind, and will include books on topics such as family, kinship and neighbourhood; welfare provision and social control; work and leisure; migration; urban growth; and legal structures and procedures, as well as more familiar matters. It will demonstrate that, for example, anthropology and economics have become as close intellectual neighbours to history as have political philosophy or biography.

For a full list of titles in the series, please see end of book

London in the age of industrialisation

Entrepreneurs, labour force and living conditions, 1700–1850

L. D. SCHWARZ

Lecturer in the Department of Economic and Social History,
University of Birmingham

CAMBRIDGE
UNIVERSITY PRESS

Published by the Press Syndicate of the University of Cambridge
The Pitt Building, Trumpington Street, Cambridge CB2 1RP
40 West 20th Street, New York, NY 10011–4211, USA
10 Stamford Road, Oakleigh, Victoria 3166, Australia

First published 1992

Printed in Great Britain by Bell and Bain Ltd., Glasgow

A catalogue record for this book is available from the British Library

Library of Congress cataloguing in publication data
Schwarz, L. D.
London in the age of industrialisation : entrepreneurs, labour force and living
conditions, 1700–1850 / L. D. Schwarz.
p.   cm. – (Cambridge studies in population, economy and society in past time : 19)
Includes bibliographical references and index.
ISBN 0–521–40365–0
1. London (England – Occupations – History.
2. Labor supply – England – London – History
3. London (England) – Population – History.
4. London (England) – Economic conditions.
I. Title.   II. Series.
HB2676.L66S38   1992
330.9421'07–dc20   91–33593   CIP

ISBN 0 521 40365 0 hardback

CE

Contents

viii   *Contents*

Figures

Tables

xi

Acknowledgements

If a future historian, seeking to analyse the process whereby his colleagues wrote their books, were to rely solely upon acknowledgements he would portray a panoply of heroic academics, unselfishly labouring against overwhelming odds to give birth to the printed word, writing with no thought of advancement, helped by ever generous and patient colleagues, wonderful telepathic secretaries and sacrificial spouses. There is a formula in these things. In my case, the Department of Economic and Social History at the University of Birmingham – or at least its successive heads – have waited for this book with a quiet impatience. Sue Kennedy and Diane Martin needed to vacate the printer regularly. Formulae apart, I would like to thank Professor Peter Mathias, the supervisor of my thesis from which this book eventually took shape, Professor Theo Barker for reading the complete typescript and for being so encouraging, and Adrian Randall for reading some of it and remaining relentlessly (if quietly) critical. Professor John Harris has been a constant source of encouragement since my first appearance at Birmingham, pressing me to write this book, keeping his interest alive as well as reading a complete draft. Of course the usual disclaimers apply.

I would like to thank the archivists of the various record offices in the London area for the efficiency and courtesy that one comes to expect from them, and especially those of the sadly long defunct Middlesex Record Office. Ralph Bailey has provided constant assistance with computing for the tax assessments, the insurance records and the servant tax. I would like to thank the editors of *Social History* and *Economic History Review* for permission to publish material that has previously appeared in those journals and Jane Dilkes for mastering the operation of CHART sufficiently to draw the graphs.

Julian Hoppit kindly gave me access to his unpublished data on bankruptcies in London and Professor Roderick Floud to the computerised insurance records of the later eighteenth century. The editors of Cambridge Studies in Population, Economy and Society in Past Time – Tony Wrigley in particular – certainly deserve thanks for regularly returning drafts with encouraging comments, as does Richard Fisher for transmitting them to me, and Mary Campbell of Cambridge University Press for raising queries on the text.

Finally, Anna and Rebecca ignored it all, and Miriam helped me more than she ever knew.

Abbreviations

Addit. MSS	Additional Manuscripts, British Library
C.D.R.	Crude death rate
C.L.R.O.	Corporation of London Records Office
Econ. Hist. Rev.	Economic History Review
Eighteenth-Century Reports	Reports from Committees of the House of Commons printed by order of the House and not inserted in the Journals (16 vols., 1803–20)
G.L.R.O.	Greater London Record Office
J. Econ. Hist.	Journal of Economic History
London Life	M. Dorothy George, London Life in the Eighteenth Century (1965 ed.)
L.W.	Lindert–Williamson
P.A.R.	Printed Acts, Reports (miscellaneous in Corporation of London Records Office)
P.B.H.	Phelps Brown–Hopkins
P.P.	Parliamentary Papers
P.R.O.	Public Record Office
R.C.	Royal Commission
R.E.A.	Royal Exchange Assurance
S.C.	Select Committee (of House of Commons unless otherwise stated)
S.G.	Schumpeter–Gilboy

Introduction

London was the largest of the great cities of the European *ancien régime*. Historians of the period invariably mention it, frequently describe it, and occasionally analyse it. But, despite their efforts, very little is known about London during the eighteenth and early nineteenth centuries. We have some knowledge of how the national economy adapted to the growth of London, of how the growth of London affected the specialisation of agriculture, industry and mining far beyond London, of London's role in banking and international trade, of the patterns of migration caused by the size and attractions of the capital. But we know much less of the reverse situation – how the national and international economy affected London, how developments in banking and trade, in law and government affected the developing economy and society of the capital. 'The capital cities', wrote Braudel when describing the eighteenth century, 'would be present at the forthcoming industrial revolution, but in the role of spectators. Not London but Manchester, Birmingham, Leeds, Glasgow and innumerable small proletarian towns launched the new era.'[1] But the nation's capital could hardly be irrelevant to the new industrial era – it was far too large and important to be 'isolated' – and much of this book will be seeking to analyse the connections. Industrial revolution or not, late eighteenth-century London had more steam engines with more horse power than Lancashire;[2] mid nineteenth-century London remained by far the largest manufacturing city in the country. It was also the largest port, even if not the fastest

---

[1] F. Braudel, *Capitalism and Material Life, 1400–1800* (1974), p. 440.
[2] A. E. Musson, 'Industrial motive power in the United Kingdom, 1800–1870', *Econ. Hist. Rev.*, 2nd ser., 29 (1976), p. 426; J. Kanefsky and J. Robey, 'Steam engines in eighteenth-century Britain: a quantitative assessment', *Technology and Culture*, 21 (1980), pp. 175–6.

1

growing: during the course of the eighteenth century England's trade quadrupled, but the trade of the Port of London trebled and the capital's shipbuilding industry expanded accordingly. Throughout the eighteenth century, over two-thirds of England's foreign trade passed through the Port of London.[3] Both at the beginning and at the end of the eighteenth century, well over four-fifths of those who lived in towns with populations of 10,000 and over lived in the capital; one in ten of the population of England and Wales lived there; it has been estimated that one in six of the population had lived there at some point of their lives.[4] For those with ambition, it was always 'the place to be'. It had more doctors than the rest of the country put together, and more lawyers. Few writers with any pretensions, few aristocrats in search of a dowry, nobody aspiring to national influence could stay away from it for too long. Dr Johnson's famous remark that a man who was tired of London was tired of life because there was in London all that life could afford was true if one was, like Johnson, much attached to tea and conversation and little attached to the virtues of clean air or a quiet environment. In the mid 1730s, London had nearly nine-tenths of the nation's dealers in tea and coffee.[5]

Yet, most of this period marked a lull in the explosive growth of London. The first heroic age had been between 1500 and 1650, when its population increased fivefold and London was the forcing house of urban-led change. It was the 'shock city' of the time: not only by far the largest, but also one of the fastest-growing cities in the country, accounting for most of the urban growth that took place in England. During the second half of the seventeenth century it overtook Paris to become the largest city in Europe. At the start of the sixteenth century one in fifty of the population of England lived there; two centuries later one in ten lived there and one person in six may have spent a part of his or her life there.

By the last third of the seventeenth century London's growth was slowing down, and it slowed down more during the first half of the eighteenth century. At the start of the seventeenth century, 59 per cent of those living in towns with populations of 5,000 or more were living in London; by the end of the century this proportion had risen to two-thirds. Then it fell: on an optimistic projection of the capital's population in 1750 the figure had fallen to 56 per cent of the total,

---

[3] P. J. Corfield, *The Impact of English Towns, 1700–1800* (Oxford, 1982), pp. 71–2.

[4] *Ibid.*, p. 8; Jan de Vries, *European Urbanization, 1500–1800* (1984), p. 64; E. A. Wrigley, 'A simple model of London's importance in changing English society and economy, 1650–1750', *Past and Present*, 37 (1967), pp. 44, 70.

[5] L. Weatherill, *Consumer Behaviour and Material Culture in Britain, 1660–1760* (1988), p. 62. Out of a national figure of 3,817, 3,415 were in London, in 1736–7.

while it was 40 per cent by 1801 and less than a third in 1851. London was no longer the forcing house for urbanisation. It would never be so again, even though by the start of the nineteenth century it was well into its second heroic age of expansion and well over four-fifths of those who lived in towns with 10,000 or more inhabitants were living there. During the succeeding century the population of London would triple. In 1851, with a population of more than two and a quarter millions, London was some six times larger than its nearest rival, Liverpool, and still the largest port.[6]

The century and a half that this book covers comprises, therefore, two periods of London's growth. The first great boom, the boom that preceded the eighteenth century, had defined the two poles of growth in London: the City and the Port. During the succeeding century and a half, the outline that had been sketched earlier was filled in and the definitions of such areas became clearer. The City and Westminster were joined up, the ring of suburbs surrounding them thickened; on the south side of the Thames the ribbon of development was lengthened, and more suburbs developed. There were many changes – in wealth, in trade and the structure of power, in the role of services – but these did not overturn the order of things that had already been established.

Such an overturning was to take place during the nineteenth century, with the explosive growth of London far beyond its eighteenth-century boundries and the merging of the City and Westminster to form a central business district, the whole forming the 'great wen' of Cobbett's nightmares. The London magistracy was strengthened, the Home Office made sure that it was kept well informed, but London ceased to be a town known to its rulers. 'What can be stable with these enormous towns?' lamented Lord Liverpool in 1819. 'One serious insurrection in London and all is lost',[7] a cry far removed from an eighteenth-century prime minister, used to having his windows broken regularly by the London mob, a mob that – at any rate before the Gordon riots – went to work frequently enough, sometimes aggressively, sometimes destructively, always assertively, but usually within careful bounds.

But, far into the nineteenth century there were many respects in which London had not changed fundamentally. The classic study of eighteenth-century London, Dorothy George's *London Life in the Eighteenth Century* – which, despite its title, encroached liberally into

[6] B. R. Mitchell, *British Historical Statistics* (Cambridge, 1988), pp. 26–7.
[7] Quoted in E. Halévy, *A History of the English People in the Nineteenth Century: II The Liberal Awakening* (1961 ed.), p. 103.

the first third of the nineteenth century – insisted that conditions were slowly improving but did not consider that there had been marked structural changes in the composition of the capital's population and economy. Like innumerable smaller towns in Western Europe that historians once considered to have been by-passed by the onward march of progress, industry and coal, London adapted itself to change that took place elsewhere and profited from such change. It remained a city of artisans, of trade, of doctors, lawyers and government. In the eighteenth century it had more lawyers than the rest of the country put together and also more doctors. It maintained its large service sector, with its role as a centre of government and empire, of shops and fashion, of sailors, of merchants and of servants. Nor was the absence of structural change in its manufacturing sector surprising – manufacturing in the capital tended to be in the finishing trades, and these did not undergo extensive mechanisation until the 1860s. Ship-building awaited the onset of steamships, which did not arrive on a large scale until the mid nineteenth century, while the wealth of the capital's upper and middle classes continued to grow, and with it the demand for servants as well as for other suitable services.

Under the apparently stable surface, however, change was constant. The first part of this book examines the structure of this economy, its occupations, its importance as a national centre for manufacturing as well as for services, and the distribution of wealth within the metropolis. The start of the eighteenth century is perhaps as good or bad a starting point as any other, but the 1850s are a good point to stop, with the old artisan economy – the traditional labour aristocracy – enjoying its Indian summer, yet under pressure, partly from new levels of mechanisation and partly from the ever growing weight of services in the City of London and in Westminster. The pyramid of wealth was steep. Few had much wealth, but most of those that did were in the service sector.

The second part of this book examines fluctuations in the economic activity of the metropolis during this century and a half. Fundamental structures may not have changed, but everything else fluctuated and usually grew. The impact of incipient trade cycles was, in the eighteenth century, much compounded by the drastic effects of the outbreak of war – and sometimes also by the outbreak of peace: crises in credit and production occurred regularly. But that should not obscure the longer-run trends. There is much evidence that conditions in London were difficult during the second third of the eighteenth century, more difficult than in much of the rest of the country. The metropolitan economy was also growing more slowly for a while from the late 1820s. Yet, all these longer-term fluctuations took place within a strong pattern of seasonality, with the annual cycle of production heavily influenced – often dominated – by the weather, the winds and the predictable peaks of London demand. It was these seasonal fluctuations that had such drastic effects on the structure of the London trades, on the attempts by the more fortunate trades to preserve a precarious gentility, on the meaning of that excessively vague term 'the standard of living', and on the composition of the labour force. Seasonality was the major influence, wars and trade cycles – so far as they can be distinguished from each other – came next.

For the lower three-quarters of the population, the experience of seasonal fluctuations did not change much during this period, but their life expectancy did. Chapter five examines this experience – more important, after all, for the populace than relatively minor changes in wage rates, while also being of considerable importance for understanding the role that London played in the national pattern of migration and doing a great deal to explain the economic stagnation of the second third of the eighteenth century. The death rate did fall during the eighteenth century, but not until quite late in the century, while the pattern of mortality and the incidence of different diseases changed drastically. For the first time, London was no longer a town that devoured the lives of an enormous proportion of its infants and children and cut deep into its rural hinterland. By 1840 its crude death rate was close to the national average: high by twentieth-century terms, but less than half that of the late seventeenth and early eighteenth centuries.

At the same time – and this is examined in part three – the conditions of life and the standard of living for the London artisinate were constantly being modified. Wage rates for a number of fairly representative London trades are presented in chapter six together with various price indices, but it is dangerous to assume that the series of real wage rates so produced gives a clear picture of some notional 'average standard of living'. Quite apart from obvious problems of unemployment, there are more serious questions, relating to the number of people who earned a money wage and depended on nothing else, which are also discussed in chapter six. A further problem, which has exercised the attention of historians to a certain degree, is that the environment of enterprise was not the same in 1850 as in 1700, even for small-scale artisan enterprises. One of the fundamental problems in the study of living standards is that the histories of living standards, as given by the indices of real wage rates, give one story; the histories of trades frequently give quite a different story. Rarely do the two coincide. This is especially true for the semi-skilled trades: benefiting from the cheap bread of the early eighteenth century, and not being affected as much as most of the other London trades by the price rise from the mid century onwards, they entered into a complex relationship with other London trades. The relationship of wage rates, earnings and the situation of trades within a mutual hierarchy is a complex matter. Average earnings mean little during a period of rapid change, they mean little during a period of industrialisation, and London was feeling the impact of industrialisation, even if only indirectly. The first half of the nine-teenth century was an age of pressure for the semi-skilled trades – the less skilled among the tailors, the shoemakers, the furniture makers and others. The defence of the precarious gentility of many in the semi-skilled trades was as noticeable and as typical a feature of the eighteenth-century trades as was their degradation in the nineteenth century. For much of this time qualitative changes and changes in status within these trades were far more important than changes in wage rates, since many experienced a change in status for the worse. Traditional means of control, such as apprenticeship regulations, guilds or the magistracy, had done little to restrain competition; during the first third of the nineteenth century these restraints finally disappeared, as they were bound to do. The altering exchanges between the capital and the provinces were at the core of the changes in the modes of production in the capital, just as they were at the core of the growth and continued predominance of the service sector.

Inevitably, this book draws heavily on Dorothy George's *London Life in the Eighteenth Century*. First published in 1926, and frequently reprinted, it will remain a classic of its kind. The labour that went into its production was prodigious; time and again one begins to write about something only to find that Dorothy George has already dealt with the subject, and done so with more authority. It is only on population that she can be seriously faulted. Nevertheless, the book reflects the interests of the time: it has many scattered figures but few tables or series of figures; its insistence that the nineteenth century was better than the eighteenth relies rather heavily on Francis Place and leads to a socially somewhat undifferentiated picture, while it does not distinguish sufficiently between different epochs within the period studied. Stressing the general awfulness of life for the eighteenth-century poor, and the discomforts of life for the less poor, may well have been necessary in 1926 but is necessary no longer. But it is because of Dorothy George that this book contains so many tables and graphs. They are not inherently superior to prose, but they point the way to the path that she left open.

PART I

Wealth and occupations in London

Seventeenth-century London was a town with two centres. The 'old' London consisted of the City, the centre of trade and finance, flanked by the Port and by the manufacturing suburbs of the Tower, Clerkenwell and Southwark. The 'new' London was in Westminster, with its Court and Parliament, with its developing squares, its aristocratic Season, its large glass-plated shops, its luxury trades and craftsmen.[1] During the course of the eighteenth century the two centres were joined together – a geographical reflection of a unity that existed economically if not always politically.[2] But at the start of the nineteenth century this duality – the different economic, administrative and geographical roles of the Port and the Court – was still clearly recognisable. The inner City, or 'City within the Walls', with a population of around 70,000 – a seventh of the capital's population – at the beginning of the eighteenth century, which fell to 56,000 – a twentieth part – in 1821, was far wealthier than the outer City, the 'City without the Walls', which had some 50,000 inhabitants in 1700 and about 65,000 during the first half of the nineteenth century. Westminster, in the meanwhile, had a population of perhaps some 70,000 in 1700, which had risen to over 150,000 by 1801 and was up to 237,000 half a century later.[3] During the eighteenth century Westminster was

[1] E. Jones, 'London in the early seventeenth century: an ecological approach', *London Journal*, 6 (1980), pp. 131–2.
[2] The classic description is J. Summerson, *Georgian London* (Harmondsworth, 1962), pp. 18–23. For the nineteenth century, F. H. W. Sheppard, *London 1808–1870. The Infernal Wen* (1971), pp. 9–17. A brief account in H. Clout, 'London in transition', in H. Clout and P. Wood (eds.), *London: Problems of Change* (1986), pp. 23–32, with a map of the built-up area, updating the map in O. H. K. Spate, 'The growth of London, A.D. 1600–1800', in H. C. Darby (ed.), *An Historical Geography of England* (Cambridge, 1936), pp. 529–48.
[3] The figures for the City are taken from P. E. Jones and A. V. Judges, 'London's population in the late seventeenth century', *Econ. Hist. Rev.*, 1st ser., 6 (1935–6),

expanding as rapidly as any of the London suburbs. During the first half of the nineteenth century it grew by over 50 per cent, but the nineteenth-century population explosion took place largely in the new 'outer' London, the ring of parishes surrounding the City, Westminster and Southwark. From Marylebone to Hackney in the north, from Richmond to Lambeth in the south, this ring contained some 300,000 inhabitants in 1700, over half a million a century later, and nearly 1,900,000 in 1851. After 1800, when the population of London was increasing at the rate of 20 per cent a decade, Westminster's expansion of some 50 per cent during the first half of the century paled by comparison with St Pancras, which expanded more than fourfold, Marylebone, which grew from 64,000 in 1801 to 158,000 in 1851, or Paddington, which increased from less than 2,000 to over 46,000.

In the eighteenth century, however, this explosion had yet to occur. Not only were the 'Port' – the City – and the 'Court' – Westminster – recognisable entities, but the Port, taken literally, and the Court, taken in the sense of London Society, were the two largest centres of employment in the capital for both skilled and unskilled labour. They were both microcosms in their own right. 'The seamen here are a generation differing from all the world', wrote Sir John Fielding in an early tourists' guide.

When one goes into Rotherhithe and Wapping, which places are inhabited chiefly by sailors, but that somewhat of the same language is spoken, a man would be apt to suspect himself in another country. Their manner of living, speaking, acting, dressing, and behaving, are so very peculiar to themselves.[4]

By the standards of its time, the Port was enormous. Defoe noted three wet docks, twenty-two dry docks and thirty-three yards for laying up, repairing and building merchant ships.[5] It was responsible for many of the food-processing trades that handled the produce imported into London, such as sugar refining and distilling, not to

---

pp. 45–63. R. A. P. Finlay and B. Shearer, 'Population growth and suburban expansion', in A. L. Beier and R. A. P. Finlay (eds.), *London 1500–1700: The Making of the Metropolis* (1986), produce a figure of 103,000 for the City Within and Without combined in 1680, which is rather low, and then have the City's population falling to 85,000 by 1700, which certainly seems too low, although it does not affect the basic argument of this chapter.

4 J. Fielding, *A Description of the Cities of London and Westminster* (1776), p. xiii. Admittedly, when Boswell visited Wapping in 1792, ten years after Johnson suggested that the exploration was worth making, he was disappointed, but after a tour of the Highlands he may have been expecting too much: *London Life*, p. 78. Also, sailors may have formed a lesser proportion of the capital's population by then, which may help to account for his disappointment.

5 D. Defoe, *A Tour Through the Whole Island of Great Britain* (Harmondsworth, 1971), p. 317.

mention shipbuilding, coopering, ropemaking, innkeeping and an infinity of other trades. Professor Ralph Davis has guessed that during the early eighteenth century, a quarter of London's population depended on the Port 'directly or indirectly'.[6] Some contemporaries believed the figure to be far greater. Patrick Colquhoun, a police magistrate as well as a self-proclaimed and highly creative statistician who managed to achieve a remarkable degree of credence both at the time and subsequently, stated in 1800 that 120,000 men were directly employed on the riverside.[7] The 1801 census had not yet appeared, or he might have reconsidered including nearly half the capital's adult males. Nevertheless, the fact that he produced such a figure shows how important he considered the river to be. Equally importantly, people believed him and it is true that a very large proportion of Londoners must, at some time during the year, have worked on the riverside.[8]

The 'Court' was the other large employer of labour. Like the Port, it employed an immense service sector, especially in transport. To a considerable degree the demands for labour of the Port and the Court overlapped and for all we know many people may have spent different seasons of the year in each of them. The West End required its share of porters, carriers and chairmen and received its share of housebreakers. Unlike the riverside, it was also a profligate employer of women.

Apart from the Port and the Court there was a large number of other trades and much manufacturing, usually in the suburbs. Silkweavers were concentrated in Spitalfields, watch makers in Clerkenwell. The more noxious trades, such as tanning, were banished south of the Thames. Potters were in Chelsea, Lambeth and Bow, brewers were in Southwark. Examples could easily be multiplied. The recent histories of eighteenth- and nineteenth-century London refer to them at some length,[9] and such descriptions are essential to a proper understanding of the metropolis. But inevitably they fail to provide criteria for comparing London with other towns. Something more systematic is required and this is provided in chapter one.

---

[6] R. Davis, *The Rise of the English Shipping Industry in the Seventeenth and Eighteenth Centuries* (1962), p. 390.

[7] P. Colquhoun, *A Treatise on the Commerce and Police of the River Thames* (1800), pp. xxx–xxxi. See appendix one of this book for a critical assessment of Colquhoun.

[8] In fact the parishes directly on the riverside and directly involved with the Port had a total population in 1801 of 89,733, a tenth of the total metropolis. This takes the parishes east of the City and Southwark and includes St Katherine Tower, Wapping, St George's-in-the-East, Shadwell, Ratcliffe, Limehouse, Poplar and Blackwall, St John Horsleydown, Bermondsey and Rotherhithe, giving a total population of 89,733.

[9] G. Rudé, *Hanoverian London, 1714–1808* (1971), pp. 1–19; Sheppard, *Infernal Wen*, pp. 7–17, 158–201.

Chapter two develops the conclusions of chapter one by examining the role of manufacturing and services within the metropolitan economy, their relationship with the production of goods and services elsewhere in England and their relationship to each other within the capital. The stress is not on the impact of the capital on provincial production[10] but on the impact of the provinces on the capital. London manufacturing existed within a national context and needed to adapt itself to changing provincial costs; since this was the age of industrialisation, these costs were changing rather drastically. Within London itself, however, manufacturing was competing with services. The relationship of the capital's manufacturing and service sectors to provincial competition and their relationship to each other were the crucial factors influencing the nature of economic activity in London during the years between 1700 and 1850.

Chapter two also examines the social structure and the distribution of incomes within London, mainly, but not only, during the last quarter of the eighteenth century. Discussions of the social pyramid in pre-industrial English towns have tended to confine themselves to extremes, pointing out the wealthiest and the poorest strata of the population and dismissing the remainder. Historians of eighteenth- and early nineteenth-century England have worked a great deal on the economic backgrounds of individual towns and on the development of their economies. While there has been some work on the economic background of urban England and on the contribution of towns to economic growth, there has been rather less investigation of the occupational structure of towns and less still on the overall distribution of incomes and social classes within towns, a surprising omission when the volume of publications on this topic for the seventeenth century is borne in mind, though less surprising when the paucity of eighteenth-century sources is considered.[11] However, for the last quarter of the eighteenth century there are some sources – tax returns of 1798 and insurance policies for the years between 1775 and 1787 – which make it possible to reach reasonably reliable conclusions on income distribution, on social segregation and even on the distribution of wealth within trades.

Essentially, part one of this book deals with structures – employment, incomes and social structure. Through all the uncertainties of life, trade and war, and the fivefold expansion of London's population, many of these structures remained unchanged.

[10] Wrigley, 'A simple model'; A. L. Beier, 'Engine of manufacture: the trades of London', in A. L. Beier and R. A. P. Finlay (eds.), *London 1500–1700* (1986), pp. 141–67.

[11] L. D. Schwarz, 'Social class and social geography: the middle classes in London at the end of the eighteenth century', *Social History*, 7 (1982), references on pp. 179–80.

1

The structure of London's economy and labour force

Employment in 1851 and earlier: the overall picture

The 1851 census is a good stopping point for this study, providing as it does the best census available throughout the period studied. It is presented in figures 1.1, 1.2 and 1.3; the criteria for inclusion in the various categories are those of the Cambridge Group, as discussed in appendix one. The detailed figures are given in appendix three and appendix four.

Some conclusions are striking. First of all, in 1851 the largest sector of employment was manufacturing, employing over 373,000 persons, thereby making London the largest manufacturing town in the country. Manufacturing occupied a third of the London labour force. Domestic service came next, with nearly a quarter, then dealing, with a ninth. Although manufacturing was by far the largest sector of employment, figure 1.2 shows that it was not manufacturing that made London unique. With 13.7 per cent of England and Wales' labour force, London had 13.6 per cent of those employed in manufacturing. Transport and dealing both occupied a proportion much higher than this – transport with 24.1 per cent of the national labour force so engaged, and dealing with 24.3 per cent – as did the smaller service sectors – government, other services and professions, and particularly banking and insurance with a figure of 41 per cent. The ways in which London was distinctive are further brought out in figure 1.3, which shows the precentage of London's labour force engaged in the various sectors of the economy, the percentage of the working population of England and Wales excluding London so engaged and, finally, the percentages for 'urban provincial England' – a hypothetical construct which removes all agriculture from England and Wales except for the 2.2 per cent that is in any case attributed to

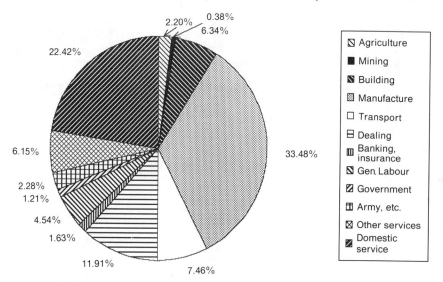

Figure 1.1 1851 census: occupations in London (both sexes)

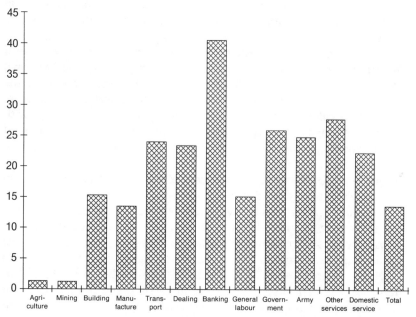

Figure 1.2 1851 census: percentage formed by Londoners of all people
engaged in that economic activity, England and Wales (both sexes)

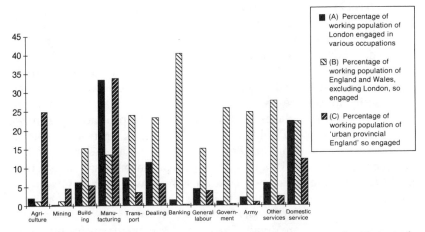

Figure 1.3 1851 census: economic activity in London compared with rest of England and Wales (both sexes)

London under the Cambridge Group classification (mainly to do with milk and market gardening). 'Urban provincial England' had 44 per cent of its working population employed in the manufacturing sector, a third more than the capital. When it came to transport and dealing, 'urban provincial England' fell somewhat behind the capital, and in the other services it fell far behind. London employed 27 per cent of those engaged in the professions, and almost a quarter of all domestic servants, male and female. Some two-thirds of its employed population were engaged in distribution, in exchange, or were employed professionally, a proportion far higher than anywhere else in the country.

To a limited extent the 1851 data can be compared with the data on occupations in London collected by Beier for the years between 1641 and 1700.[1] The drawbacks of doing so are fairly technical, and this has therefore been relegated to appendix one, as have the detailed results, which are difficult to interpret with much confidence. However, we can be reasonably confident that during the succeeding century and a half the proportion of the population engaged in transport and distribution increased, as did the professions, while the importance of manufacturing fell. More interesting is when Beier's data are connected with that of Earle. Beier suggests that some 60 per cent of the labour force were engaged in production. Earle considers this too

---

[1] Beier, 'Engine of manufacture', p. 148.

high, possibly as a result of bias in the parishes chosen, and suggests a 'very approximate' figure of around 40 per cent, which is in any case considerably more than the 33 per cent of the 1851 census.[2] Such a fall over a century and a half is consistent with what is known of the rise of the services, especially the professions but also shopkeeping. These will be discussed in this chapter and in chapter two. The great increase in the services was over by the 1730s: it may be significant that the insurance policies for the years 1775–87 produce a figure of one-third of the policy holders involved in manufacturing, the same as the total population in 1851, but less than at the start of the eighteenth century.[3] Whatever the precise chronology, it is quite likely that during these two centuries there was a shift towards a labour force more orientated towards the production of services. However, such a shift is only visible when the sexes are examined separately and in more detail. The employment patterns for men and women were very different. Whatever changes there were, they did not really affect women. Their opportunities for employment were limited at the beginning of this period, and they were limited at the end.

The employment of women

There are two approaches to women's employment in the eighteenth and nineteenth centuries. The first is to argue that it was very limited to begin with and remained limited. The second is to argue that while it was limited, it became even more limited during the nineteenth century. The latter argument has tended to find more favour, even when the impact of industrialisation is not under consideration. The tradition, which was begun by Ivy Pinchbeck, was continued by, for instance, Eric Richards who stated that 'in the pre-industrial framework, women were absorbed in a broad range of activity which was subsequently narrowed by the structural changes associated with the Industrial Revolution'. Recently, Dr Snell has argued that while the 'male' trades were indeed male dominated, 'they were not exclusively male as so often is supposed; that there did indeed exist opportunities for women to be apprenticed to these trades; and, in particular, that such opportunities were more noticeable before the nineteenth century'. Earle has recently taken issue with Snell, arguing that

[2] P. Earle, *The Making of the English Middle Class. Business, Society and Family Life in London, 1660–1730* (1989), pp. 19, 342 n.6.
[3] See appendix two.

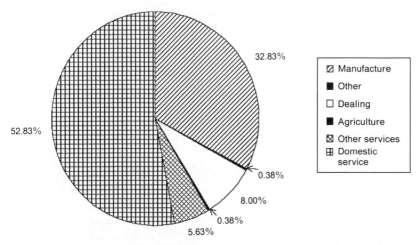

Figure 1.4 1851 census: female occupations in London

women's occupations were highly restricted, at any rate by the end of the seventeenth century.[4]

As figures 1.4, 1.5 and 1.6 show, the nineteenth-century situation was certainly distinctive. In 1851, over half the female labour force in London was returned as being employed in domestic service – much more than was the case nationally. Another third was engaged in manufacturing, mostly clothing – significantly less than the national average – while less than 6 per cent were employed in the professions.

The fact that a quarter of the women in England and Wales who were engaged in the professions, or in services other than domestic service or dealing, were employed in London must not blind one to noticing how few such women there were. Over 93 per cent of those London women who declared a job in 1851 were employed in domestic service, manufacturing or dealing. The question is whether this is a substantially different picture from that of the eighteenth century. It will be argued here that – at any rate in the case of London – it was not very different. The protagonists of female decline do not deny that women are to be found in all kinds of jobs during the nineteenth century, but argue that there were not very many of them outside their fortresses of service and needlework, and that during the eighteenth century their direct contribution across a wide range of

[4] K. D. M. Snell, *Annals of the Labouring Poor. Social Change and Agrarian England, 1600–1900* (Cambridge, 1985), p. 311; P. Earle, 'The female labour market in London in the late seventeenth and early eighteenth centuries', *Econ. Hist. Rev.*, 2nd ser., 42 (1989), pp. 328–53.

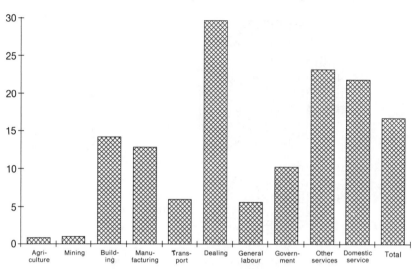

Figure 1.5 1851 census: percentage formed by London females of all females
engaged in that economic activity, England and Wales

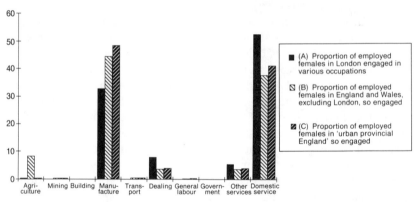

Figure 1.6 1851 census: economic activity in London compared with rest of
England and Wales (females)

occupations was more significant than subsequently. In the case of
London, however, there is a considerable amount of evidence that
suggests otherwise.

In the first place, the 1851 census is particularly inaccurate about
women. It is inconceivable that out of a total male workforce of
700,000 some 300,000 could have earned enough to have supported
their wives. Victorian artisans would hardly have entered their wives
as 'laundresses' on the census form and only 'tailor's wife' and

'shoemaker's wife' were entered in this fashion, it being so well known that the wives of tailors and shoemakers helped their husbands at home that there was no point pretending otherwise.

On the fringes of society there would be a minority of occupations not recorded in the census at all: Mayhew's entertainers, scavengers, mudlarks and prostitutes, for instance.[5] More numerous would be street traders and market workers – virtually none of them recorded – and, more numerous still, part-time service and laundry workers. Such work was usually hard, back-breaking and involved long hours and low pay. To quote a study of women's work in nineteenth-century London:

A mixture of washing, cleaning, charring as well as various sorts of home- or slop-work in addition to domestic labour occupied most women throughout their working lives. The diversity and indeterminacy of this spasmodic, casual and irregular employment was not easily condensed and classified into a Census occupation.

Women's work, it is concluded, fell into four main categories:

Firstly, all aspects of domestic and household labour – washing, cooking, charring, sewing, mending, laundry-work, mangling, ironing, etc.; secondly, child care and training; thirdly, the distribution and retail of food and other articles of regular consumption; and, finally, specific skills in manufacturing.[6]

These specific skills were relatively few – mostly needlework in its various forms. The significant point is that there has not been much change from the eighteenth century. Service was the largest occupation in 1851, but as far back as the 1690s, and probably a long time before then, the proportion of women in service was two or three times as great in London as it was in provincial towns (table 1.1).

It must be emphasised that table 1.1 shows the proportion that female servants formed of the entire population. Obviously they would form a much higher proportion of adult females. They formed a quarter of Earle's sample, drawn from among the poorer women of London between 1695 and 1725.

When they were no longer employed in service, eighteenth-century women were reputed to crowd into the few available jobs that paid any money worth earning, and to compete with each other for work and for pay. With the exception of the laundry and, to some extent, of needlework, there was in London rather little demand for part-time

5 See the various descriptions scattered around H. Mayhew, *London Labour and the London Poor* (4 vols., 1861).
6 Sally Alexander, 'Women's work in nineteenth-century London: a study of the years 1820–50', in A. Oakley and J. Mitchell (eds.), *The Rights and Wrongs of Women* (Harmondsworth, 1976), pp. 65, 73.

Table 1.1. *Female servants as percentage of total population, late*
seventeenth century[7]

	%
Bristol, 1696	3.5
Norwich, 1696	5.6
Gloucester, 1696	5.9
Lichfield, 1696	4.7
Southampton, 1696	6.7
London, 1695[8]	11.3–13

female work, so essential to a mother with young children. In the mid
eighteenth century, Sir John Fielding accounted for the prevalence of
prostitution by claiming that the only opportunities for employment
available to women were to become dressmakers or to open a board-
ing school; as for poor widows, their only resources were 'the
wash-tub, green-stall, or barrow'.[9] He was exaggerating of course,
partly because he was campaigning for a reformatory for penitent
prostitutes – a reformatory that, it should be noted, would take the
shape of a laundry – but he was not exaggerating unduly. There are
three useful contemporary lists of the jobs available to women: that of
Campbell in 1747, Collyer in 1761, and Colquhoun in 1806.[10] The most
striking feature of all these lists is that, although they differ from each
other in detail, they are very similar, both to each other, and to the
situation that existed in 1851. Of the twenty trades mentioned in 1747,
thirteen were connected with needlework, as were eleven of the
nineteen mentioned in 1761. Colquhoun's 1806 list mentions, in
typical Colquhoun fashion, as many as thirty-two trades, some of
which were noteworthy only by their total unimportance, such as

[7] Taken from D. Souden, 'Migrants and the population structure of later seventeenth-
century provincial cities and market towns', in P. Clarke (ed.), *The Transformation of
English Provincial Towns 1600–1800* (1984), p. 150.
[8] R. Wall, 'Regional and temporal variations in English household structure from
1650', in J. Hobcraft and P. Rees (eds.), *Regional Demographic Development* (1977),
pp. 101, 107, takes seven City parishes, carefully distributed between rich and poor,
and finds servants of both sexes coming to 20.9 per cent of the local population; S. M.
Macfarlane, 'Studies in poverty and poor relief in London at the end of the seventeenth century', Oxford University, D.Phil. thesis, 1982, p. 68, examines five other
City parishes and reports servants at 23.5 per cent of the population.
[9] J. Fielding in *London Chronicle*, 11–14 February 1758. See also his *An Account of the
Origin and Effect of a Police set on Foot by the Duke of Newcastle* (1758), pp. 49–55.
[10] R. Campbell, *The London Tradesman* (1747), *passim*; J. Collyer, *The Parents' and Guardians' Directory* (1761), *passim*; P. Colquhoun, *A Treatise on Indigence* (1806), pp. 167–70.

paste board making, while others involved agricultural work or trades not carried out in London, such as spinning, but a very large proportion of the remainder involved needlework. In short, according to these sources, between 1747 and 1851 there appears to have been no significant expansion or contraction in the variety of trades open to women. Ribbon weaving, button making and shoebinding entered the list in 1761, while pin-making and hat binding appeared in 1806, but these were no better paid than the trades hitherto available to women. In addition, there is the list provided by Earle of the occupations of some of the poorer London women who came before the church courts between 1695 and 1725, all remarkably similar to those of the 1851 census, with 25 per cent of the sample engaged in domestic service, 20 per cent in making or mending clothes, another 11 per cent in charring and laundry work, 9 per cent in nursing and medicine, 7 per cent in hawking and carrying and another 8 per cent in shopkeeping.[11]

Those who argue to the contrary, among whom Dr Snell is a notable exponent, point to many examples of women being employed in particular occupations during the eighteenth century. It is true that it is not difficult to come across women engaged in various 'male' trades – that is to say, trades not connected with clothing. There are examples of female carpenters, butchers, goldsmiths, furniture makers, stone masons, engravers, oculists, surgeons and others. The problem, however, with such examples is that they are merely examples.[12] A better approach is to examine lists of apprentices. In the City, the apprenticeships that were worth having – those that provided serious training for a well-paid job – usually involved one of the London Companies, and such Companies left registers of their apprentices. What is particularly noticeable in these registers is the paucity of female apprentices. There were, of course, female drapers, but they are difficult to spot in the printed Roll of their Company, which occupies three columns a page for 200 pages.[13] There appears to have been a small flurry of female apprentices between 1690 and about 1720, but it was fairly small and it did not last.[14] In any case, out

---

[11] Table in L. D. Schwarz, 'Conditions of life and work in London, c. 1770–1820, with special reference to East London', Oxford University, D.Phil. thesis, 1976, p. 339; Earle, 'The female labour market', p. 339.

[12] Snell, *Annals*, pp. 273–6. One should surely not take the domestic iron workers of the Black Country as examples of a nineteenth-century male trade. Earle, 'The female labour market', n. 39, likewise considers such women to be exceptions.

[13] P. Boyd (ed.), *Roll of the Drapers' Company of London* (1934).

[14] M. J. Walker, 'The extent of the guild control of trades in England, c. 1660–1820: a study based on a sample of provincial towns and London Companies', Cambridge University, Ph.D. thesis, 1985, pp. 207–8.

of a total of 1,590 persons admitted the freedom of the City of London by apprenticeship in 1690, there were only twelve women.[15] Moving away from the possibly biased City Companies, an extensive list of about 7,000 goldsmiths active in London between 1200 and 1800 refers in its index to only thirty-two female goldsmiths, at least four of whom succeeded to their husbands' businesses, while another four were working with their husbands.[16]

At the other end of the scale the lists of pauper apprentices do not make very promising reading. Parishes did indeed apprentice many girls. Many overseers simply wrote down 'housewifery' opposite the girl's name; alternatively, a list with such typically female occupations as millinery proceeded to mix the questionably female occupations of butcher, baker and wire drawer with the even more questionable female occupations of 'gent', 'butler', 'spinster' and even (on one occasion) 'labourer', obviously implying that a seven-year contract as an unpaid domestic servant to a male so described was at issue. It is perfectly true that the modern concept of housewife is extremely narrow and meant much more when domestic production was so common,[17] but that is not to say that the female apprentice – especially if she was from the workhouse – would necessarily learn the whole of the trade practised by the head of the household where she was living.

In support of his argument that female employment contracted, Dr Snell summarises the parish apprenticeship register of St Clement Danes for the years between 1803 and 1822. This enables him to refer to 'the unprecedented acuteness of the early nineteenth-century sexual specialisations of apprentices by trade ... the sexual segregation of occupations was almost total, with only 5 trades out of 74 indicating both male and female apprenticeship'.[18] This conclusion can be significantly modified by showing that in fact 36 per cent of boys and 39 per cent of girls were apprenticed to occupations common to both sexes. But even so, is it the case that 'such a marked occupational division earlier would have been unlikely for parish apprentices'? Such a division is precisely what did take place in Shoreditch between 1770 and 1789, where the parish apprenticed 156 boys and 158 girls into a total of fifty-nine trades, of which only nine were

[15] D. V. Glass, 'Socio-economic status and occupations in the City of London at the end of the seventeenth century', in A. E. J. Hollaender and W. Kellaway (eds.), *Studies in London History* (1969), pp. 385–6.

[16] Sir A. Heal, *The London Goldsmiths, 1200–1800* (Cambridge, 1935), pp. x, 280.

[17] Snell, *Annals*, p. 283 n.

[18] *Ibid.*, pp. 287–9.

Table 1.2. *Female employment: insurance registers 1775–87 and 1851 census*

	Insurance registers			% women, 1851
	Number	Number of women	%	
Apothecaries[a]	240	3	1.2	1.0
Bricklayers	366	3	0.8	–
Butchers[b]	578	28	4.8	25.7
Cabinet makers and upholsterers	618	7	1.1	13.2
Carpenters	1,255	7	0.6	–
Chandlers[c]	870	151	17.4	52.4
Clock and watch makers	356	5	1.4	–
Coopers	261	2	0.8	–
Drapers	676	28	4.1	28.8
Glaziers	111	2	1.8	–
Goldsmiths, silversmiths and jewellers	402	7	1.7	2.5
Grocers and greengrocers	624	39	6.2	12.5
Pawnbrokers	215	28	13.0	–
Peruke makers	254	3	1.2	n.a.
Plumbers	114	3	2.6	–
Shoemakers	520	9	1.7	39.1
Stationers	147	9	6.1	17.0
Tailors	943	9	1.0	26.9
Haberdashers[d]	529	58	11.0	–
Milliners	265	227	85.7	26.3[e]

Notes: [a] Apothecaries in 1851 include druggist.
[b] Butchers in 1851 include 'butcher's wife'.
[c] Chandlers in 1851 = shopkeeper and 'shopkeeper's wife'.
[d] Haberdashers' insurance policies – thirty-four 'haberdashers and milliners' excluded from haberdashers as already included under milliners. For 1851, 'hosiers and haberdashers' were taken.
[e] 'Haberdashers and milliners' taken as milliners.

shared, and four of which were connected with clothing.[19] And would a workhouse girl apprenticed to a sawyer or a cooper for a pittance have been taught the trade in all its details?

A good indication of the spread of females in the higher reaches of employment in the late eighteenth century is to be found in the insurance registers. Table 1.2 lists twenty of the larger occupations in the metropolis, giving the proportion of women employed in the

[19] G.L.R.O., P/91/1335: *Register of the Workhouse, St Leonard Shoreditch.*

particular trade between 1775 and 1787, and also the proportion so employed according to the 1851 census. The census is obviously not an ideal point of comparison since it deals with the entire labour force, while insurance policies were taken out by those who could afford them, but the conclusions to be drawn from such a comparison are nevertheless illuminating.

A source that excludes servants and tends to exclude needlewomen will naturally show the majority of women as employed in retailing. But it is remarkable that during the late eighteenth century the only branch of retailing in which women were dominant was millinery, with over four-fifths of the trade in their hands. Elsewhere they formed only 17.4 per cent of the chandlers, 13 per cent of the pawn-brokers, falling to 6 per cent of the stationers and less for other trades. During the first half of the nineteenth century, female involvement does not seem to have fallen – on the contrary, it rose. The insurance records and the census are, of course, very different sources and not really compatible, but it is interesting to note that the percentage of female stationers rose from 6 to 17 per cent and drapers rose from 4 to 29 per cent – which more than counteracted the fall from 38 to 26 per cent for haberdashers and milliners. A few trades had no women registered for them at all in 1851, but the numbers of women in these trades had already been minimal in the insurance registers three-quarters of a century before, the maximum being 2.6 per cent in the case of the plumbers, and less than 1 per cent of the carpenters and coopers.

Finally, in a handful of cases – 266 in total – the insurance registers specifically state the occupation of a person's wife. Over half of the wives were laundresses, another quarter were mantua makers and another tenth were milliners. Nineteen of the remaining twenty-eight occupations were connected with clothing, leaving two chandlers and seven individuals variously described as fishwomen, shop-keepers, silk fan painter, artificial flower maker, dealer in glass and earthenware.

It can therefore be concluded that although eighteenth-century London saw women employed in quite a wide variety of occupations, the great bulk of women were in the same occupations as they were to be in the mid nineteenth century: service, needlework, the laundry and branches of retailing. In some respects their position may even have been inferior to what it became in the mid nineteenth century. The range of occupations was narrow and remained narrow. Women formed a large proportion of the army of casual labour in the capital, an army examined further in chapter two.

The employment of men

Male employment in the metropolis followed a very different pattern. Men had a much larger choice of occupations than did women, and most of these occupations were much better paid. Manufacturing was by far the largest sector, employing a third of the labour force, but it was itself divided into a very large number of individual trades. As will be shown in chapter two, the areas in which London specialised did not, on the whole, employ a very significant proportion of its labour force because the labour force itself was so large that it prevented individual trades, however important, from standing out much. Manufacturing was, on the whole, small scale, its capital requirements were not usually high, its productivity was not particularly high, and it did not usually change its nature much during this period. Growth took place through capital widening and greater division of labour, not predominantly through capital deepening. Manufacturing provided a large core of employment and an enormous influence on the social structure: when the winds of change blew over it during the 1860s and later, the effects were devastating. That it did not suffer unduly from these winds before the 1860s was crucial. But manufacturing was not what made London unique. Figures 1.7, 1.8 and 1.9, breaking down the 1851 census in the manner described earlier in this chapter, make this clear.

Although the largest single sector of employment in 1851, manufacturing employed only a third of the male labour force, little more than the national average, and significantly less than in 'urban provincial England', where the figure was two-fifths. The building sector was similarly comparable in size to the rest of the country, while labourers were present in as great numbers as they were in other towns. What was different was the importance of transport on the one hand, and the service sector – meaning the professions, domestic service and retailers – on the other. Within the professions this distinctiveness was characterised not so much by those working for the central government, which employed only 1.6 per cent of the capital's males, but rather by the other professions, which together employed 6.5 per cent of the labour force, double the proportion of 'urban provincial England'. Domestic service was not far behind with 5.2 per cent, but transport and dealing overshadowed both of these. The extensive transport sector, at 11.6 per cent of the labour force, or nearly a quarter of all those in England and Wales who claimed on the census form that they were involved with transport, might be expected in view of the importance of the Port as well as the sheer size of London.

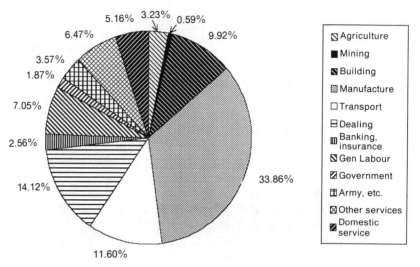

Figure 1.7 1851 census: male occupations in London

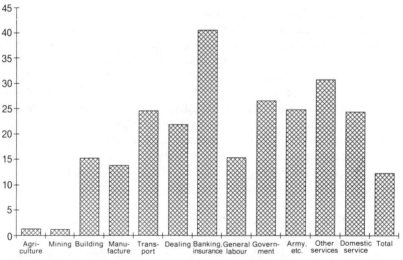

Figure 1.8 1851 census: percentage formed by London males of all males
engaged in that economic activity, England and Wales

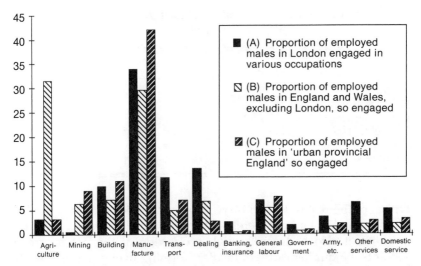

Figure 1.9 1851 census: economic activity in London compared with rest of England and Wales (males)

It is probably inflated compared with rural regions where a labourer who spent most of his time driving cattle to market would presumably not come under this category. Nevertheless, it is double the national proportion, as well as being significantly above the 7.1 per cent for 'urban provincial England', where the census categories are more likely to be comparable. This proportion may in fact be less than it had been in the early eighteenth century, when Earle believes that there were at least 30,000 persons involved in inland carriage, or some 18 per cent of the adult male population.[20] But dealing increased. It was particularly important in London; by its nature it was widespread across the town, it contained an extremely large part of the capital's wealth, and it was destined to grow and to become more important still.

The other sectors of the metropolitan economy were also less

[20] Earle, *Making*, p. 357, n. 187. There is also a suggestion from another source that the importance of sailors declined. The Customs reported some 12,000 Londoners involved in international trade in 1703, which would be some 7 per cent of the adult male population. In 1851 the number was 18,000 or only 2.6 per cent. The increase of some 59 per cent during the course of a century and a half seems suspiciously low, but it is not unlikely that the importance of sailors declined as the population of the East End grew. For the 1703 figure, see 'An account of the English ships with the number of men cleared...by ye officers of the Customs House, between the 1 December 1702 and 1 December 1703', British Library, Additional MS 5459, fo. 104, quoted in M. Rediker, *Between the Devil and the Deep Blue Sea* (Cambridge, 1987), p. 24.

Table 1.3. *Male servants as percentage of total population, late seventeenth century*[21]

	%
Bristol, 1696	2.7
Norwich, 1696	4.5
Gloucester, 1696	4.1
Lichfield, 1696	3.2
Southampton, 1696	3.7
London, 1695	9.5–11

typical of the rest of the country. Domestic service provides an illustration. London had not merely a disproportionate number of female servants; it also had a very high proportion of the nation's manservants – a quarter of them in 1851, forming over 5 per cent of the employed male population, a proportion more than twice as high as the rest of the country, and two-thirds higher than 'urban provincial England'. This was of long standing: the 13,000 manservants in London and Middlesex in 1780 were 28 per cent of England and Wales' manservants,[22] a proportion remarkably similar to 1851. In the 1690s, male servants were two or three times more numerous in London than in other towns, as table 1.3 shows.

However, before the principle of table 1.1 is followed and London's proportion of 9.5–11 per cent doubled or even trebled, it must be borne in mind that this figure includes male apprentices, as is made clear by the fact that there were some eighty-five male servants for every 100 female servants. (By contrast, in 1851 there were only seventeen per hundred.) However, this was also the case in some of the towns in table 1.3, especially larger towns such as Norwich or Bristol, and London was so far ahead of them as to put aside all doubt as to how far the difference was caused by a greater propensity to have apprentices in the capital.

London also had considerably more than its fair share of lawyers, other professionals and services. It had done so throughout the eighteenth century, and doubtless long before. However, the great increase in the professions, both in numbers and as a proportion of

[21] As nn. 7, 8.
[22] This is culled from P.R.O. T47.8 by ESRC grant No. B00232228. The only use of this source that I know is by L. Martindale, 'Demography and land use in the late seventeenth and eighteenth centuries in Middlesex', London University, Ph.D. thesis, 1968, p. 155.

the population, came not during the nineteenth century but during the half century after 1680. Thereafter, the professions as a whole tended merely to keep pace with the growth of population, though obviously specialised groups, such as civil engineers, would peak at later times. In the mid nineteenth century, as in the seventeenth or eighteenth centuries, the major professions were the church, the law, medicine, government service and the armed forces.[23] It was only the church that did not increase its numbers much during these fifty years. Law and medicine increased a great deal, government service increased somewhat and the armed forces increased erratically.

Between 1660 and 1690, the number of lawyers was mushrooming. The output of the Inns of Court peaked and then fell during the succeeding war years – not surprisingly in view of the demands of the armed forces and civil service – but recovered again during the 1720s.[24] King estimated 10,000 'persons in the law', Massie 12,000 and in 1851, with what is probably a looser definition (clerks, etc. appear to be included more liberally), they numbered 32,500, meaning that during the preceding century their numbers had grown at about the same rate as the population.[25] At all times, however, their sheer weight of numbers dwarfed the provinces: London had at least a quarter of the national stock of attorneys and solicitors in 1729, according to a very incomplete list; it had a third of them in 1800. One has to look at other towns to realise what this means: detailed figures for 1790 show that London had more than six times as many registered attorneys as Liverpool, Bristol, Manchester, Norwich, Chester, Newcastle and Leeds combined.[26]

The number of doctors was likewise growing during the early eighteenth century, helped by a spate of hospital building in Walpole's unhealthy capital. The foundations of what was to become the Westminster Infirmary were laid in 1719; Guy's Hospital opened in 1725, St George's Hospital in 1733, the London Hospital in 1740, the Middlesex Hospital in 1745, and there were others.[27] What eighteenth-century hospitals did for the sick is open to debate, but they did wonders for doctors. The para-medical professions,

---

[23] The professions have been examined recently in some detail, by Holmes nationally: G. Holmes, *Augustan England: Professions, State and Society, 1680–1730* (1982), and by Earle, *Making*, for London.

[24] Holmes, *Augustan England*, p. 137.

[25] Another of Colquhoun's unbelievable figures: he came up with 11,000 (*A Treatise on Indigence*, p. 23) 'including judges, barristers, attornies, clerks etc.'.

[26] P. Mathias, 'The lawyer as businessman in eighteenth-century England', in D. C. Coleman and P. Mathias (eds.), *Enterprise and History. Essays in Honour of Charles Wilson* (Cambridge, 1984), pp. 157–8.

[27] *Ibid.*, p. 200.

especially apothecaries, many of whom achieved a genuine degree of status during the early eighteenth century, also did well. Apothecaries had, it was claimed, multiplied eightfold during the last sixty years of the seventeenth century and at the end of the century were supposed to number about 800.[28] The 240 apothecaries who took out new fire insurance policies with the Sun Fire Office and the Royal Exchange Assurance between 1775 and 1787 outnumbered the 169 members of the legal profession to form one of the capital's largest professional groups. This does not mean that there were more apothecaries than lawyers in the capital – apothecaries had more stock in trade to invest while lawyers may have put down their occupation as 'gentleman' or 'esquire' – but it does indicate that they were a significant group in the population.

Central government, on the other hand, grew more slowly throughout this period. Gregory King estimated that government service occupied some 10,000 persons in 1680. Professor Holmes has estimated that by the mid 1720s the central government's permanent employees numbered some 12,000 'and many more auxiliaries of one kind or another' such as dockyard workers. In 1759 Massie increased the figure to 16,000, and by 1851 they numbered 27,000 nationally, with a third of them in London.[29]

The relatively slow growth of the legal profession after about 1730 may not have been exceptional: it is by no means obvious that in the capital the importance of the professions as a whole increased drastically between 1730 and 1851, when London employed 12 per cent of the town's employed males and 28 per cent of the nation's professions. Deducting the armed forces reduces the figure from 12 per cent to 8.5 per cent, which may be comparable to the 1730s, a decade for which Holmes has estimated that there were some 55,000–60,000 permanent jobs in the professions nationally.[30] London should have had at least a quarter of these. If, around 1720, London had a population of some 600,000, or some 200,000 adult males, the professions would therefore be employing some 7–8 per cent of the total. The slower progress of the professions in the capital after 1730 may well have been typical of the rest of the country: the figure of 55,000–60,000

[28] Holmes, *Augustan England*, p. 191.
[29] Holmes, *Augustan England*, pp. 19, 255. Patrick Colquhoun produced a totally incredible figure of 12,500 for 1803 (*A Treatise on Indigence*, p. 23).
[30] Holmes, *Augustan England*, p. 16. This is for permanent jobs. This estimate, based on detailed counting and detailed knowledge, is near enough to Massie's estimate of 57,000 for the clergy, law, civil officers and liberal arts for 1759, a figure accepted by P. H. Lindert and J. G. Williamson, 'Revising England's social tables 1688–1812', *Explorations in Economic History*, 19 (1982), p. 396.

employed in the professions in 1730 was about 3 per cent of adult males at the time; in 1851 the professional classes – which is a significantly looser definition than that employed by Holmes, including many clerks in solicitors' offices, and so forth – came to about 5 per cent of adult males.

Nor did the older professions show a great increase during the later part of the nineteenth century. Numbers employed in the 'three ancient professions' of law, medicine and the church barely kept pace with the general rise of population. Teachers, of course, increased considerably in numbers, though it is doubtful how far the mass of teachers, many of them female and working in primary schools, should be considered 'professional' in the nineteenth-century meaning of the term.[31] General clerical jobs increased very substantially indeed throughout the nation, though commercial clerks were already one of the largest occupational categories in London in 1851. What is applicable nationally is also applicable to London and is borne out by Stedman Jones' manipulation of the 1861 and 1891 census returns for the capital: his 'professional and teaching' category employed 4.5 per cent of adult males in 1861, but only 3.7 per cent in 1891. 'Administration' rose, but only from 1.66 per cent to 1.8 per cent, while 'clerical' increased from 3.2 per cent to 5.7 per cent of adult males.[32]

More significant than the professional classes, at any rate in numbers, were shopkeepers. In 1851, distribution occupied 14.1 per cent of the employed population. It has been estimated that shopkeepers formed between 11 and 14 per cent of the capital's employed population in 1798.[33] One would expect this proportion to increase during the century and a half covered by this book, but the evidence for such an increase is rather indecisive. Beier's category 'transport and distribution' covers 9 per cent of the occupied population of both sexes for the seventeenth century; Earle has suggested that some 15–20 per cent of the adult male population of late seventeenth-century London were involved in transport, which, if correct, would leave little for distribution.[34] However, the burial registers of St Giles without Cripplegate – a large and none too wealthy parish, and

[31] W. J. Reader, *Professional Men* (1966), p. 155.

[32] G. Stedman Jones, *Outcast London* (Oxford, 1971), pp. 358–9.

[33] L. D. Schwarz, 'Income distribution and social structure in London in the late eighteenth century', *Econ. Hist. Rev.*, 2nd ser., 32 (1979), pp. 250–9.

[34] This figure is biased towards the low side by being based upon the palpably incorrect assumption that only males were involved in transport and that the adult sex ratio was parity. However, if females outnumbered males – which seventeenth-century historians suggest was the case – then the figure is even higher.

unlikely to be overburdened with purchasing power – show 11 per cent of its 12,140 burials between 1654 and 1693 as being of those involved in distribution,[35] and this statistic does not include small artisans such as cordwainers or tailors who sold the goods they made, but only 'retailers' (with the exception of bakers, who are included). They formed 13 per cent of burials between 1729 and 1745.[36] Baptism registers for a large number of parishes in East London in 1770 and 1813 show 'provisioners' as forming between 9 and 12 per cent of the entire population.[37] So the evidence does not point either way. Many artisans during this period would have kept shops to sell their wares. There was always a specialised retailing sector and this would have increased, perhaps at the expense of the 'artisan retailer'.

The analysis of occupations is only a starting point. It describes, but it does not explain. The next stage is to examine the distribution of wealth, and the context in which this wealth was made and held.

[35] T. R. Forbes, 'Weaver and cordwainer: occupations in the parish of St Giles without Cripplegate, London, in 1654–1693 and 1729–1743', *Guildhall Studies in London History*, 4 (1980), pp. 119–32.

[36] Women, by contrast, taking the most favourable definition of retailing possible – assuming that female goldsmiths, ironmongers and pewterers, and the like, were involved in distribution – did not form more than 8 per cent of the total for their sex during the earlier period – and they only reached 8 per cent out of a total that excludes all single women, spinsters, wives and widows. They moved into their husbands' shops: *ibid.*

[37] L. D. Schwarz, 'Occupations and incomes in late eighteenth-century East London', *East London Papers*, 14 (1972), pp. 93–4.

2

Manufacturing, services and the London bourgeoisie

Manufacturing and services in London

Despite the stress on the importance of services in the previous chapter, it would be a great mistake to underestimate the role of London as a manufacturing town. With over 370,000 of its inhabitants in 1851 employed in the manufacturing sector, London was the largest manufacturing town in the country and in Europe. This section will not seek to describe all of London's manufactures, or their geography, but will enquire into the nature of manufacturing in London, why it took place there at all, and the effects that the salient characteristics of manufacturing in London had on the nature of London's workforce.[1]

Naturally, those who chose to manufacture goods in London needed to adapt themselves to the advantages and drawbacks of operating in the nation's capital. There were three large drawbacks. In the first place, land cost more, so rents were higher than elsewhere. Secondly, labour cost more, and had a disconcerting tendency to organise itself into trade unions. Thirdly, coal cost more than it did on or near coalfields. On the other hand, there were three large advantages. Proximity to the largest and most concentrated market in the country meant both low transport costs for the finished product and a good observation point for consumers' tastes. The labour may have cost more, but there was a great deal of it, and it came in almost any degree of skill required. Thirdly, London was not only the largest consumer centre in the country; it was also the country's largest port, and for many trades involved in international commerce it was useful to be in London.

---

[1] For brief descriptions of this, see Sheppard, *Infernal Wen*, ch. 5, which can certainly be used retrospectively; P. G. Hall, *The Industries of London since 1861* (1962), which can also be used retrospectively, and, to a certain extent, Rudé, *Hanoverian London*, ch. 2.

31

As a result of this situation there were comparatively few factories, large-scale works, or works requiring much space to be found in London, and those that were to be found, such as tanning, hat-making, woodcutting, brewing or vinegar-making, tended to be south of the Thames where the land was cheaper while the supply of water – an essential factor – happened to be plentiful.[2] These firms still had high London overheads with which to contend, but the advantages more than compensated for this: brewers were in the centre of the London market, tanners used the hides of cattle slaughtered at Smithfield, while woodworkers set to work at the port where their wood entered the country and had built up an infra-structure to ensure that it continued to do so. Engineers were also usually south of the river: the larger engineering works required quite considerable space and the smaller works, with hopes of subcontract-ing, would not wish to be too far away. In the nineteenth century, South London had its own distinct labour market which had little connection with North London, and there is no reason to believe that this had not been the case during the eighteenth century when crossing the Thames was no easier.[3]

North of the Thames were the smaller-scale, less capital-intensive concerns, and it was for these – the luxury trades of Westminster, the clock makers of Clerkenwell, the silkweavers of Spitalfields and a myriad of others – that London manufacturing was best known, and in which so many of its workmen were to be found. There was an obvious advantage from the abundant skilled labour, there was often an advantage from the Port, but the crucial entrepreneurial role came from London being at the centre of the national market, so that its fashions could be watched closely. Since fashions were liable to change suddenly and with little warning, the tendency would be to produce comparatively small quantities, often in very short runs. Large-scale factory production, even had the technical means for it existed, might well have entailed real diseconomies. Geographical localisation can be an effective means of increasing the economic size of an industry and achieving the gains of specialisation while reduc-ing transaction costs. When the division of labour is practised over a particular locality, individual firms do not need to develop expensive

---

[2] R. J. Hartridge, 'The development of industries in London south of the Thames', London University, M.Sc.(Econ.) thesis, 1955.
[3] E. J. Hobsbawm, 'The nineteenth-century London labour market', in E. J. Hobs-bawm, *Worlds of Labour* (1984), pp. 131–51.

specialisms.[4] There are, of course, drawbacks, mainly arising from there being so many independent links in the production chain, but these were not decisive during this period and production units usually failed to become vertically integrated, even when price competition became more intense from the 1860s. A major reason why they failed to do so was that there was so much labour available that the price and quality of the finished product could be controlled while the ability of the disorganised outworkers to cause trouble was very limited.[5]

The forces of the market, therefore, as well as the technology of the time, reinforced domestic production. Nor did domestic production require much fixed capital. Using little machinery, and not requiring very specialised premises, it was flexible, and even if wages were higher than in other parts of the country these included the rent of the outworker's premises and the expenses of the machinery he or she was using. As a result, the disintegration of production was carried very far. In Peter Hall's words, the assembly line ran through the street, where the material, in its different stages of completion, was carried from one manufacturer to another.[6] The watch makers of Clerkenwell found around them all the different workmen and the specialised machinery into which mechanisation had divided the watch industry, as well as a machine-tool industry. In Spitalfields lived not only the silkweavers but also the sellers and repairers of looms, the dyers, many of the employers as well as the warehouses. Outside Clerkenwell or Spitalfields the infrastructure would be lacking.[7] Once established, an industry was likely to stay in the same part of London unless it departed from London entirely.

[4] Much has been written on this: for a classic example see G. J. Stigler, 'The division of labour is limited by the size of the market', *Journal of Political Economy*, 59 (1951), pp. 185–93. See also Hall, *Industries*, p. 119.

[5] This will be recognised as drawing on the theory of the firm as originated in Coase, comparing transaction costs (i.e. the cost of relying on the market) with the organisational (or opportunity) costs of increased integration within the firm: R. H. Coase, 'The nature of the firm', *Economica* (1937). More specifically it relates to the discussion of quasi-rents by B. Klein, R. G. Crawford and A. A. Alchian, 'Vertical integration, appropriable rents and the competitive contracting process', *Journal of Law and Economics* (1978), pp. 297–326.

[6] Hall, *Industries*, p. 119; P. G. Hall, 'Industrial London: a general view', in J. T. Coppock and H. C. Prince (eds.), *Greater London* (1964), p. 228.

[7] Some trades did move – furniture making, for instance, began the eighteenth century around St Paul's Churchyard, but moved to Long Acre and St Martin's Lane by the 1730s; during the second half of the eighteenth century the West End increasingly replaced Long Acre. This was a trade where the large practitioners had most of what they needed in their own workshops: the Linnells moved to Berkeley Square itself in 1754, where they were employing around fifty people: P. Kirkham and H. Hayward,

Such departures took place in the nineteenth century but very infrequently before then. Transport costs were an important factor in protecting the capital from regions which in later years would be competing successfully. Tariff barriers excluded competing foreign goods, such as Lyons silk. Most important of all, a mass market of the extent that would exist in the late nineteenth century did not yet exist. With the exception of shipbuilding and the industries on the South Bank, London tended to specialise in the finishing trades, and the finishing trades were themselves orientated predominantly towards the luxury market or towards individually specified products, such as clothes. The mass production of goods – even under the domestic system – tended to be performed outside London. In the course of the nineteenth century the situation would change. Provisional competition would become more intense, tariff barriers would be removed, and a stable mass market would develop. Many industries, such as tanning or shoemaking, would then leave London or lower their overheads as much as possible, a process that might well involve cutting down on wage costs. The 1860s were the years of reckoning.[8]

But already at the end of the eighteenth century the signs of effective competition were visible, although few would have noticed them at the time. Framework-knitting, which had been practised in seventeenth-century London on quite a large scale, had already been driven out by the middle of the century[9] – only two framework knitters took out insurance policies later in the century – and it was around the mid eighteenth century that London shoe retailers began the practice of sending to Northampton to have their shoes made.[10] A hat manufacturer informed a House of Commons committee in 1764:

that the Price of Labour in France is about one Half cheaper than in London; but that in the North of England Labour is much cheaper; that he had, on that Account, established his Manufactory there, as several other Hatters of London had done.[11]

Even shipbuilding, despite – or perhaps because of – the boast that London produced the best ships in the country, was specialising, concentrating increasingly on complex ships for the East India trade and for the navy, and leaving easier work to the Tyne and else-

William and John Linnell: *Eighteenth-Century London Furniture Makers* (2 vols., 1980), I, pp. 4, 31, 45.

[8] Stedman Jones, *Outcast London*, pp. 19–32, 99–111, 152–3.

[9] W. Felkin, *A History of the Machine-Wrought Hosiery and Lace Manufactures* (1867), pp. 74–6; J. D. Chambers, *Nottinghamshire in the Eighteenth Century* (1932), pp. 94, 106, 109, 113–15. *Journal of the House of Commons*, 26, 19 April 1753.

[10] *London Life*, p. 368; see below, p. 195.

[11] *Journal of the House of Commons*, 29, 5 March 1764.

where.[12] The 1785 Eden Treaty with France, in many respects a foretaste of things to come, was welcomed by the Northern and Midlands cotton, woollen, iron, pottery and hosiery trades, which expected to benefit from the reduced French tariffs on their produce and duly contributed towards depressing the economy of northern France during the succeeding years, but it was opposed by the smaller, more traditional trades, many of which were concentrated in London – trades such as tanning, clock making, silkweaving and hat making (with the notable exception of the Lancashire hatters).[13] So the General Chamber of Manufacturers – the first attempt to combine the nation's manufacturing interests into a single pressure group – was paralysed because, as Wedgwood complained, 'a man who should get a delegation from the toothbrush makers of London would have a vote equal with a delegate from Birmingham and Manchester'. It duly broke up.[14]

What is noticeable is the number of trades for which London was *the* national centre of production at the start of the eighteenth century but was, by the 1750s or 1760s, only *one* centre of production. Silkweaving is a good example. During the course of the seventeenth century it took over from fustian weaving, in typical London fashion. Fustian weaving had been practised on some scale: fustian was a heavy, hard-wearing material, the manufacture of which would not be expected to remain in London, and it was losing its place to silk-weaving even before the arrival of Huguenot silkweavers taking refuge in England after the Revocation of the Edict of Nantes in 1685.[15] However, it was the Huguenots who established silkweaving very firmly in the capital.[16] There it stayed, and it was large. The suggest-

[12] *S.C. to whom the several petitions of shipbuilders and others . . . were referred*, P.P. 1813–14, 8, pp. 376, 431.

[13] W. Bowden, *Industrial Society in England towards the End of the Eighteenth Century* (New York, 1925), pp. 183–93; J. Ehrman, *The British Government and Commercial Negotiations with Europe, 1783–1793* (Cambridge, 1962), pp. 44–8.

[14] Bowden, *Industrial Society*, p. 191.

[15] A. Plummer, *The London Weavers' Company, 1600–1970* (1972), pp. 9–11.

[16] The best account of Spitalfields before 1766 is N. K. A. Rothstein, 'The silk industry in London, 1702–66', London University, M.A. thesis, 1961. From 1760, the best account is M. Bondois-Morris, 'Spitalfields: unité économique et diversité sociale dans "l'East End" londonien, 1760–1830', Université de Paris, I, thèse pour doctorat du Troisième Cycle, 1980. It is to be hoped that there will be a copy available at the Institute of Historical Research in London. Otherwise there is the still acceptable M.A. thesis by W. M. Jordan, 'The silk industry in London 1760–1830, with special reference to the condition of the wage earners and the policy of the Spitalfields Acts', London University, M.A. thesis, 1931. On the Spitalfields Acts, the classic article by J. H. Clapham, 'The Spitalfields Acts, 1773–1824', *Economic Journal*, 6 (1916), remains authoritative. There is some information in Plummer, *Weavers' Company*. For the context of all this, there remains only Sir F. Warner, *The Silk Industry of the United*

ion is that it employed some 10,000 looms in the early eighteenth
century and perhaps more in the mid century, which, on the assumption that a loom employed more than one person and including the
various dependent trades such as gold and silver threadmakers,
lacemakers and silk throwers, produces a figure of some 40,000–
50,000 persons, nearly a tenth of the population.[17] In 1719 the industry had not yet moved much beyond London, to judge from the
absence of provincial silkweavers among the petitions flooding Parliament from virtually all the important textile centres of the country
protesting against the import of calicoes.[18] But, in that same year the
Lombe brothers set up their silk twisting mill near Derby, and when,
in 1766, the Spitalfields silkweavers were complaining to Parliament
of French competition, they were joined in their chorus by workers in
other parts of the country: not only the silk throwers in Macclesfield
and Derby but also 'the users of thrown silk' in Manchester, the 'silk
and worsted weavers' of Kidderminster, and 'the hosiers, framework
knitters, manufacturers of and dealers in framework-knitted silk
stockings and silk mitts' in Nottingham.

That the first part of the operation, silk twisting, should have left
London during the first half of the eighteenth century is unsurprising.
Silk twisting was an early stage of the production process, the product
was undifferentiated, the work was not skilled, the transport costs for
silk were not high and it was notoriously a job for the poorest women
and children. One of these was being paid 3s. a week in the 1760s, or a
quarter of a labourer's wage. Dorothy George found that it became a
common occupation in London workhouses from the 1730s.[19] This
was not the sort of thing for which London, with its high cost of
living, was suitable – the labour of women and children was best used
either in the service sector, where there was no provincial competition, or in the finishing sector of manufacturing, where there was
little. Silk twisting accordingly left London.[20] However, the spread of
silk manufacture itself from Spitalfields took a little longer. Unsurprisingly, it appears to have begun with those goods that could be
produced on a larger scale and for which the precise whims of the
London market were not so important. Manchester began to produce

Kingdom. Its Origins and Development (1921): we have to await what promises to be an
impressive history of the English silk industry by N. K. A. Rothstein. However,
there is an interesting article on the changing technology in the industry by S. R. H.
Jones, 'Technology, transaction costs and the transition to factory production in the
British silk industry, 1700–1870', *J. Econ. Hist.*, 47 (1987), pp. 71–96.

[17] Earle, *Making*, p. 20.
[18] *Journal of the House of Commons*, November–December 1719. N. K. A. Rothstein, 'The
calico campaign of 1719–1721', *East London Papers*, 1964.
[19] *London Life*, p. 185.   [20] *Ibid.*, p. 186.

handkerchiefs, Coventry ribbons.[21] The process probably accelerated during the 1760s, especially after 1766, when Parliament obligingly placed a prohibition on the import of French manufactured silks.[22] Over the next sixty years the London trade increasingly maintained itself by concentrating on the latest London fashions. In 1821, when a committee of the House of Lords specifically asked 'Are there any [silk] manufactures that can be carried out more profitably at Spital-fields than elsewhere?', they received the answer, 'The branches more immediately connected with the fashion of the day, and with the higher fashions of the day'. Broad silks were made at Spitalfields, but also at Macclesfield and Manchester, ribbons chiefly at Coventry, mixed silk and worsted at Kidderminster and Norwich, hosiery at Nottingham and Derby; the last handkerchiefs had, it was claimed, finally departed from Spitalfields for Manchester within the last twelve years, but while 'the country manufacture' produced goods more cheaply than did London, 'they have not the taste in the country; and as long as the principal manufacturers remain in London, there will always be a demand for their goods; they have more taste, and there are certain articles that I think they will be a long time before they can accomplish in the country . . . Are these articles of great sale? Yes'.[23] But moving upmarket still left the silk manufac-turers with what they considered more than their fair share of prob-lems. They blamed the Spitalfields Act of 1773 – it had let the magis-trates impose agreed piece rates – for these problems, while failing to notice that the wages of the better weavers had fallen from those of an artisan during the early 1760s to those of a labourer by the early 1820s.[24] 'The repeal of the Act means the end of the domestic system in Spitalfields and the establishment of factories' was the confident assertion of one of their more important members to a House of Lords committee in 1823.[25] This seems doubtful, considering the unsuit-ability of London for factories, not to mention the difficulties of mechanisation for a fabric that was so fragile, was produced in short runs and was – given its up-market appeal and the high cost of the raw material – not particularly price elastic, at any rate to small falls in the price of the finished product. But the experiment was not made, at

21 *Journal of the House of Commons*, 30, 4 March 1766, pp. 208–19.
22 *Ibid.*, 34, 5 April 1773, p. 239.
23 *Second report of the House of Lords Committee on Foreign Trade*, P.P. 1821, 6, evidence of Durant, Gibson, and Davison.
24 See below, pp. 204–5. Technically they blamed the Spitalfields Acts: the original Act was extended on several occasions.
25 Bondois-Morris, 'Spitalfields', p. 111; *House of Lords Sessional Papers*, P.P. 1823, 13, p. 113.

least not on any scale: the Spitalfields Acts were repealed in 1824, but in 1826 the import prohibition was replaced by a 30 per cent tariff. Proximity to the market was no guarantee that the market would not prefer French fashions, which it duly did. This was no time to introduce machinery, although a silk factory was in fact opened in London in 1824. During the five years after 1826 the piece rates of Spitalfields silkweavers fell by half.[26] In 1840 only 3 per cent of the 10,500 looms in the capital were in shops with more than five looms. Spitalfields still had a quarter of all the silk looms in England during the late 1830s, but essentially the Spitalfields silk industry was limping from 1826. In 1851, fewer than 10,000 men, and only 11,000 women, were returned as involved in the silk industry in the capital. The Cobden–Chevalier Treaty finished it off in 1860.[27]

The Spitalfields silk industry was unusual in being unable to cope with French competition. But the process that it underwent was not so untypical. At the start of the eighteenth century it dominated the nation, by the 1760s it was facing provincial rivalry to which it had to adapt. It did so, increasingly, by concentrating on the final stage of manufacture, by adapting itself to a specialised metropolitan demand – a demand that was very seasonal, very changeable, very unpredictable. The entrepreneurial response was usually to invest in width, not in depth. It was safer.

Of course, not all the nation's most skilled manufactures began the eighteenth century in an unchallenged position in the capital. That could hardly have been expected. Watch making, for instance, was taken up in Lancashire on a large scale from the late seventeenth century.[28] The many parts that comprised a watch were separately manufactured by very precise machines and highly skilled labour, and many of the parts were sent down to London to be assembled and put into cases with the London watch maker's name on them. The

---

[26] For piece rates, see below, p. 205.

[27] Jones, 'Technology, transaction costs', table 12 for the distribution of looms in England, c. 1838. For the effects of the 1860 treaty see Plummer, *Weavers' Company*, pp. 368–9, Warner, *Silk Industry*, pp. 84–99. Jones, 'Technology, transaction costs', p. 28, points out that inferior work suitable for factory production by the less skilled was frequently sent to factories or outworkers in the provinces, where labour was cheaper; what remained in Spitalfields, to be paid at reasonable rates, was the most skilled work on the most intricate patterns. Of course, what factories would not do, Jacquard looms might manage, and these were being introduced during the 1820s: N. K. A. Rothstein, 'The introduction of the Jacquard loom to Great Britain', in V. Gervers (ed.), *Studies in Textile History in Memory of Harold B. Burnham* (Toronto, 1977).

[28] F. A. Bailey and T. C. Barker, 'The Seventeenth-century origins of watchmaking in south-west Lancashire', in J. R. Harris (ed.), *Liverpool and Merseyside. Essays in the Economic and Social History of the Port and its Hinterland* (1969).

relationship of the Clerkenwell watch makers to those of Lancashire and, subsequently, Coventry is unclear. They all seem to have achieved a tolerable *modus vivendi*, with a rapidly expanding market at home and abroad, though London workers seem to have concentrated more on the finishing and assembly end of the process. In 1797, when the London trade was probably at its peak, about 7,000 persons around Clerkenwell were, it was claimed, dependent upon it.[29]

Other industries, of which engineering is an example, lost their dominance later. Engineering was not particularly large by London, or national, standards, but it exemplified London's dominance. The capital's engineers stood at the peak of their profession, their work in such high demand that their high wages – half as high again as the wages of most artisans – could easily be afforded. 'All Proprietors of Mines and Collieries which are incumbered with Water', announced Thomas Savery in 1702, 'may be furnished with Engines to drain the same at his Workhouse in Salisbury Court, London.' However, in 1825 there were only between 400 and 500 engineering employers in the capital, and not more than 10,000 workers; in 1851, only 168 employers returned information on the number of their employees for the census: a few were large, such as Maudsley, Sons and Field with 800 employees, but only twenty-six employed more than twenty men.[30] Along with the other capital-intensive industries that needed land, engineering was mostly carried out south of the Thames.[31]

In retrospect, it is clear that many London trades were vulnerable to provincial competition, but this was by no means clear at the end of the eighteenth century, and would not become obvious until the 1860s, when shipbuilding collapsed in the 1866 depression and failed to revive significantly thereafter. Shipbuilding had been a traditional London concern of a classic kind, with its well-paid and frequently militant shipwrights, and it had done well in the age of wood and sail

---

[29] At least they did in the eighteenth century. See D. S. Landes, *Revolution in Time* (1983), pp. 230–4, and C. Ellmers, 'The impact of the 1797 tax on clocks and watches on the London trade', in J. Bird, H. Chapman and J. Clark (eds.), *Collectanea Londiniensia. Studies in London Archaeology and History presented to Ralph Merrifield* (London and Middlesex Archaeological Society, special paper no. 2, 1978), pp. 388–400. S. E. Atkins and W. H. Overall, *Some Account of the Worshipful Company of Clockmakers of the City of London* (1881), p. 269, which is sometimes quoted, mistakes the population of Clerkenwell – 20,000 – for the number of watch makers in the parish.

[30] T. C. Barker, 'Business as usual? London and the Industrial Revolution', *History Today*, 39, February 1989, pp. 45–51; K. Burgess, 'Technological change and the 1852 lock out in the British engineering industry', *International Review of Social History*, 14 (1969), pp. 218–22; G. Crossick, *An Artisan Elite in Victorian Society. Kentish London, 1840–1880* (1978), pp. 77–81.

[31] Hobsbawm, 'London labour market', pp. 140, 149–50.

but had few advantages in the age of steam and coal. Its departure led the way: during the succeeding decades, other manufactures either departed from London or moved to its new periphery.[32]

However, until the 1860s changes in London's manufacturing had tended to be gradual. During the eighteenth and for much of the nineteenth century, the nature of London's manufacturing produced a distinct working population, a distinctiveness that shows itself clearly when examining the capital's trades in more detail. Male occupations in the capital were divided into a large number of relatively small trades, very few of them employing as much as 2 per cent of the male labour force, and usually very much less. The occupations that were the most concentrated in London, with the highest location quotients, were not, on the whole, among London's largest. Furthermore, the largest occupations in London were not those in which London held a particular advantage as measured by its location quotient. The forty-five most concentrated trades in 1851 (with location quotients higher than 2.0) are listed in table 2.1, and together they formed 37 per cent of the male labour force. However, the seventeen largest occupations in the capital, in table 2.2, employing 10,000 males or more employed 48 per cent of the labour force; if the two categories of 'general labourers' and 'messengers, porters' are excluded as being excessively imprecise – the former means little, while many messengers were children – then the remaining largest fifteen occupations formed 36 per cent of the labour force and only seven of them appear in both table 2.1 and table 2.2: domestic servants, commercial clerks, bakers, painters, plumbers, lawyers, civil servants and printers. This was 14.6 per cent of the male labour force. Only two of the eight were in the manufacturing sector – bakers and printers, and these formed less than 4 per cent of the male labour force, and only 10 per cent of the manufacturing sector.[33]

Not only was manufacturing not outstandingly important, but there were few London trades that combined a superiority over the rest of the country with the employment of a large number of Londoners. The largest occupations in 1851 – tailor, shoemaker and such like – had low location quotients. Hall found the same in a more restricted analysis of London manufacturing in 1861, as well as in

[32] Stedman Jones, *Outcast London*, pp. 152–5; S. Pollard, 'The decline of shipbuilding on the Thames', *Econ. Hist. Rev.*, 2nd ser., 3 (1950–1); Crossick, *Artisan Elite*, pp. 48–50; I. J. Prothero, *Artisans and Politics in Early Nineteenth-Century London. John Gast and his Times* (1979), pp. 24–5, 46–50, 305–6.

[33] Stedman Jones, *Outcast London*, pp. 69–70, for the juvenile labour market. Some occupations in tables 2.1 and 2.2 are composite, but they are also composite in the other tables in this chapter, so they remain comparable.

Table 2.1. *1851 male occupied population: the most concentrated trades*

	% of national labour force in category	% of London labour force	L.Q.	Number
1. Oil and colourmen	83.89	0.23	6.90	1,632
2. Musical instrument makers	83.69	0.41	6.72	2,929
3. Gold, silver and jewellery manufacturers	80.37	0.80	6.46	5,706
4. Cheese and butter sellers	75.42	0.38	6.06	2,715
5. Paper stainers	71.86	0.20	5.78	1,438
6. Glue, tallow makers,	65.32	0.61	5.25	4,311
7. Sugar refiners	60.00	0.17	4.82	1,200
8. Scientific instrument makers	54.41	0.22	4.37	1,578
9. Bookbinders	50.00	0.40	4.02	2,850
10. Tobacconists	47.25	0.11	3.80	756
11. Printers	46.69	1.46	3.75	10,365
12. Greengrocers	44.66	0.55	3.59	3,885
13. Commercial clerks	43.79	2.31	3.52	16,420
14. Hosiers, haberdashers	41.06	0.18	3.30	1,314
15. Publishers, booksellers	40.57	0.34	3.26	2,435
16. Umbrella makers	40.05	0.12	3.22	841
17. Lawyers	39.73	1.79	3.19	12,794
18. Stationers, bookbinders	39.54	0.68	3.18	4,824
19. Police	38.82	0.89	3.12	6,367
20. Messengers, porters	37.19	4.67	2.99	33,214
21. Milksellers	36.80	0.55	2.96	3,938
22. Fishmongers	36.21	0.36	2.91	2,571
23. East India Company employees	35.71	0.17	2.87	1,214
24. Commercial travellers	34.61	0.41	2.78	2,907
25. Coal heavers	32.68	0.57	2.64	4,020
26. Wine and spirit merchants	32.51	0.30	2.61	2,142
27. Hair, quill, feather, brush manufacturers	32.10	0.42	2.58	2,954
28. Carriage makers	32.10	0.70	2.58	4,948
29. Poulterers	31.55	0.09	2.53	631
30. Civil servants (central government)	30.04	1.62	2.41	11,535
31. Warehousemen	29.51	0.58	2.38	4,108
32. Watch and clock makers	28.35	0.68	2.28	4,847
33. Plasterers	27.92	0.62	2.24	4,378
34. Household utensils, ornament makers	27.78	0.63	2.23	4,500
35. Drink manufacturers	27.39	1.07	2.22	7,604
36. Domestic servants	27.39	2.86	2.20	20,348
37. Plumbers, painters, glaziers	26.36	2.16	2.12	15,369
38. Accountants	26.93	0.22	2.18	1,530
39. Hatters	26.85	0.29	2.16	2,084
40. Post office employees	26.40	0.47	2.12	3,326
41. Cabinet makers and upholsterers	26.30	1.34	2.11	9,558
42. Fur and leather dealers	25.88	0.88	2.08	6,263
43. Bakers and confectioners	25.77	1.93	2.07	13,762
44. Auctioneers	25.63	0.13	2.06	897
45. Medical workers	25.58	1.22	2.05	8,698
Total		36.96		261,706

Table 2.2. *The largest London male occupations, 1851*

	Number	% of male labour force (national)	L.Q.	% or male labour force (London)
1. General labourers	50,173	15.46	1.24	7.05
2. Messengers, porters	33,214	37.19	2.99	4.67
3. Boot and shoemakers	30,855	14.62	1.17	4.34
4. Carpenters	23,453	15.00	1.21	3.30
5. Tailors	22,479	18.47	1.48	3.16
6. Domestic servants	20,348	27.39	2.20	2.86
7. Armed forces	19,047	22.23	1.79	2.68
8. Mariners	18,193	23.47	1.89	2.56
9. Commercial clerks	16,420	43.75	3.52	2.31
10. Servants: non-domestic	16,392	21.74	1.75	2.30
11. Plumbers, painters, glaziers	15,369	26.36	2.12	2.16
12. Woodworkers	14,202	19.14	1.54	2.00
13. Bricklayers	13,919	20.74	1.67	1.96
14. Bakers and confectioners	13,762	25.77	2.07	1.93
15. Lawyers	12,794	39.73	3.19	1.80
16. Civil servants	11,535	30.04	2.41	1.62
17. Printers	10,365	46.69	3.75	1.46

Total for nos. 1–17 = 342,520 = 48.1 per cent of employed male population.
Total for nos. 3–17 = 259,133 = 36.4 per cent of employed male population
(i.e. excluding labourers, porters and messengers).

1951.[34] London was so large that many industries that would stand out in smaller towns were hidden. It was otherwise with the service sector. Services were particularly concentrated in the capital, especially the non-tradable services such as government, armed forces, domestic service and medicine – all professions that were so important to the capital's bourgeoisie, and which expanded so much between 1680 and 1730.[35]

The nature of manufacturing in the capital thus meant that the best jobs employed relatively few people. The rest had to go somewhere; the only question was where. For many the answer was sweated or casual labour. For others, the path to employment led through retailing. The next section considers both these paths.

[34] Hall, *Industries*, pp. 24–5.   [35] See above, pp. 26–9.

The London labour force: manufacturers, services and the residual

For those engaged in the non-tradable services, such as lawyers, civil servants or doctors, in professions that expanded greatly between 1680 and 1730, life in London was reasonably comfortable and secure. Those supplying tradable services were in another world. They fell into three categories: a minority of the comfortable – those few involved in finance, overseas trade and some wealthy shopkeepers – a fair number of 'middling' persons, some rather more precariously poised in life than others, and a large number of the extremely uncomfortable – those whom a later age would label the residuum.

The position of the capital's wealthier shopkeepers will be discussed later in this chapter. They required extensive capital to set up with much security, which did not prevent them from relying heavily on credit, both for starting their business and for maintaining it, but the greater the credit the greater the capital required to support it. Those who could not obtain the necessary capital found themselves in the position of John O'Neill, an Irish-born shoemaker who had saved £10 and used it to buy a chandler's shop in 1842. He could hardly have chosen a worse year; nevertheless, his description is perfectly applicable to all chandlers' shops during the eighteenth and nineteenth centuries:

We soon found out that a chandler's shop was no sinecure; but a comfortless drudgery, where one is obliged to be the servant and liable to the abuse of the most degraded, while the profits, if articles are honestly sold to your customers, are so small, and in some cases, are actual losses, that there is not a living to be got at it, while the keeping of the chandler's shop is marked out as fair game for all the swindlers in the neighbourhood. If he refuses to give credit, the shop is avoided, as if marked with a plague spot . . . Whatever evils befall the regular customers of the chandler's shop is sure to fall upon the chandler; if a wife is confined, the week's score cannot be cleared off on the Saturday night; if a man gets drunk and is robbed of his wages, the week's score must lay over; if an accident happens, or a child dies, or a thousand other ills that flesh is heir to, the chandler's shop must stand the brunt.[36]

Such tight margins, with such a temptation – amounting virtually to necessity – for adulteration meant that the poor did not much like the chandler's shop either. 'The more respectable poor deal with the baker; the lowest order deal with the chandler's shop', was the view of the assistant overseer of the poor of Lambeth in 1834. 'Where I find that a man is not to be heard of at a baker's or butcher's, and I find that

---

[36] J. O'Neill, 'Fifty years' experience of an Irish shoemaker in London', St Crispin, 1–2 (1869–70).

he only deals with the chandler's shop, I take that as a sign that he is a man who is trusted nowhere else.'[37]

Perhaps O'Neill's mistake had been to go for a fixed shop. Below the shopkeeper came a fluctuating mass of street traders. More than a century before Mayhew, they were described by a person calling himself Don Manoel Gonzalez, probably an Englishman seeking to increase his sales by posing as a foreign visitor to the country:

> I must not forget the numbers of poor creatures, who ... maintain their families by buying provisions in one part of the town, and retailing them in another, whose stock perhaps does not amount to more than 40 or 50s. and part of this they take up (many of them) on their cloaths at a pawnbroker's on a Monday morning, which they make shift to redeem on a Saturday night, that they may appear in a proper habit at their parish churches on a Sunday. These are the people that cry fish, fruit, herbs, root, news, etc. about town.[38]

The *Spectator* in 1711 listed street sellers of milk, coal, glasses, brick-dust, barrels, pickled dill and cucumbers (but only for two months), pastry, powder and washballs, apples, gingerbread, bellows, as well as tinkers and knife grinders.[39]

It was all very flexible. 'In January and February the costers generally sell fish', wrote Mayhew. The supply of fish tended to be erratic in March and April, but good in May. However,

> in June, new potatoes, peas and beans tempt the costermonger's customers ... In July cherries are the principal article of traffic. On my inquiry if they did not sell fish in that month, the answer was, 'No, sir; we pitch fish to the —; we stick to cherries, strawberries, raspberries and ripe currants and gooseberries. Potatoes is getting good and cheap then and so is peas' ... In August the chief trading is Orleans plums, greengages, apples and pears ... In September apples are vended ... in October 'the weather gets cold and the apples gets fewer ... we then deals most in fish' ... In November fish and vegetables are the chief commodities ... In December the trade is still principally in fish.[40]

The high rents in London, compounded by the high cost of setting up a shop in a reputable part of the town, meant that a significant proportion of the underemployed 'residual' service sector found some employment for itself in street trading. A large and rapidly growing volume of services is considered as one of the hallmarks of a modern industrialised economy, but eighteenth-century London consumed

---

[37] R.C. on the Poor Laws. Appendix A. Reports of Assistant Commissioners (E. Chadwick), P.P. 1834, 29, p. 178.
[38] 'The voyage of Don Manoel [sic] Gonzalez in Great Britain', in J. Pinkerton (ed.), A General Collection of the Best and Most Interesting Voyages and Travels in all parts of the World (1808–14), II, p. 94. Dorothy George, England in Transition (1953), p. 24, considers Gonzalez to be English.
[39] Spectator, no. 251, 18 December 1711.   [40] Mayhew, London Labour, I, pp. 54–5.

services in a manner that would do honour to the most profligate post-industrial society. The volume of tradable services was enormous; unlike manufacturing, the growth in the supply of such services was not necessarily closely correlated with the growth in the demand for them. Considering the ease with which this sector could employ the labour of women, children and underemployed labour in general the supply of these services may well have expanded faster than the output from manufacturing. To most of its practitioners it was a residual group of occupations,[41] into which they moved every now and then, depending on the trade cycle, the season and a host of other factors. The reserve army of labour was available to all, although subject to strong cultural constraints about hours of work, festivals and sexual stereotyping. Men and women worked in services because services required the least capital: merely sufficient strength and a skill that could be learnt on the job, whether it be the riverside, the laundry or domestic service.

For a young woman, especially a young woman newly arrived in London, it was best to become a domestic servant. This provided some security and an opportunity for saving; historians have also suggested that it provided an opportunity to learn some arts of looking after a household that a potential suitor might value. But not everyone could become a servant – servants were, on the whole, supposed to be young and unmarried, and in addition they required certain qualifications not always to be found: hence the paradox of a mass of female poverty amidst the continuous clamour of respectable householders that they could not obtain a suitable servant. In the nineteenth century, when the rage for having a servant of one's own was no less than a century earlier, many households excluded the Irish as a matter of principle.[42]

William Morton Pitt reported some of the problems in 1797 when he described a school for poor girls aged between nine and thirteen lately established in Chelsea: three quarters of the girls could not sew,

and not one of the best could sew so well as to make a single article of dress. They were equally ignorant of knitting and spinning. Being thus wretchedly unskilful in the common and most useful arts of life, they are plainly disquali-

---

41 P. K. O'Brien, 'The analysis and measurement of the service economy in European economic history', in P. K. O'Brien and R. Fremdling (eds.), *Productivity in the Economies of Europe* (Stuttgart, 1983), pp. 82, 85.

42 T. M. McBride, *The Domestic Revolution. The Modernisation of Household Service in England and France, 1820–1920* (1976), p. 45, for the age structure of the servant population of London in 1851: 27 per cent were aged between fifteen and nineteen, another 27 per cent between twenty and twenty-four, and 15 per cent between twenty-five and twenty-nine.

fied for domestic servants, and for most other offices in society, and have few means in their power to earn an honest maintenance.[43]

The restrictions on female employment were one of the major causes of the poverty and exploitation suffered by women. The reasons for such restrictions were very varied. Sheer physical strength was unlikely to have been a major factor: traditional cultural and sexual norms were more important. In addition, the effort by skilled workers to restrict the free flow of labour into their trade was sure to rebound principally against women. By the 1830s such efforts were not meeting with much success. From their point of view, the men were quite right: the breakdown of barriers to entry led to an invasion of women and a great reduction in the wage rate: the process is discussed in some detail in part three of this book. There was, however, an additional reason for the pattern of female employment, and this was the age at which women sought particular employments. The age distribution of employed women was as distinctive as their concentration into a handful of trades, and the situation of 1851 is likely to have been duplicated a century and a half earlier. A breakdown of these two characteristics is given in table 2.3. Service, needlework and laundry employed by far the largest number of women – in total nearly 60 per cent of the female labour force, as many as 73 per cent of all working girls between the ages of fifteen and nineteen, and two-thirds of those aged between twenty and twenty-four.

Domestic service was, of course, by far the most popular occupation for girls, employing almost half of those aged between fifteen and nineteen, and accounting for the large number of girls who migrated to London at this period of their lives. When servants reached their late twenties and early thirties they tended to marry and leave service altogether, while those that remained found the career prospects poor. The proportion of employed women in service fell sharply from its peak of 49.1 per cent of those aged between fifteen and nineteen to 31.8 per cent of those aged between twenty-four and twenty-nine, and to 19.4 per cent of those aged between thirty-five and thirty-nine. Needlework offered a more permanent, if limited, standby employing between a fifth and a quarter of all working women between the ages of fifteen and forty-four. Above this age it employed a smaller number of women, and the laundry became more important – it is interesting to note that laundry work was by far the most common employment for women over the age of fifty. This was not very different from

---

[43] W. M. Pitt, *An Address to the Landed Interest on the Deficiencies of Habitation and Fuel for the Use of the Poor* (1797), p. 34.

Table 2.3. *1851 census: women's occupation by age*

Age	Total employed as % of total female population	% of employed engaged in Service	Needlework	Laundry	Service, needlework and laundry as % or total female employment	Service, needlework and laundry as % of total female population
10–14	13.0	45.1	16.9	1.4	63.5	8.2
15–19	58.6	49.1	21.0	2.8	73.0	41.3
20–24	60.7	40.3	22.6	3.7	66.7	40.4
25–29	47.7	31.8	23.3	5.1	60.1	28.6
30–34	39.8	23.8	23.3	8.3	55.4	21.9
35–39	38.2	19.4	22.5	11.3	53.2	20.3
40–44	39.9	16.7	20.3	14.3	51.2	20.4
45–49	41.3	15.4	18.7	16.0	50.1	20.6
50–54	42.9	14.1	16.4	17.7	48.1	20.7
55–59	42.9	13.0	16.3	18.2	47.5	20.3
60–64	43.2	13.3	14.5	18.4	46.2	20.0
65–69	42.1	13.4	15.7	17.1	46.3	19.4
70 and over	35.3	16.1	14.2	16.2	46.5	14.8
All women aged 10 and over	43.1	29.8	20.7	8.6	59.1	25.5

Earle's early eighteenth-century sample, in which 60 per cent of those aged under twenty-five were servants, but less than 30 per cent of the women aged between twenty-five and thirty-four were in this situation. On the other hand, a quarter of those employed between the ages of twenty-five and thirty-four were in the needle trades; over a quarter of those aged thirty-five to forty-four were working as charwomen, laundry or nursing, while the proportion of those in hawking, shopkeeping or victualling rose steadily.[44]

The danger of an analysis such as this is that it suggests a misleading degree of precision. When they ceased to be domestic servants, women might well cease to have distinct occupations. This put them into the same category as most men in the labour market, but they earned much less. The most dramatic examples of residual employment come with women, especially women too old (or too burdened with children) for employment as full-time servants;

> By enquiry an honest chairwoman, to support the place of a woman-servant, may be procured for 1/- a day. If such are hired to wash, their wages are larger: 1/6 with tea and a dram twice a day, and strong beer and supper; but for this they slave hard, will begin to work at 2 in the morning, and continue it till 9 of the next evening.[45]

And this at a time when a labourer was paid 2s. a day for a fourteen-hour day.[46] Laundry work was something that women usually began doing in their late thirties, and they continued doing it for as long as they needed the money or were physically capable of the labour. Francis Place's mother, at the end of the eighteenth century, nearly sixty years old and facing 'what for a moment seemed irremediable poverty and misery', promptly took in washing. 'Not at all ashamed of honestly earning her living as she considered it her duty to her family to do she used to bring home large bundles of cloaths upon her head and take them back again in the same way. Often did she labour till twelve o'clock at night, and rise again at four in the morning to pursue her occupation.'[47]

The concept of a single occupation, carried on throughout the year, was by no means universal during this period. It is very difficult to track down the development of specialisation. There is the obvious danger of exaggerating how complete the process was by the nineteenth century: the nineteenth-century census, by its nature, was

[44] Earle, 'The female labour market', p. 343.
[45] G. Kearsley, *Kearsley's Table of Trades* (1786), p. 97. See also Anonymous, *Low Life* (1764), p. 91: women still at work at 1 a.m.
[46] See below, p. 170 for wage rates.
[47] *The Autobiography of Francis Place (1771–1854)*, ed. M. Thale (Cambridge, 1972), pp. 98–9.

constrained to give a single job to individuals. There was a long-term process of specialisation, which is discussed in Part III. But we must never forget that multiple occupations were commonplace and necessary. Once we move below the level of the most skilled members of a trade – or, in the case of women, once they were no longer domestic servants – we are moving into a world where very many people, perhaps the majority, no longer had distinct occupations. The occupational tables so carefully assembled by historians are snapshots of a shifting world. Even when, as with a census, they were taken on a particular day, they reflect only the occupations of that day. A census taken in Westminster at the height of the London Season would be as different from one taken in midsummer as a census taken in the countryside during the harvest would differ from midwinter. This was not a world where people had the *same* jobs all the time. The skilled artisan might do so, but he was very much in a minority. London consisted of a mass of people – men, women and children – technically untrained but willing to learn any job that required a relatively short period of training. This was only to be expected in a world of underemployment and mass poverty. With the possible exception of a period during the second quarter of the eighteenth century (and even that is doubtful), it was a case of an economy with a virtually unlimited supply of labour. More precisely, it was an economy where large masses of underemployed labour would switch jobs frequently. There were islands of steady employment, inhabited by colonies of skilled workmen; there were some profitable retailers but, by and large, the world was in a state of flux.

Historians should, therefore, be careful when saying that a certain percentage of the population were tailors, carpenters, and so forth. Quite a number would have been tailors at the peak of the Season, but not for the rest of the year. They might have called themselves tailors, rather than labourers, but for nine months of the year they would have been labourers. Work was too seasonal for anything else. There were jobs, and people took them, so what an occupational census does is to give an indication of the nature and extent of these jobs. Taking one year with another, there were quite a number of jobs for tailors and shoemakers and builders, fewer for shipwrights and coachpainters. For the most skilled trades a job description can be taken fairly literally. A certain proportion of skilled craftsmen would, of course, be laid off once the peak of seasonal demand had passed, but their numbers would probably not vary much; their job description would be meaningful. For the semi-skilled trades such a description would be weaker, while for the unskilled jobs it would be virtually meaningless. For women, of course, it did not mean much. Few would *choose* to be a sempstress and fewer still to hawk goods from a barrow in winter.

It is, however, possible to discern a certain pattern from all this. An occupational census for East London, derived from a sample of baptism registers for 1770 and 1813, shows that in 1813 some 14–20 per cent of the local population fell into the category of general labourer. We can expand this more by allowing for seasonality of work and allowing for 25 per cent of semi-skilled labourers as being marginal and laid off once the peak of demand had passed. This produces a figure of almost one-third of the adult male population of East London, or 40 per cent of the working population who would have been in extreme poverty if they had families, and with little enough spending power if single.[48] They would take any job that they could for most of the year, though the semi-skilled trades at least knew what they would be doing during the peak of demand for their product. This is the meaning to attach to the fact that over half the parents of children baptised in Spitalfields in 1770 gave their occupation as weaving, compared with less than 1 per cent of the riverside.

This figure is remarkably close to Booth's estimate of 35 per cent of the population of East London living in poverty during the late nineteenth century, though of course changes in the local economy during the intervening period make a direct comparison impossible.[49] But, in both periods, and doubtless for many centuries previously, London was awash with semi-skilled labour. Its industries, large by provincial standards, were inevitably not large enough to absorb all its labour. Its trades, seasonal and erratic at the best of times, could not employ so many at any one time and, as will be shown in chapter four, the very seasonality created a surplus reserve labour force. The enormous service sector reinforced this, by attracting female servants to London and then leaving them without occupations when they chose to set up their own households, by the casual earnings that it gave to its porters, carriers, cleaners and others, by the low wages given to so many of those who worked in the lower reaches of the services. London had a reputation of being a high-wage town. For skilled workmen this was true. For those with low productivity, living in the interstices of the service and manufacturing economy, the fact that earnings were higher than in the provinces was little compensation for the higher cost of living in London and the very irregular

[48] Schwarz, 'Occupations and incomes', pp. 87–100.
[49] W. Booth, *Life and Labour of the People in London* (1902), i, pp. 33–61.

earnings to be made there. So it had always been in the capital, and so it would remain.

The social structure at the end of the eighteenth century

Professor Rudé has attempted to estimate the size of the upper- and middle-income groups in eighteenth-century London. In very general terms, he guesses at there being some 3,000–4,500 aristocratic and gentry families living in the metropolis at some time of the year.[50] In addition, there were about 1,000 families in high finance and large-scale trade,[51] making a total upper-income sector of about 4,000–5,000 families, forming 2–3 per cent of the population of London in 1801. But when going further down the social scale, Rudé becomes more tentative. He describes and attempts to enumerate those to whom he applies the eighteenth-century term 'middling classes' – a very broad social and economic group indeed, of great political importance in the London of its time, but a group whose bounds stretched very far up and down the income scale. In pre-industrial urban society, the 'middling classes' consisted, broadly speaking, of anyone below an aristocrat or very rich merchant or banker, but above a journeyman worker or a small-scale employer in one of the less prestigious trades, such as a butcher. They are the subject of Earle's book.[52] The term encompassed both moderately wealthy merchants and small employers working in their own shops with only two or three men under them.

Occupationally, the 'middling classes' in London comprised three different groups: the tradesmen and shopkeepers of the City of London and of Westminster; the manufacturers, carrying and servicing trades based on the Port and the outparishes of Surrey and Middlesex; and finally, belonging to the 'middling classes' by reason of status if not always of income, professional men and artists.[53] Unfortunately, Rudé does not say what he believes to be the minimum income necessary to belong to this class.

As the 'middling classes' are such a broad category, Rudé has problems in enumerating them. He estimates some 10,000–15,000 'merchants' and 'principal tradesmen',[54] but realises that this is too narrowly defined a category for the 'middling classes'. He therefore quotes an alternative figure from *Holden's Triennial Directory* of 1805–7 (the fullest yet to appear) which listed just under 50,000 business and

---

[50] Rudé, *Hanoverian London*, p. 48.   [51] *Ibid.*, p. 53.
[52] And are discussed in *ibid.*, pp. 56–63.
[53] *Ibid.*, p. 58.   [54] *Ibid.*, p. 53.

professional men. Many of these belonged, however, in Rudé's opinion, to the working trades, while others were too wealthy for the 'middling classes'.

If we deduct [he argues] an adequate proportion for those higher and lower [income] groups and take note of the number of voters in London, Westminster and the outparishes (about 20,000 at this time), we may arrive at a figure of some 30,000 families of the 'middle sort', accounting for perhaps 125,000 persons, or 1 in 7 of the population of London according to the census of 1801.[55]

While Rudé does not indicate the income of those belonging to this group, he does give some suggestions about the rent they paid for their houses. As the group itself is so large, it comes as no surprise to learn that in the middle of the eighteenth century the rents of this group varied between £8 and £10 per annum at the lower end of the scale and between £40 and £50 at the upper end,[56] compared with the nobility and gentry, who generally paid more than £40 a year for their town houses.[57] The assessed tax returns to a government enquiry of 1798 provide the basis for a comparison and a check on these estimates. The information requested by the government has survived for only a very few parts of the country, but among these parts London is very well represented, with returns from parishes which together accounted for some 75 per cent of the population of London in 1801.[58] The collectors – there appears to have been at least one for each parish, sometimes more – were asked to divide the houses in their areas into two groups: those that had retail shops in them, and those that did not. Each of these groups was then further subdivided, specifying houses with lodgers, houses whose owners found it difficult to pay their assessed taxes, and houses where warrants had been issued compelling the owners to pay. Furthermore, all houses were divided into five categories, depending on the total amount of assessed tax they paid each year: those paying less than £1 per annum, those paying more than £1 and less than £2, from £2 to less than £5, from £5 to less than £10, and those paying more than £10. Of course, the assessed taxes were evaded, but the categories employed are sufficiently broad to allow for some evasion. The taxes were, however, fairly heavily progressive, so it is impossible to move directly and accurately from the amount of assessed tax paid to an estimate of annual income. Fortunately, some of the collectors provided impressionistic accounts of income according to the amount of

---

[55] *Ibid.*, pp. 57–8.   [56] *Ibid.*, p. 58.   [57] *Ibid.*, pp. 50–1.
[58] P.R.O., PRO/30/8/280–1. The detailed statistics are in Schwarz, 'Conditions of life', pp. 343–57.

Table 2.4. *Median incomes according to the amount of assessed tax paid annually*[59]

	Amount of tax	Income per annum
I	Under £1	£61
II	£1–under £2	£66
III	£2–under £5	£79
IV	£5–under £10	£128
V	£10 and over	over £200

taxation paid, from which a rough indication of median incomes, the midpoint in the scale, can be attained. It is shown in table 2.4.

While table 2.4 would make no pretence at considerable accuracy, it does suggest that, roughly speaking, classes III and IV, whose income was thought by the various collectors to range between £70 and £200 a year, and with median incomes of £79 and £128, can be considered as middle class, at least as far as their incomes were concerned, while class V, earning over £200 a year, would quite probably be upper class. Whether those in tax categories I and II, with incomes of £61 and £66 a year, should be considered middle class is open to doubt. In this chapter, however, they are included, not because persons with incomes exceeding £60 a year were intrinsically 'middle class' – a skilled artisan could earn as much – but because, comprising some 10–12 per cent of London's population, they formed a group between the 'comfortable' middle classes of the higher tax categories and the two-thirds or more of London's population too poor to be liable to assessed taxes at all, while they merged with neither of them. For convenience, they will be referred to as lower-middle class – to refer to their incomes and *not* to make implications about class consciousness or related factors. It is simply more convenient to use this term than to have 'lower-middle income group'. Similarly, classes IV and V are referred to as upper-middle class.[60]

Before presenting the assessed tax figures, it is important to point out that of the 92,654 houses outside the City for which there are figures, 49,479, or 53.4 per cent, did not pay assessed taxes at all,

---

[59] There is a graph in Schwarz, 'Income distribution', p. 253.
[60] For the original estimate of the size of London's middle classes, where the intention was to compare the results with Patrick Colquhoun's estimate of the 'comfortable' middle classes, they were not specifically considered, although some allowances were made: Schwarz, 'Income distribution', p. 256, n. 1. If included, the London middle and upper classes formed some 30 per cent of the population; excluded they formed 25 per cent.

Table 2.5. *Distribution of taxed houses by amount of assessed tax paid*

		%
I	Under £1	19.1
II	£1–under £2	17.8
III	£2–under £5	30.2
IV	£5–under £10	22.0
V	£10 and over	10.9
Total		100.0
Number		51,828

having no more than seven windows, or not being worth more than £5 a year in rates, the point at which a householder became liable for such taxes.[61] For the inner part of the City of London, the City Within, it is not possible to give precise figures of the proportion of houses excused tax, as the tax figures are provided by wards, while the census figures are for parishes, whose boundaries were different from those of wards.

Table 2.5 shows that the overall division of those houses that did pay assessed taxes was spread widely across the spectrum. In the area covered by the tax returns, there were just over 5,600 fifth-class houses. Allowing for a family of five, their inhabitants would come to about 3 per cent of the population of London in 1801; with a family of four they would form about 2 per cent – very similar to Rudé's estimate of 2–3 per cent for the wealthiest class.

There were 27,000 third- and fourth-class houses for the 'middling classes', who would thus form 16–21 per cent of the population, depending on family size, comparing very well with Rudé's estimate of around 17 per cent. The combined upper and 'middling' classes therefore formed up to a quarter of London's population.

In examining the adult male working population, which formed some 75 per cent of the total adult male population, one has to move away from the relatively firm ground of the tax returns. Some of them were householders paying assessed taxes, but most of them were not. Without a great deal of detailed research it is impossible to estimate with any accuracy the proportion of better-off working men – skilled artisans, and the higher ranks of the less skilled trades, such as shoemakers or tailors. However, by using the data on shops, it is possible to make a rough estimate of the number of artisans who were

[61] S. Dowell, *A History of Taxation and Taxes in England* (3 vols., 1884), II, pp. 169–70; III, p. 206; 37 Geo. III c. 30.

actually self-employed.[62] Except for a very few who would be working for a factor of some sort, most of them would require a shop of their own, unless they were in the building trades; such a shop would probably belong to the first two tax classes, paying less than £2 a year in taxes, but some might belong to the third class. The shopkeepers in these three classes of shops formed only about 6–7 per cent of the population, or 8–10 per cent of the working population, but not all of them were skilled artisans – many sold food and drink – and to arrive at the number of artisan employers we must deduct these from the total number of shops.

However, the only type of shop that can be specifically pinned down is the public house. In 1803, Patrick Colquhoun estimated that there were 820 of them in the City and 990 in Westminster;[63] applied to the 1798 figure this comes to 12.6 per cent of the shops in the City and 17.2 per cent of those in Westminster.[64] For the East London parishes there are figures available for 1816,[65] which compare fairly closely to the figures left by a few East London tax collectors in 1798, reflecting the strictness of licensing policy during the intervening eighteen years.[66] Except for outlying parishes, the number of public houses in East London may not have been substantially greater in 1816 than in 1798, and applying the 1816 figures to the number of shops in the 1798 returns reveals a proportion much higher than further to the west, often as high as a quarter of all shops.

A more difficult problem is that of distinguishing the sellers of food from other shopkeepers. A rough estimate can be made for East London, where there are some indications of the occupational structure.[67] In 1813, 'provisioners' – a term which would include publicans – formed about 11 per cent of all the heads of families in East London, so far as baptism registers can be relied upon. The 1798 tax figures give the proportion of shopkeepers to the total population as being also roughly of this order of magnitude. Even after making allowance

---

[62] The tax commissioners appear to have found no difficulty in distinguishing shops from other houses; presumably they defined a shop as being a building 'any part of which shall for the time being be . . . publickly kept open for carrying on any trade, or for selling any goods, wares or merchandize by retail' as they had done during Pitt's short-lived attempt to tax shops from 1785 to 1788: Dowell, *Taxes*, III, pp. 16–19; 25 Geo. III c. 30.

[63] Colquhoun, *A Treatise on Indigence*, p. 284.

[64] P.R.O., PRO/30/8/281, fo. 144 provides figures for the total number of shops both taxed and untaxed, in the City and in Westminster.

[65] *S.C. on the Police of the Metropolis*, P.P. 1816, 5, p. 116.

[66] P. Mathias, *The Brewing Industry in England, 1700–1830* (Cambridge, 1959), pp. 125–8. For detailed figures see Schwarz, 'Conditions of life', p. 190.

[67] Schwarz, 'Conditions of life', pp. 226–7; Schwarz, 'Occupations and incomes', pp. 92–9.

for errors, especially in the baptism figures, the number of retailers selling items other than food and drink must have been small. This might be expected: in a poor area there would be little surplus spending power, especially after the traditional demands for drink had been met, so there would only be a small role for the artisan shopkeeper except in a few specialised regions: along the riverside he could help to provide for the shipbuilding industry, in Whitechapel and Shoreditch for the metal workers.

A similar picture may well have existed in other parts of London, especially south of the Thames. Shops selling food and drink may well have formed at least half of the total number of shops in London. This would reduce the proportion of self-employed artisans in the manufacturing trades to around 3–4 per cent of the male population, or 5–6 per cent of the working-class population. In poor areas, where the proportion of shops to the total number of houses was below the average, and the proportion of public houses and food shops was above the average, the proportion of independent artisans would be even smaller. In East London they probably formed only 2–3 per cent of the population; in Westminster they might have come to 8 per cent.

So, despite its reputation as 'the Athens of the artisan',[68] London turns out to have contained a much larger employed population than might be supposed. Some 90 per cent of the male working population, or two-thirds of the total male population, are likely to have been employed.

The number of highly skilled artisans among the employed cannot be estimated with very much accuracy. They did mostly belong to friendly societies, but so did many other working men. However, since membership involved a fixed weekly subscription, it could be afforded only by those in receipt of a steady income, so that the figures of friendly society membership do at least serve the function of distinguishing the better-off working men from the rest. With this qualification, taking the various estimates, and the evidence of the 1803 parliamentary return, about one-third of the adult male population, or some 40 per cent of the working population, belonged to a friendly society.[69]

This leaves some two-thirds of the employed male population falling into the general categories of unskilled and semi-skilled. Without the benefit of very detailed local work, there is no way of arriving at even a rough idea of the different sizes of these two groups. This work has been done for East London and mentioned in

[68] E. P. Thompson, *The Making of the English Working Class* (1968 ed.), p. 284.
[69] This is discussed in more detail in Schwarz, 'Conditions of life', pp. 192–4.

the previous section: making various assumptions about seasonality of employment, about 30 per cent of the working population were found to be in considerable poverty if they had families, and with little enough surplus spending power if they were single – though obviously the marginal semi-skilled man was likely to be a little better-off over the entire year than the totally unskilled man.[70] To move from East London to the rest of London without the benefit of previous detailed work on the occupational structure brings us into a terrain where we have unfortunately to abandon even the most general attempt to distinguish between unskilled and semi-skilled labour.

At this point, the argument can be summarised. The upper income group in London, with an average income of over £200, formed only 2–3 per cent of London's adult male population; the 'middling classes', with average incomes between £80 and £130, formed another 16–21 per cent, while the working population formed 75 per cent. About 9–10 per cent of the latter were self-employed in the sense that they were shopkeepers, but only about 5–6 per cent of them were self-employed artisans outside the building trades. More impressive are the figures for artisans, who may have formed as much as 35 per cent of the working population. But two-thirds of the working population and half of the entire adult male population were unskilled or semi-skilled.

The London bourgeoisie: shopkeepers and other tradesmen

There are no less than three separate descriptions of the hierarchy of occupations within London during the late seventeenth century: that of Elliott, which is based on marriage patterns, that of Earle, based on wills, and that of Alexander, based on the 1693 tax assessment.[71] Those of Earle and Alexander are based on wealth; Elliott's is not primarily so, but shows clearly that as far as the marriage market of late seventeenth-century London was concerned, if wealth and status were in conflict, it was unusual for wealth not to win. Elliott shows, unsurprisingly, that within a hierarchy that broadly reflected wealth (although with obvious exceptions such as the clergy – and clergymen were wealthier in London than elsewhere[72]) there was a definite tendency for those who worked in manual trades to remain lower in

---

70 Schwarz, 'Occupations and incomes'. See below, p. 122.
71 Vivien Brodsky Elliott, 'Mobility and marriage in pre-industrial England', Cambridge University, Ph.D. thesis, 1978, pp. 73, 79; Earle, *Making*, pp. 32, 36; J. M. B. Alexander, 'The economic and social structure of the City of London, c. 1700', London University, Ph.D. thesis, 1989.
72 Earle, *Making*, p. 64.

status and income than retailers, themselves less wealthy and less prestigious than wholesalers; while manufacturers who could delegate would have a higher status (and usually more wealth) than manufacturers who could not delegate.[73]

At the top, obviously, were the aristocracy, the gentry and the larger merchants, and at the bottom, in Elliott's fifth group, were labourers. Between the two were three clusters, and it is the nature of these three clusters that is of interest. Above the labourers came a group comprising porters, coopers, bakers, butchers, tailors, weavers, sailors, gardeners and masons: these were hard-working manual jobs, some were quite skilled but all low in status, the pay usually rather poor and irregular. Above them, at the third level, were the smaller retailers and some manufacturers with the opportunity to delegate: innholders, feltmakers, mercers, chandlers, clothworkers, bricklayers, maltsters, tanners and joiners. And above them, second in the hierarchy, and being led only by the aristocracy and the larger merchants, were the lesser gentry and merchants, clergy and doctors, but also apothecaries, clothiers, skinners, brewers, ironmongers, salters and vintners – in other words the professionals, wholesalers, the larger retailers and the larger manufacturers.

For a longer period which covers the years between 1670 and 1730, Earle has provided information on the money left at death by persons operating in quite a large variety of London trades but, by virtue of leaving property at death, belonging to the middle classes. It is solely a hierarchy of wealth, not status, so the clergy will usually be omitted. All trades had their rich and poor practitioners, but one can note the wealthiest members of a particular trade, and thereby construct a hierarchy of wealth which is not very different from that of Elliott, but which sub-divides Elliott's top three groups, especially the second and third groups. So, at the top of the scale, leaving £10,000 or more on their death, were merchants and bankers but also some of the larger wholesalers – a haberdasher, a draper, the largest organiser and distributor of bodices in the country – as well as a distiller and a builder. All these trades re-appear at many points lower down the scale in Earle's list of worth at death, but confectioners, chandlers, coalmen, joiners, cutlers, candlemakers, hatters, tailors and brass founders only appear in the lowest category, leaving property worth less than £500.

Five hundred pounds was the usual ceiling for artisan accumu-

---

[73] Elliott, 'Mobility and marriage', p. 63. Not surprisingly, in seventeenth-century London there is clear evidence that non-manual occupations commanded more prestige than manual occupations.

lation. A very few of the more successful and fortunate artisans might accumulate up to £1,000: a glazier, a currier, a plumber, a tortoise-shell maker, but they were exceptional. Above that, worth between £1,000 and £2,000, were the wealthier of the smaller manufacturers and retailers – a timber merchant, a bookseller, a yarn dealer, a coachmaker, a gunmaker, a looking-glass maker, a putting-out silk manufacturer. Between £2,000 and £5,000 were the larger manufac-turers and retailers, and also some wholesalers – grocers, iron-mongers, mercers, pawnbrokers, coalmerchants, brewers, printers, coopers, sugar refiners. Those worth between £5,000 and £10,000 were usually wholesalers such as cheesemongers, or very large retailers verging on wholesale, such as leather sellers.[74]

This is all very compatible with Alexander's analysis of the 1693 tax returns for large parts of the City of London, a tax based on the value of stocks. Alexander shows clearly that the dealing sector was con-siderably wealthier than the manufacturing sector: the average value of the stocks of the former being more than three times that of the latter. When examined in a little more detail there is the – by now – familiar pattern: 'overseas and general traders' with average (mean) stocks of £258, were ahead of mercers and drapers – at £196, while the lesser dealers in apparel, retailers rather than wholesalers, worth only £98, were far less wealthy than mercers or drapers. Salters, whose retail role was 'almost negligible', were far ahead of the rather up-market confectioners at £47, themselves worth more than double the fruiterers at £21.[75] The rough division between wholesalers and retailers was, however, far less significant than the fact that, with the sole exception of the manufacturers of drink and chemicals, all those with stocks of £60 or more were in the dealing sector. Makers of apparel were only worth £24, dealers in apparel were worth four times as much. Booksellers had stocks of £122, printers £37.[76] Distributors would keep larger stocks than manufacturers, but the difference would not be so great.

The remainder of this section takes this further by analysing two sources from late in the eighteenth century: the assessed tax data of 1798 and the insurance returns for 1775–87. These provide quite a considerable degree of precision about the distribution of wealth within the bourgeoisie, the importance of shopkeepers and manu-facturers as well as information on the distribution of wealth within

[74] *Ibid.*, pp. 32, 36 and 352 n. 116.
[75] Alexander, 'Economic and social structure', pp. 127–8.
[76] *Ibid.*, pp. 77–8. Dealers in apparel are a miscellaneous group, ranging from haber-dashers to bodice sellers: *ibid.*, p. 117.

trades. They also show the importance of shopkeepers within the bourgeoisie, the distribution of wealth between shopkeepers and the trades, and much else.

Wholesalers may have been wealthier and more important than retailers, but in any examination of the capital's bourgeoisie it is the shopkeeper who stands out. In 1798, the 'dealing' sector comprised 37 per cent of households paying taxes, but this is lower than other estimates: the sector formed 52 per cent of households in the City paying the poll tax in 1692 and 48 per cent of the insurance policies taken out in the capital between 1775 and 1787.[77] These figures should be handled carefully: for instance we do not know how many of the seven silversmiths and thirteen goldsmiths who paid taxes in certain parishes of the City Within in 1692, or the 176 silversmiths and 125 goldsmiths who took out fire insurance between 1775 and 1787, were simply retailers as opposed to manufacturers who perhaps also kept a shop. Nevertheless, the importance of dealing is clear. If, in 1798, a quarter of the capital's shopkeepers were not liable for assessed taxes – not an unreasonable assumption – then, as a group, shopkeepers, taxed and untaxed, formed between 11 and 14 per cent of the population in that year: a remarkably high proportion by the standards of the present day, and a reflection of the small-scale artisanal mode of production so prevalent in London. This is not to deny the existence of many small chandlers' shops whose owners lived on the breadline, not to mention the street sellers described in an earlier section of this chapter, but to warn against exaggerating their numbers. 'Shopocracy' was not an empty term, and the importance of shopkeepers in metropolitan politics is not difficult to explain. When Pitt imposed a tax on shops in 1785, protests from London were the principal cause of the tax being abolished only a few months later.[78] After all, more than one-third of those earning in excess of £75 a year were shopkeepers.

More significant than their numerical importance among the more comfortable of London's population is the fact that the wealthier the group, the more important the shopkeepers. This phenomenon only declined at the very top of the ladder. It was clearly the case in 1692, when distribution was producing wealthier men than was production. Professor Glass has provided various categories of taxpayers, depending on the amount of tax and surtax paid in that year, although

---

[77] For 1798, Schwarz, 'Social class and social geography', p. 176. For insurance data, see appendix two. Alexander ('Economic and social structure', pp. 178–9), using slightly different criteria, gives a figure of 48 per cent for the 1692 poll tax.

[78] Dowell, *Taxes*, III, pp. 16–19; J. Ehrman, *The Younger Pitt. The Years of Acclaim* (1969), pp. 258–61.

Table 2.6. *Shops per 100 taxable houses, 1798*

Assessed tax class I	27.3
Assessed tax class II	44.1
Assessed tax class III	60.7
Assessed tax class IV	58.7
Assessed tax class V	38.5

unfortunately forced to exclude professional groups such as lawyers and clergy.[79] In the highest category, where all were liable to surtax and which includes merchants, as many as 84 per cent were shop-keepers. A second, less wealthy category, where the majority paid surtax, had 68 per cent of its members involved in distribution. A third, poorer, category where less than half the members paid surtax had only 37 per cent of its members involved in distribution, while only 16 per cent of those who paid no surtax at all were so involved. Alexander's data for 1693 shows this in more detail, with the dealing sector having average stocks of £123 and the manufacturing sector of £38.[80]

The same pattern is clearly visible in 1798 (table 2.6). The number of shopkeepers for every hundred other households that paid assessed taxes in 1798 was only twenty-seven for tax class I, rising to forty-four for class II, and reaching sixty-one for class III and fifty-nine for class IV, before falling to thirty-eight for class V. As many as 73 per cent of the shopkeepers who paid the assessed taxes were in the three highest tax categories, compared with 57 per cent of other taxable households. In 1798, 37 per cent of those liable for assessed taxes were shopkeepers, as were more than one-third of those earning more than £75 a year. There is justification for Stedman Jones, who in his analysis of the 1861 census, placed the smallest traders into the same socio-economic class as artisans, and then placed retailers alongside small employers and the larger dealers in the highest class. No dealers – unless they were street traders – went into his two lowest classes.[81]

Setting up a respectable shop required considerable capital. By the end of the seventeenth century it cost £50–£60 to do so in most towns, but it cost at least £100 in London.[82] The cost rose inexorably. In 1747,

[79] D. V. Glass, 'Socio-economic status and occupations in the City of London at the end of the seventeenth century', in A. E. J. Hollaender and W. Kellaway (eds.), *Studies in London History* (1969), pp. 382–3.

[80] Alexander, 'Economic and social structure', pp. 78–9.

[81] Stedman Jones, *Outcast London*, pp. 44–5.

[82] R. Grassby, 'Social mobility and business enterprise in seventeenth-century England', in D. Pennington and K. Thomas (eds.), *Puritans and Revolutionaries*.

Campbell listed what, in his opinion, was the necessary sum to set up independently (table 2.7). Well informed though Campbell was, his figures were obviously intended to be indicative rather than definitive, and they cover a broad range, such as £50–£500 for fruiterers or £500–£5,000 for booksellers. However, Earle has found that the rough orders of magnitude are in accordance with evidence on the wealth of shopkeepers obtained from other sources.[83] What is significant is the expense, usually far greater than £100.

Table 2.7. *Campbell's estimate of the cost of setting up a shop in London,* 1747[84]

Apothecary	£50–£200
Baker	£100–£500
Bookseller	£500–£5,000
Butcher	£20–£100
China shop	£500–£2,000
Confectioner	£100–£300
Fishmonger	£100–£1,000
Fruiterer	£50–£500
Grocer	£500–£2,000
Haberdasher	£100–£2,000
Hosier	£500–£5,000
Jeweller	£100–£5,000
Mercer	£1,000–£10,000
Pawnbroker	£500–£2,000
Stationer	£100–£2,000
Tobacconist	£100–£5,000
Woollen-Draper	£1,000–£5,000

If one started with too little, all one's access to credit and reputation for reliability failed to produce an escape from the problems faced by Francis Place:

I was obliged to give credit even in my small way and to charge low prices. I could not from want of capital enlarge my trade beyond the point to which I had brought it. Had I increased the number of my customers and consequently the credit I must have given I should have gone deeper into debt, and should not have receivd payment from my customers fast enough to enable me to make my payments to the mercers and drapers as regularly as I had hitherto done, and thus have injurd my credit and put an obstacle in the way of my getting into business as I wished. Had I enlarged my business I

Essays in Seventeenth-Century History presented to Christopher Hill (Oxford, 1978), p. 366.
[83] Campbell, *London Tradesman*, pp. 330–40; Earle, *Making*, pp. 107–9.
[84] Campbell, *London Tradesman*, pp. 331ff.

should have had to purchase the things to fit up the garments for ready money, as I had all along been obliged to do, as the quantities were small, and I should have been also obliged to employ a journeyman occasionally. These things were beyond my ability.[85]

Imprecise though Campbell's figures are, they do reveal a familiar clustering into three groups: the wealthiest, who were mostly wholesalers but also did some retailing, such as drapers, mercers, hosiers; those in the middle, who were mainly retailers of the more expensive consumer goods – haberdashers, stationers, keepers of china shops – and those at the bottom, who sold food for mass consumption – fishmongers, bakers, fruiterers, confectioners, butchers. Grocers fitted into the middle group, as the poor did not deal with them. So,

The Woollen-Draper . . . buys his Goods from Blackwell-Hall Factory, or from the Clothiers in the West of England. They buy their Cloths of one Colour, white from the Hall, in long or short Pieces, and have them dressed and dyed in Town . . . They not only serve the Taylor here in London, by Retail, but the Country shops Wholesale.[86]

The Business of a Mercer requires a very considerable Stock; Ten Thousand Pounds, without a great deal of prudent Management, makes but a small Figure in their way.[87]

The mercer, however, was but

the Twin Brother of the Woollen-Draper, they are as like one another as two Eggs, only the Woollen-Draper deals chiefly with the Men, and is the graver Animal of the two, and the Mercer traficks most with the Ladies, and has a small Dash of Effeminacy in his Constitution.[88]

In the middle rank came haberdashers, who purchased from the wholesale drapers,[89] and stationers, who purchased from the paper makers[90] – these were wholesale stationers, who were wealthier than retail stationers. There were pawnbrokers, keepers of china shops, and grocers. There were also booksellers – who were publishers as well as booksellers and paid for printing the book as well as selling it – and did not escape Campbell's disapproval: 'I do not reckon every man a Bookseller who keeps a Stall in Moorfields, or a Shop in a more eminent Part of the Town, more than I esteem a Chandler's Shop a Merchant's Warehouse: Those who do not understand their Business,

---

[85] *The Autobiography of Francis Place*, pp. 173–4.
[86] Campbell, *London Tradesman*, p. 194.
[87] *Ibid.*, p. 198.   [88] *Ibid.*, p. 134.   [89] *Ibid.*, p. 199.
[90] *Ibid.*, p. 127. Most of the larger stationers appear on pp. 164–9 of D. C. Coleman, *The British Paper Industry 1495–1860: a Study in Industrial Growth* (Oxford, 1958).

are to me but Quacks, and Book-Worms, whatever Name they assume.'[91]

At the bottom came keepers of the various food shops – fishmongers, bakers, fruiterers, confectioners, butchers and, misleadingly, the profitable trade of apothecary. 'There is no Branch of Business in which a Man requires less Money to set him up, than this very profitable Trade: Ten or Twenty Pounds, judiciously applied, will buy Gallipots and Counters, and as many Drugs to fill them with as might poison the whole Island. His Profits are unconceivable; Five Hundred per Cent is the least he receives. The greatest Part of his Out-laying is in Viols, small Boxes, and cut Paper; and these are often worth ten Times what they contain.'[92] Nevertheless, apothecaries required some training, otherwise everybody would have become one, and training was more than Campbell allowed for many of the assistants in the food shops. These he put at the bottom of the heap: they made little money (unless they cheated or adulterated) and they required little capital.

The insurance policies on property insured against fire with the Sun Fire Office and the Royal Exchange Assurance between 1775–87 provide a useful means of checking on Campbell, albeit a generation later. They are only a very approximate check, however, because of the problem, of multiple insurance policies. This is a problem that is discussed in appendix one: briefly, it is impossible, without a great deal of further work (and sometimes not even then), to know whether a man taking out a policy of £500 on his property in 1776 and another policy of £500 in 1778 was substituting the second policy for the first, so was only worth £500, or was adding to his first policy, and therefore worth £1,000. If the policies are for different addresses, they are more likely to be cumulative, but then one cannot always be sure that one is dealing with the same person. So the insurance data should, strictly speaking, be regarded as referring not to persons but to policies. The likelihood is that the wealthier the trade the more policies wealthy individual members of that trade took out on different properties so that the bias of using individual policies would be to produce greater equality between and within trades. Wealthy merchants are likely to have insured more than one warehouse, poorer merchants less likely; chandlers are not likely to have owned more than one shop. But one cannot measure the extent of this.

Since the insured values for trades stretch far across the spectrum, from £200 to several thousand pounds, the best guide is not the mean but the median, the mid point in the series. Table 2.8 compares

[91] Campbell, *London Tradesman*, p. 64.   [92] *Ibid.*; Earle, *Making*, pp. 72, 108.

Table 2.8. *Comparison of Campbell's estimate of the cost of setting up shop in London with median and top of third-quartile insurance policies, 1775–87*

	Campbell	Insurance Median	75%
Apothecary	£50–£200	£450	£700
Baker	£100–£500	£300	£500
Bookseller	£500–£5,000	£800	£1,400
Butcher	£20–£100	£300	£400
Fishmonger	£100–£1,000	£200	£400
Grocer	£500–£2,000	£500	£900
Haberdasher	£100–£2,000	£500	£1,000
Jeweller	£100–£5,000	£300	£500
Mercer	£1,000–£10,000	£1,200	£2,200
Pawnbroker	£500–£2,000	£600	£1,000
Stationer	£100–£2,000	£550	£1,000
Woollen-Draper	£1,000–£5,000	£1,000	£2,000

Campbell's estimates of the cost of setting up shop in London with the median value of the policy for that trade, as well as the top of the third quartile of such policies. They compare quite well, but suggest that Campbell's own figures were on the high side: there had been a generation of mild inflation after Campbell, and most trades were still tending towards the lower end of his estimates.

Table 2.9 extends this to the top forty London trades, as measured by the number of insurance policies. In the process, the forty were reduced to thirty-eight by adding together silversmiths and gold-smiths on the one hand, and clock and watch makers on the other, necessary because people often entered both trades opposite their name. It shows the value of the policy attained by the median of the trade as well as the highest point reached by the poorest three-quarters of the trade. The Gini coefficient (a standard measure of inequality) is also included, for later discussion.

Quite a number of conclusions can be drawn from table 2.9. In the first place, it shows that there remained some validity in the threefold distinction between wholesalers, up-market retailers, and the rest. At the top of the table came drapers, mercers, merchants and brewers. Apothecaries, grocers and victuallers (i.e. publicans) were in the middle, as were pawnbrokers and stationers, while at the bottom came those who sold their wares – especially food – through retail outlets, such as chandlers, fishmongers, cheesemongers. Only 15 per cent of butchers insured property worth more than £500 – of all the

Table 2.9. *Insurance policies for London trades, 1776–85: mean, median, upper-quartile values and Gini coefficients*

Trade	Number	Median	75%	Mean	Gini
		£	£	£	
Mercers	159	1,200	2,200	1,700	0.43368
Drapers	530	1,000	2,000	1,539	0.47283
Merchants	566	1,000	2,300	1,993	0.53017
Distillers	73	1,000	2,300	1,993	0.55585
Booksellers	129	800	1,400	1,064	0.47653
Brewers	282	700	1,500	1,398	0.59611
Vintners	282	600	1,000	988	0.45284
Pawnbrokers	243	600	1,000	1,025	0.50842
Upholsterers	48	550	1,000	908	0.51290
Haberdashers	504	500	1,000	729	0.47095
Grocers	625	500	900	682	0.43292
Corn dealers	225	500	1,000	908	0.52391
Goldsmiths and silversmiths	235	500	1,000	680	0.45274
Stationers	152	500	1,000	845	0.50188
Apothecaries	248	450	700	544	0.32742
Printers	187	400	1,000	826	0.30479
Coachmakers	138	400	1,000	712	0.49037
Bricklayers	453	400	600	586	0.49313
Victuallers	4,031	400	600	469	0.29070
Coopers	309	400	1,000	891	0.61749
Glaziers	181	400	500	458	0.38537
Plumbers	109	400	600	541	0.37963
Milliners	355	400	600	516	0.42098
Smiths	227	300	600	479	0.46805
Carpenters	1,492	300	600	516	0.47915
Clock and watch makers	322	300	500	381	0.,39605
Jewellers	110	300	500	414	0.42723
Tailors	947	300	500	402	0.43386
Cabinetmakers	481	300	700	554	0.49238
Turners	118	300	500	420	0.37596
Bakers	609	300	500	420	0.33090
Cheesemongers	405	300	500	424	0.34359
Butchers	554	300	400	364	0.40941
Poulterers	81	300	500	409	0.39588
Shoemakers	540	200	400	319	0.40687
Peruke makers	270	200	300	273	0.33704
Fishmongers	62	200	400	384	0.48035
Chandlers	983	200	300	235	0.29517

thirty-eight trades examined, only the shoemakers came below, at 14 per cent, while with haberdashers the figure was 42 per cent, with apothecaries it was 48 per cent and with grocers 35 per cent.

Secondly, the insurance figures tend on the whole to bear out the argument that 'dealers' were better off than manufacturers. Capital-intensive breweries come high on the list, but there were not many breweries, while the far more populous building trades had medians of £400, as did coopers. Smiths, clock and watch makers were only at £300, with the wealthiest quarter of their number entering the scene at £500–£600, compared with £2,000 or more for mercers, drapers or merchants, but wealthier than shoemakers at £400.

Where the insurance figures give a more qualified answer is the question of the inequality between trades. Was there, for instance, a threshold of wealth above which most people could not go? Reproducing the distribution of insured property for all the trades in table 2.9 is impractical for reasons of space, but it bears out what is already shown in that table – that everywhere between two-thirds and three-quarters of the members of a trade were concentrated in the lower range of policy values. In only nine trades was the median value of the policy higher than £500; in fifteen trades it was less than £400. Figure 2.1 demonstrates the pattern for members of four reasonably typical trades: tailors, coopers, coachmakers, and goldsmiths and silversmiths.

Thirdly, the Gini coefficients show that, taking the London trades as a whole, while some trades were wealthier than others, they were not necessarily wealthier because there was a greater proportion of wealthy people at the top of the trade than was the case with poorer trades. The statistics are likely to be particularly misleading in this respect, especially in regard to multiple policies, while others would have had wealth that would not have been insured against fire. Nevertheless, the correlation between the rank order of median wealth for the thirty-eight trades and the rank order of the Gini coefficient of inequality is significant at 0.508, but not very high.[93] This does not apply to all activities covered by the insurance records and in some cases there was a definite tendency that the higher the median the more unequal the trade and the more concentrated the wealth at the top. In the food trades, the median policy value for brewers was £700 with a Gini coefficient of 0.596, while at the bottom came chandlers with a median policy of £200 and a coefficient of 0.295.

---

[93] If mean policy values are taken, thereby taking the wealthiest policy holders into account, then the coefficient is higher, but still only 0.63, which is not high enough to prove the point.

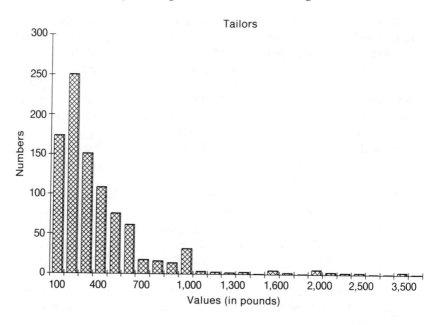

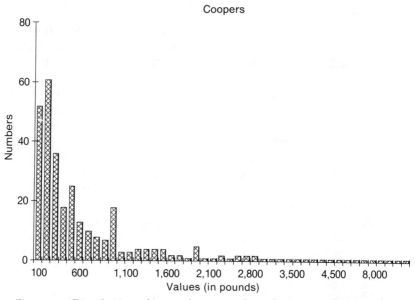

Figure 2.1 Distribution of insured property by value among four London trades, 1775–87

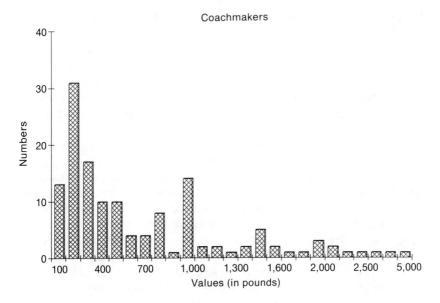

Coachmakers

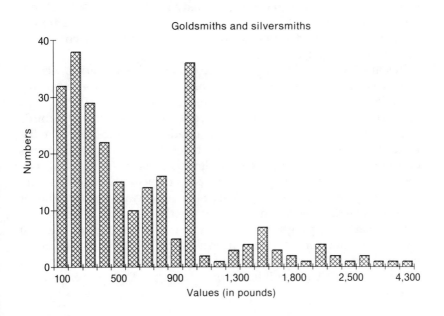

Goldsmiths and silversmiths

Drapers, with a median policy of £1,000 and a coefficient of 0.473, compare with peruke makers at £300 and 0.337. Not many with much money were in peruke making. In other trades, however, the progression was more patchy. Tailors were at £400 and 0.434, which was the same coefficient as mercers, with a median policy value of £1,200. Some trades might not lend themselves to much inequality. Apothecaries stood at £450 and 0.327, one of the lowest coefficients in the list. The pattern is unclear.

In many of the trades there is quite clearly a break in the progression of insured property. Silversmiths are a good example. There were not many of them, but sixteen insured themselves for £400 or less, none insured themselves for £500, one for £600, one for £700, one for £800, none for £900 but as many as five for £1,000. The sample is small but indicative. With printers and with bookbinders the fastest progression of wealth was up to £500, then there was little increase until £900 was reached. Of the printers, 59 per cent, or 110 out of 187, insured themselves for £500 or less. Only sixteen took out policies between £700 and £900, while twenty were insuring themselves for £1,000. Of the 345 bookbinders, 192 went for £500 or less, with well over thirty taking out insurance at the levels of £200, £300, £400 and £500 respectively. The number then dropped. At £600 there were only sixteen, at £700 there were eighteen, at £900 only seven while at £1,000 there were as many as thirty-five. A fair number of bookbinders and printers got as far as £500, and not many got beyond that level, but there was a new threshold of £1,000, which *may* indicate a different order of activity and capitalisation, though future research will be needed to show this.

In some trades the break was not so obvious. Apothecaries, victuallers or watch makers, for instance, had fairly regular progressions, declining gradually in numbers as the figure of £1,000 was approached. What is clear is that everywhere, between two-thirds and three-quarters of the members of a trade were concentrated in the lower range of policy values. One could get into the bottom two-thirds of a trade, but getting beyond that level was difficult, and few succeeded. People clustered on the left side of the various trades in figure 2.1, usually far on the left side. Those that got away were spread over a wide range of values, and stand out clearly.

However, the progression of these trades as regards median wealth was not very different from what it had been in the 1690s, when there is information on those who, in 1692, paid a surtax in addition to their basic poll tax of one shilling.[94] The surtax has been

[94] As n. 79.

mentioned briefly earlier in this chapter, when stressing the importance of shopkeepers. We have information on four groups: where all
paid the surtax, where the majority paid surtax, where less than half
paid surtax and where none paid the surtax. Of the trades considered
by Professor Glass for 1692, thirty-one are listed in table 2.10. Out of
this number, there were fifteen trades where more than half of the
members paid the surtax in 1692, and thirteen of them were in the
wealthier half of the trades during the late eighteenth century. Of the
sixteen trades where, in 1692, the minority of members paid surtax, or
nobody paid surtax at all, fifteen were in the lower half for the
eighteenth century.[95] The detailed fit is of course not so good,
although to a certain extent this is due to the small size of Professor
Glass' samples. The only coachmaker to appear in 1692 paid a surtax,
and no other coachmaker lived in the parishes that were sampled, so
the fact that the insurance policies for coachmakers placed them
sixteenth in rank order does not prove a decline in the status of
coachmakers. The majority of jewellers paid the surtax: they ranked
24th a century later, but there were only three jewellers in the 1692
sample. Furthermore, the insurance records are biased because multiple policies have been omitted. Taken all in all, the overall match is
reasonable enough to lend support to the argument that there was no
enormous overturning of the hierarchies of wealth during these three-
quarters of a century. The hierarchies of the insurance policies also fit
reasonably well with the Elliott and Earle hierarchies.

The pyramid of incomes in London was steeply angled, with a wide
and shallow base, but becoming progressively steeper. The upper
income groups formed only 2–3 per cent of the population; the middle
income groups some 16–21 per cent but, within the latter, the divisions of income were very marked. Most members of the trades
whose insurance policies for the late eighteenth century were examined had little opportunity to rise, possessed the lower limits of capital
necessary to practise their trade; in all the trades examined, the
wealthiest 10 per cent of the members held over a quarter of the
insured wealth (and, considering multiple policies, probably more).
In almost all the trades, the top quarter of the membership held over
half the property insured. The limit on insured property for most
London tradesmen was around £400–£600. To rise above this limit
was unusual. The assessed tax figures, which give 30 per cent of the
taxpayers as being in class III and 22 per cent in class IV, give a false
impression of the progress of the London bourgeoisie. During the late
eighteenth century, some two-thirds of them were at the lower end of

[95] *Ibid.*

Table 2.10. *London occupations: liability for surtax in 1692 compared with rank order of insurance policy values, 1775–87*

All paying surtax			Less than half paying surtax		
	Insurance policies			Insurance policies	
Trade	Rank	Median	Trade	Rank	Median
Coachmakers	16	£400	Bakers	24	£300
Distillers	2	£1,000	Carpenters	24	£300
Haberdashers	10	£500	Glaziers	16	£400
Merchants	2	£1,000	Milliners	16	£400
Vintners	7	£600	Tailors	24	£300
			Victuallers	16	£400
Majority paying surtax			Watch makers	24	£300

Majority paying surtax			None paying surtax		
	Insurance policies				
Trade	Rank	Median			
Apothecaries	15	£450		Insurance policies	
Brewers	6	£700	Trade	Rank	Median
Drapers	2	£1,000	Blacksmiths	24	£300
Goldsmiths	10	£500	Booksellers	5	£800
Grocers	10	£500	Bricklayers	16	£400
Jewellers	24	£300	Cabinetmakers	24	£300
Mercers	1	£1,200	Chandlers	35	£200
Plumbers	16	£400	Coopers	16	£400
Stationers	10	£500	Peruke makers	35	£200
Upholsterers	9	£550	Poulterers	24	£300
			Shoemakers	35	£200

their occupations. Of course, some occupations were wealthier than others. Wealthy barristers, doctors or merchants were very wealthy indeed, but the foothills of these occupations were enormous.

We lack the data for the progression of incomes during the first half of the nineteenth century, but the progression of the late eighteenth century is likely to have been of long standing and not lightly overturned. It did not become easier to set up in business. The figure quoted nationally for the 1830s – and therefore far too low for London – was between £400 and £600 for most trades. Haberdashers, with a higher ratio of capital to turnover, needed between £400 and £800. However, to purchase a really good business would cost at least £1,000. It was all an inexorable rise from the eighteenth century,[96] but

---

[96] D. Alexander, *Retailing in England during the Industrial Revolution* (1970), p. 207. A large sample of insurance policies for industrial and commercial properties in

this was itself a rise from the seventeenth century. Things may have been different in the sixteenth century, if we are to believe Rappaport, but by the late seventeenth century if one wanted to make money one had to begin with money.[97] A century later one had to begin with more money, and by the middle of the nineteenth century one needed yet more.

London produced an arithmetic mean of £233 for 1750–1800 and £298 for 1801–50: S. Pollard, 'The insurance policies', in C. H. Feinstein and S. Pollard (eds.), *Studies in Capital Formation in the United Kingdom, 1750–1920* (Oxford, 1988), pp. 240, 253. This needs to be broken down more before many conclusions can be drawn,

97 Earle, *Making*, pp. 106, 108; S. Rappaport, 'Social structure and mobility in sixteenth-century London', *London Journal*, 10 (1984), pp. 115–23.

PART II

Fluctuations and mortality in the metropolis

The first part of this book has sought to show the composition of the population, its occupations and its wealth. It presents a structural view, stressing continuities. The continuities are indeed striking, whether one is examining the economy, the distribution of wealth, or the social structure in general. During this century and a half London's population increased fivefold, the – retrospectively – compact dual-centred town of 1700 would have appeared to an inhabitant of London in the year of the Great Exhibition to be far distant. But the essential structures of production, the nature of manufacture, the stress on the services had not changed. Neither – industrial revolution or not – had the importance of the Port and the Court, now translated as the City and Westminster.

Nevertheless, the stress on continuities, important though it is, obscures much that took place during this period. This was an era of the 'Second Hundred Years War' with France, an era that began when fear of the plague was still strong – as late as 1720 a particularly horrifying plague would erupt in another port, Marseilles. It was the era when the trade cycle emerged, as well as periodic slumps as strong as anything that the nineteenth century could produce. That is why the second part of this book examines these changes. London changed a great deal. But it was not steam that changed London. By the late eighteenth century London was the fifth or sixth largest user of steam power in the country, but the engines were mostly confined to waterworks, docks, flour mills, breweries and distillers. Some smaller engines were used by foundries and machine makers.[1] They did not spread far from these confines, because there was little demand for them to do so. Economic growth continued, as it did in

[1] Musson, 'Industrial motive power', p. 426; Kanefsky and Robey, 'Steam engines', pp. 161–86.

most of the country, with little reference to steam engines. Seasonal fluctuations and the trade cycle continued unabated, and to Londoners these mattered much more. So did the death rate: the seventeenth-century sink of mortality that called itself London was a much healthier city by the mid nineteenth century. These are the factors that are discussed in the three chapters of part two.

The background to such a discussion is of course the capital's role within the national economy. By European standards England was unusual in having an urban system that was so particularly dominated by London, driven from London and directed towards London: the product, presumably, of an unusual degree of economic integration as well as other factors. This dominance was declining throughout the eighteenth century, but it was still overwhelming.[2] Provincial cities grew rapidly, equalling the population of London in 1750 and having more than double the capital's population in 1801,[3] but London's dominance was such that this cannot – at any rate beyond a point – be analysed in isolation from London as something provincial and autonomous. We may be fairly well acquainted with the effect of cotton on Lancashire and of Lancashire on the national economy, but we know much less about the effect of London on the national economy, about the fluctuations in the capital's growth or – no less important – about the effects of the fluctuations in the national economy on prosperity in London. Throughout the century and a half covered by this book fluctuations in London's prosperity were of much more than local interest and quite capable of moderating national trends. If the capital's economy was depressed and the rest of the country was managing to grow despite the depressing influence of the capital, this might show in national terms as stagnation; conversely, growth in London and stagnation elsewhere would also distort the statistics.

Hence the significance of the urban growth of the second third of the eighteenth century, which affected not only manufacturing towns but also, as Borsay has shown, spas, and towns offering leisure services,[4] and which coincided with slow overall national growth. This was once ascribed to agricultural depression, more recently it has been ascribed to war.[5] It also happened to coincide with a slow period of growth of the capital's economy.

---

[2] de Vries, *European Urbanization*, pp. 28–77; Wrigley, 'A simple model', pp. 44–70.
[3] Corfield, *English Towns*, pp. 10–11.
[4] P. Borsay, *The English Urban Renaissance: Culture and Society in the Provincial Town, 1660–1770* (Oxford, 1989), particularly pp. 16–37. One searches in vain in this book for serious evidence of any long-term depression during this period.
[5] W. A. Cole, 'Factors in demand, 1700–80', in R. Floud and D. N. McCloskey (eds.), *The Economic History of Britain since 1700* (2 vols., Cambridge, 1981), I, p. 53.

Not that this mattered very much to the day-to-day life of most Londoners, whose lives were dominated by the seasons. Production, services and earnings in the capital were obviously not as much dominated by the time of the year and the weather as was agriculture, but the difference was one of degree rather than kind. For many trades there was not even a difference in degree and many hopeful immigrants found that they had exchanged seasonal unemployment in the country for seasonal unemployment in the capital. The matter is important enough to merit a chapter.

Underpinning all the longer-term trends was the growth of population. The long-term growth of pre-industrial cities, with their high death rates and inability to maintain their numbers without massive immigration, depended on the relationship between trade cycles and rural immigration. Rural immigration, in its turn, depended on the production and maintenance of a population that – insofar as foreign trade did not suffice – was sufficiently large to maintain a food surplus for the cities, and a market for the produce of the cities, as well as being able to release labour for immigration to the cities. The preservation of a reasonable level of prosperity for the mass of the inhabitants depended, in its turn, on the migration being dominated by pull rather than push factors, at least in the long run. The maintenance of such a balance was not inevitable. During the sixteenth and much of the seventeenth centuries, most of the immigration appears to have been pushed rather than pulled towards the capital; by the late seventeenth century the catchment area for immigration to London narrowed and pull factors became more important, but it was by no means obvious during the first half of the eighteenth century that this could be combined with continued urban prosperity. This was the last crisis of the demographic *ancien régime*; it faded away in the 1760s as population growth accelerated and London gradually entered a new state of existence, no longer the sink of mortality of the nation.

3

Trends, cycles and wars

The long-run trends

An analysis of long-run trends in the development of the capital's economy for this period must begin with the better statistics that become available during the second decade of the eighteenth century, after the Peace of Utrecht. This appears to have inaugurated a boom; the effect of the bursting of the South Sea Bubble was relatively short-lived, and Defoe, writing during the mid 1720s, would wax eloquent on London's growth:

New squares and new streets rising up every day to such a prodigy of buildings, that nothing in the world does, or ever did equal it, except old Rome in Trajan's time ... We see several villages, formerly standing, as it were, in the country and at a great distance, now joined to the streets by continued buildings, and more making haste to meet in the like manner; for example Deptford ... Islington ... Newington ... Westminster is in a fair way to shake hands with Chelsea, as St. Gyles's is with Marybone ...

It is ... to be observed, as a particular and remarkable crisis, singular to those who write in this age, and very much to our advantage in writing, that the great and more eminent increase of buildings in, and about the city of London, and the vast extent of ground taken in, and now become streets and noble squares of houses, by which the mass, or body of the whole, is become so infinitely great, has been generally made in our time, not only within our memory, but even within a few years.[1]

Even as he was writing, the building boom in London was breaking. Building deeds reached their peak in Middlesex in 1725 and did not return to that level for forty years. Building stagnated between 1724 and 1738, fell quite sharply until 1745, and remained at a very low and depressed level until 1761,[2] as figure 3.1 shows. This pattern was not

---

[1] Defoe, *A Tour*, pp. 286–8, 295.
[2] F. H. W. Sheppard, V. Belcher and P. Cottrell, 'The Middlesex and Yorkshire deeds registries and the study of building fluctuations', *London Journal*, 5 (2), (1979), pp. 176–217.

very obvious in the rest of the country: the index of imported timber – which obviously includes London – does indeed stagnate between 1725 and 1750, but it fails to reflect the fall in London building during the 1740s, suggesting quite vigorous growth in the provinces, while it is climbing steadily from the mid century.

The depression in the capital's building is well known to historians. Summerson had the impression that 'the war period of 1743–8 seems to have witnessed building activity at its lowest ebb'[3] and Chalklin, along with Parry Lewis, suggested – quite correctly – that building in London was at a higher level for a part of the 1720s than it was to be again until the 1760s.[4] What these writers were not in a position to do was to bring other data to bear: coal imports, beer production, and especially the statistics of London's foreign trade. These all show a pattern of stagnation and often depression between the late 1720s and the 1760s. The most significant of them all is that of retained imports. Figure 3.2 separates London and the outports of England and Wales, and it is similar to the building index.[5] There is stagnation in London between 1725 and 1740, a sharp decline between 1740 and 1745, a return to the old level during the next decade, erratic growth from the 1760s, but a higher level is not really achieved until the 1770s. The 21-year moving index is fairly stable from the 1720s until the late 1750s. The outports showed a different pattern: their retained imports were increasing fairly steadily until the 1750s, and faster thereafter. Further support for the view that bad times for London came in 1726 was the peaking of beer production in the metropolis in 1724, with a steady fall thereafter until the early 1740s. It then stabilised for the next three decades, not showing a sustained increase until the 1770s. Of course, beer consumption may well have been affected by the gin mania, so it is an unreliable indicator in itself, but it does fit in with the other evidence.[6]

The specific downturn of 1726 has been explained by Ashton as a routine downturn in the trade cycle, soon coinciding with a war with Spain that began in 1727.[7] What was remarkable was that the subsequent upswing took so long to arrive. The 'great depression' of the

---

[3] Summerson, *Georgian London*, p. 112.

[4] C. W. Chalklin, *The Provincial Towns of Georgian England* (1974), pp. 258–9; J. Parry Lewis, *Building Cycles and Britain's Growth* (1965), pp. 16–17.

[5] C. J. French, 'The trade and shipping of the Port of London, 1700–1776', Exeter University Ph.D. thesis, 1980, pp. 339–54. Retained imports are defined as imports minus re-exports.

[6] The statistics on metropolitan beer production are taken from Mathias, *Brewing Industry*, pp. 544–5.

[7] T. S. Ashton, *Economic Fluctuations in England 1700–1800* (Oxford, 1959), pp. 59, 121–2, 144.

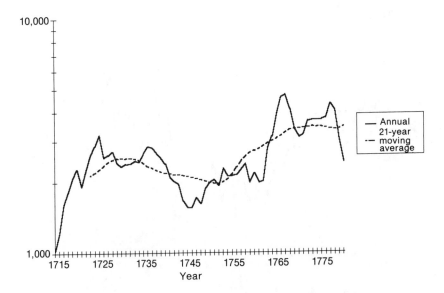

Figure 3.1 London building deeds, 1715–80

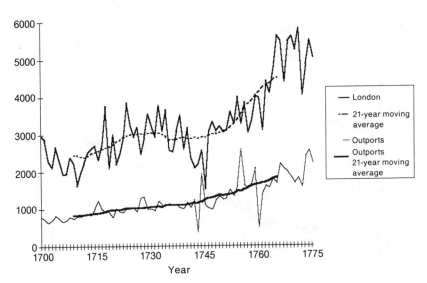

Figure 3.2 Net imports, London and outports, 1700–76 (official values, in thousands of pounds)

D

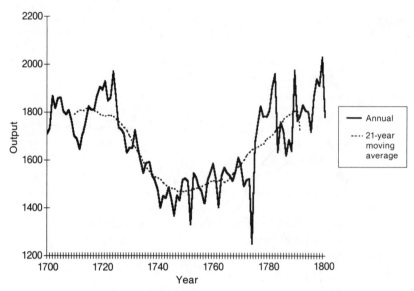

Figure 3.3 Beer production in London, 1700–1800 (thousands of barrels)

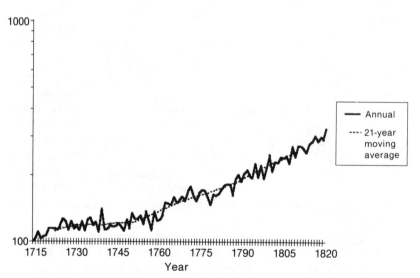

Figure 3.4 Coal imports to Port of London, 1715–1820 (1715 = 100)

eighteenth century has not been studied, and one can only speculate on its causes. The 'agricultural depression' presumably played its part here, but so did London's population. What seems to have happened during the late 1720s and succeeding decades is that the capital's population failed to grow.[8] The reasons for this appear to have been a particularly high death rate during the first half of the eighteenth century – a death rate that may well have been higher than for the generation that followed the Great Plague and was almost certainly higher than for non plague years before the Great Plague – and a reduced catchment area for immigrants to the capital. Figure 3.4, showing coal imports to the capital, supports this argument.[9] In the short run, coal imports were a reflection of the weather, but in the longer run they reflected the size of London's population. They were increasing steadily until 1725, and then stagnated until the 1760s. The pattern is of a general stagnation that began during the 1720s and lasted until the 1760s, if not later, when the capital's population began to grow faster. This is, of course, to some extent compatible with the picture elsewhere. The trade of Liverpool appears to have grown more slowly between the 1720s and the mid century; Chambers found little growth in the Vale of Trent, while Deane and Cole found little growth in the entire country during the two decades ending around 1740–5. Trade grew but slowly between 1720 and 1745; Cole has recently confirmed his original supposition that 'the home market was relatively depressed for much of the period between 1730 and 1750': according to his estimates, domestic per capita consumption was stagnant between 1730 and 1735, declining until 1745 and not exceeding the 1730 level until 1755.[10] One may, however, suspect that the aggregate statistics are biased by the sheer weight of London. Some regions away from London may have been experiencing slow growth, but others did not: this was the period when many of London's staple manufactures, such as framework-knitting or silk twisting, left the capital. The index for imports to London is stagnating or at times even declining, but the combined index for exports and re-exports from the capital shows a steady rise, although the slope for London is a little less steep than for the outports.[11]

London's retained imports were stagnating from 1726, while the outports were expanding. But the stagnation turned into a decline with the outbreak of war in 1739 and the bad harvest, not to say

[8] See below, chapter five.   [9] Mitchell, British Historical Statistics, p. 244.
[10] A. J. Little, Deceleration in the Eighteenth-Century British Economy (1976), p. 56 and refs.; W. A. Cole, in R. Floud and D. N. McCloskey (eds.), The Economic History of Britain since 1700, I, p. 53.
[11] Drawn from French, 'Trade and shipping', pp. 339–54.

dearth, of 1740. Building had begun its decline earlier, falling steadily from 1737 to 1745; imports (whether retained or not) at the Port of London were falling precipitously from 1741 until 1745. This seems to have been a depression that hit London particularly heavily. The national index for imported timber rose steadily during this period; the net imports that came through the outports continued, on the whole, to rise. Furthermore, the recovery took time to come to London. Figure 3.1 shows that building took until the 1760s to recover to the pre-slump levels; net imports recovered a little earlier, but not before the late 1750s. As Summerson wrote, with regard to building, 'a revival was foreshadowed during the fifties, but did not really gather strength until the Peace of Paris, in 1763'.[12] Indeed, much of the increase in retained imports during the 1760s marks a return to the higher level of two decades previously, while a sustained increase in beer production in London awaited the 1770s.

The building revival was clearly underway by the 1760s, though its chronology followed that of the rest of the metropolitan economy. This was the third great wave of building in Georgian London (Georgian, as defined generously by Summerson): the first wave came with the Restoration, the second after the Peace of Utrecht – clearly visible in figure 3.1 – and the third began during the Seven Years War. 'It was slow in breaking, and the peak came ten to fifteen years later. The demand in this instance came from two quarters – from the country gentleman getting a foothold in town and from the citizen migrating to the west end.'[13] Ashton has demonstrated the remarkable extent of the building boom, both in London and elsewhere, from 1764,[14] and the statistics of building deeds do indeed bear this out. It was during this boom that the demand for bricks outran the supply. Their price had increased so greatly, said the *London Chronicle* in 1764, 'that the makers are tempted to mix the slop of the streets, ashes, scavenger's dirt and everything that will make the brick earth or clay go as far as possible'.[15] Or they did the opposite:

The rage or at least hurry of building is so great at present that the bricks are often brought to the bricklayers before they are cold enough to be handled, so that some time ago the floor of a cart loaded with bricks took fire in Golden Lane, Old Street, and was consumed before the bricks could be unloaded.[16]

Net imports, likewise, continued their fairly steady growth, slowly during the 1750s, faster after the Peace of Paris, and stabilising after 1766. The supposed depression in the Atlantic economy is none too

---

[12] Summerson, *Georgian London*, p. 163.   [13] *Ibid.*, p. 24.
[14] Ashton, *Economic Fluctuations*, p. 98.
[15] Quoted *London Life*, p. 84.   [16] *Ibid.*, p. 335, n. 52.

obvious in London's retained imports: it would be more promising to look for it in the outports, whose net imports collapsed during the Seven Years War and had barely regained their pre-war level by the time of the American War. Coal imports to London were rising steadily from the 1760s, and even brewing was on the increase by the 1770s.

This growth was interrupted, but not greatly interrupted, during the 1790s. Before then, building showed a cyclical downturn during the late 1770s, but soon recovered. Beer production fell a few years later. It was a pattern that was repeated in the 1790s. But the depression during these years appears to have been confined to individual sectors – the slumps in building and brewing, for instance, did not coincide – while for most of the time trade was continuing to grow. Building obviously did suffer during wartime; in London it did not return to its level of 1790–2 until 1804, and it fell to that level again in 1815. However, trade seems to have suffered less. There are no figures for retained imports comparable with the early years of the eighteenth century, although figure 3.5, giving the much interrupted data for tonnage entering the Port of London, suggests reasonable long-term growth, even at a slower rate than previously. None of this is very out of line with what is known of national trends.

The depression during a large part of the second decade of the nineteenth century, and the strong boom of the early 1820s, is likewise unsurprising. What is surprising, however, is the extent of the stagnation that followed the collapse of the 1826 boom. Nationally, the years between 1826 and 1842 were rather dismal: strong downswings in 1826, 1837 and 1842, indifferent recoveries between 1827 and 1832 and between 1838 and 1840, with reasonable booms only in 1833–7 and, in some regions, 1839.[17] London appears to have been one of the regions that suffered this period particularly badly. The stagnation did not last as long, or descend as deeply and long into actual depression, as during the early eighteenth century, but the similarities are obvious with trade, as well as with building.

The trade statistics for the Port of London are rather inadequate. There is a Parliamentary Paper summarising the tonnage of ships entering and leaving the Port[18] but it cannot distinguish re-exports from exports and – needless to say – it does not give values. However, it has its uses and figure 3.6 shows the movement in the volume of imports between 1816 and 1850, along with Imlah's figures of the total

---

17 R. C. O. Matthews, *A Study in Trade-Cycle History* (Cambridge, 1954), p. 2.
18 P.P. 1851, 52, pp. 214–17. *Returns Showing the Number of Vessels and Tonnage Entered Inwards and Cleared Outwards at Each of the Twelve Principal Ports of the United Kingdom.*

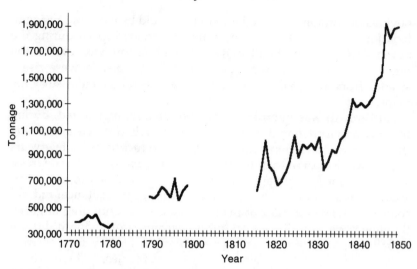

Figure 3.5 Tonnage of shipping entering Port of London, 1772–1850

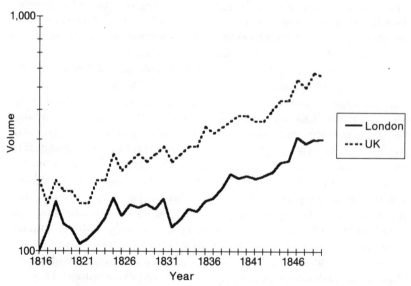

Figure 3.6 Inward volumes, Port of London and UK, 1816–50 (London
1816 = 100, UK 1816 = 200)

volume of UK imports.[19] The figures show clearly, first of all, that foreign trade in the rest of the country was growing faster than in London and, secondly, the stagnation in imports to London between 1825 and 1836. As is well known, the movement in the volume of trade during this period is a questionable device, the terms of trade moving so steadily against the UK. Other things being equal, this would have been deflationary. In London other things were not equal. They tended to be worse.

Cairncross and Weber analysed the building statistics in 1956 and one cannot do better than to repeat their summary:

> The main feature of the series for London is the extraordinarily sharp depression which followed the boom of 1825. The upswing from 1817 to the peak of 1819 was similar to that in the rest of the country. The ensuing depression in London was apparently relatively mild ... and it was followed by a boom of dimensions even larger than elsewhere. The reaction, however, was far more severe, and apart from a slight check in 1828–9 continued until 1832. By contrast the worst appears to have been over in the rest of the country by 1828, although a slight fall took place before the trough was reached in 1832. The decline in London over the years 1825–32 amounts almost to a secular drop to a lower level of activity, so much so that even in 1847 brick production did not regain the level reached from 1822 to 1826.[20]

Figure 3.7 slightly modifies this picture: there is little in the way of a recovery in 1828–9, and the upswing began not in 1832 but in 1836, although the 1825 level was regained in 1848. Cairncross and Weber suggested that the slump was caused by overbuilding during the 1820s.[21] The trade statistics suggest that the depression was more deep seated and again invite comparison with the 1740s. This time population growth was rapid and continuous: there is no obvious monocausal culprit.

We should be wary of overdoing the extent of the boom in London after 1835–50. First of all, the rest of the country was growing more quickly. Secondly, London's growth rates were, over the long run, unimpressive by the standards of the late eighteenth century. The war marked a watershed. Figure 3.8, showing a 21-year moving average for annual growth rates, makes the argument clearer. Ignoring the cyclical pattern (which may be partly the fault of the statistical method employed) there are two clear troughs in growth rates: 1730–50 and 1818–38. The first period was the worse, because growth rates were

[19] A. H. Imlah, *Economic Elements in the Pax Britannica* (Cambridge, Mass., 1958), pp. 94–8, 205–7.
[20] A. K. Cairncross and B. Weber, 'Fluctuations in building in Great Britain, 1785–1849', reprinted in E. M. Carus-Wilson (ed.), *Essays in Economic History* (1962), III, pp. 326–7.
[21] *Ibid.*, pp. 330–1.

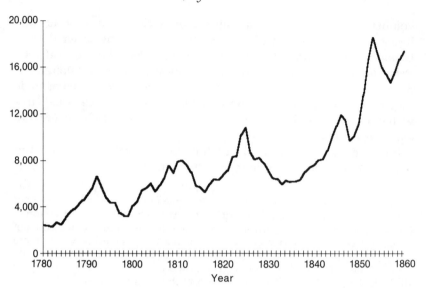

Figure 3.7 London building deeds, 1780–1860

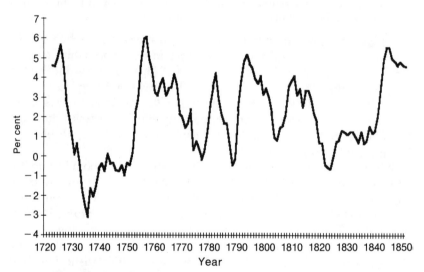

Figure 3.8 Growth rate of London building deeds, 1720–1850
(21-year moving average)

negative for much of the time; during the nineteenth century growth rates were positive, if low. But it took until the 1840s for growth rates to return to a level common during the second half of the eighteenth century. The crude statistics of tonnage entering the Port of London show a similar pattern: volumes were increasing, but the growth rate fell rapidly after 1800, and did not return to that level until the 1840s.

That the metropolitan economy was growing more slowly between 1800 and 1840 than during the second half of the eighteenth century is not an argument that is easy to accept. The latest figures of national output show a persistent acceleration in growth: from 1700 to 1780 national production was growing at 0.7 per cent per annum, between 1780 and 1801 at 1.32 per cent and between 1801 and 1831 at 1.97 per cent.[22] If the figures quoted above were to be taken at their face value, one would expect more contemporary evidence and discussion on the subject. So the argument is not strong, but it does suggest a certain caution in making assumptions about accelerating growth rates in all major regions of the country during the nineteenth century.

What is less surprising is that the rest of England should be growing faster than the capital. The national brick index (the only one long enough for 21-year moving averages) suggests a continuous divergence between the growth rates of building in the capital and the rest of the country – but only from 1818. Figures 3.5 and 3.6 suggest – likewise – that foreign trade grew at a similar rate in London and the outports between the 1790s and the battle of Waterloo, and then diverged. This is quite compatible with other evidence. By 1850 the Port of Liverpool was handling as great a volume of foreign trade as London. The recent calculations of McCloskey suggest that productivity in the 'modernised sectors' of cottons, worsted, woollens, iron, canals, railways and shipping was expanding between 1780 and 1860 at an annual average rate of 1.8 per cent per annum, agriculture at 0.45 per cent and 'all other sectors' at a mere 0.65 per cent.[23]

The main outlines of the capital's growth are reasonably clear. What must now be analysed in more detail is the nature and frequency of cyclical fluctuations. Life was not lived in the long run: how frequent were the years of slump, the years of boom, how intense were the year by year fluctuations and what lay behind these fluctuations? As the next section illustrates, the answer lies in the

---

22 N. F. R. Crafts, *British Economic Growth during the Industrial Revolution* (Oxford, 1985), p. 45.
23 Floud and McCloskey, *Economic History of Britain*, I, p. 114.

relationship of an incipient trade cycle with regular financial crises and, more particularly, with wars.

Cycles and wars

During the nineteenth century there was a reasonably clear trade cycle which usually applied to London as much as to the rest of the country; during the eighteenth century incipient cycles were so frequently interrupted by the outbreak of war as to be much more difficult to discern, while the national economy was less integrated. The various indices – trade, building, high finance – share the obvious drawback of relating only to their own sector of the economy; the index of bankruptcies constructed by Hoppit for the eighteenth century is the sole index to give a more general picture. Separate figures are available for London.[24] Since the number of firms at risk from bankruptcy was increasing, the series must be detrended and Hoppit has done so by a 61-quarter moving average. The drawback of a moving average of this length is, first of all, that since the data ends in 1800 the crises of 1793 and 1797 are omitted. Secondly, there is a methodological problem: if there are two crises within the sixty-one quarters – and this was usually the case – the larger crisis may well swamp the smaller crisis. For this reason, figure 3.9 shows the annual variations from a 7-year moving average. Acceptable data begins in 1708, so detrended years are available between 1711 and 1797. These point to a very high peak of bankruptcies in 1726 as well as periods with relatively high levels of bankruptcy during the early 1740s, the mid 1750s, the early and late 1770s. For something a little more systematic, figure 3.10 has followed Wrigley and Schofield's principle of dividing crisis into three categories, depending on the extent of their deviation from the trend, but has not followed their categorisation precisely: in this case a one-star peak or trough of bankruptcy is defined when bankruptcies were 15–19 per cent above or below trend, a two-star crisis when 20–29 per cent above or below trend and a

[24] J. Hoppit, *Risk and Failure in English Business, 1700–1800* (Cambridge, 1987). I would like to thank Dr Hoppit for kindly making available to me his processed data on bankruptcies in London and the provinces. For high finance, see P. E. Mirowski, 'The rise (and retreat) of a market: English joint stock shares in the eighteenth century', *J. Econ. Hist.*, 41 (1981), pp. 559–77 and P. E. Mirowski, 'Adam Smith, empiricism, and the rate of profit in eighteenth-century England', *History of Political Economy*, 14 (1982), pp. 178–98. The whole question of the existence of a trade cycle in eighteenth-century England is discussed by Hoppit, *Risk and Failure*, pp. 116–21, where the arguments of Mirowski are particularly criticised.

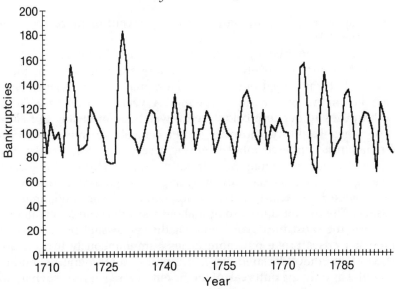

Figure 3.9 Bankruptcies in London, 1710–97 (annual percentage deviation from 7-year moving averages)

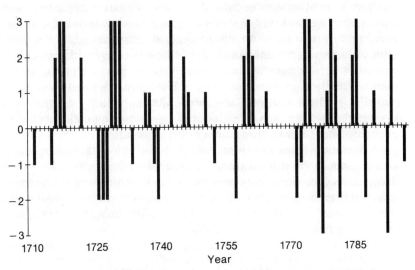

Figure 3.10 Peaks and troughs in London bankruptcies (1–3 stars), 1710–97

three-star crisis when the figure was 30 per cent or more above or below trend.[25]

Figure 3.10 must be regarded with some care. In the first place, a peak in bankruptcy is likely to be followed by a trough, with the more vulnerable firms wiped out; the survivors may not necessarily have been booming, but merely surviving. A year such as 1794, with bankruptcies 19 per cent below trend, was therefore likely to follow 1793, when bankruptcies were 51 per cent above trend. Such an alternation is rendered more likely by a second factor, namely the choice of a moving average to detrend the series. Thirdly, the data is missing for 1723 and 1724. However, the overall pattern is fairly clear. There were two factors that produced crises – wars and financial crashes. The former often brought about the latter: the outbreak of a war was the most important cause of the major slumps. Wars and three-star crises broke out more or less simultaneously in 1739–40, 1778 (when France declared war in support of the Americans) and in 1793. It was only the outbreak of the Seven Years War in 1756 that did not produce such a crisis, with bankruptcies being precisely on trend, but this was a war that had been anticipated for some time.[26] If a three-star crisis erupted in peacetime it was usually financial in origin, but there were at least three financial crises that barely caused a ripple in the aggregate bankruptcy statistics: 1745, which was only a one-star crisis, 1761, which rated no star at all, and – surprisingly – the most notorious crisis of all, the South Sea Bubble of 1720, which does not appear either – reflecting the relatively weak links of public sector finance with the rest of the economy.[27] However, the financial crisis of 1726 did produce a three-star crisis – although the 1726 crisis was precipitated by fear of war with Spain[28] – as did the crashes of 1772 and 1788. That of 1797 produced a two-star crisis.

While the outbreak of a war tended to produce a three-star crisis, recovery could be quite rapid, although rarely to the extent of a three-star boom. There was only one such boom during wartime, in 1780, but there were eight in peacetime: 1717–18, 1729–31, 1774–5 and 1786. Two-star booms occurred about as often in war – 1743, 1760, 1761 – as in peace – 1718, 1722, 1785–6.

---

[25] E. A. Wrigley and R. S. Schofield, *The Population History of England, 1541–1871. A Reconstruction* (1981), p. 333; see below, p. 145; Wrigley and Schofield use a 25-year moving average, and their one-star crises are 10 per cent or more above trend.

[26] Hoppit, *Risk and Failure*, pp. 122–30.

[27] Hoppit, *Risk and Failure*, pp. 130–9; J. Hoppit, 'Financial crises in eighteenth-century England', *Econ. Hist. Rev.*, 39 (1986), pp. 47–8.

[28] Hoppit, 'Financial crises', p. 49.

Table 3.1. *Peaks of bankruptcy in London and provincial England,*
1708–1800

3-star			2-star (120–9%)			1-star (115–19%)		
(130% and more) London	Provinces		London	Provinces		London	Provinces	
1726	136	111	1711	120	80	1719	117	87
1727	140	114	1715	124	48	1745	115	73
1728	133	114	1734	121	92	1748	118	107
1740	131	88	1739	120	79	1773	119	121
1772	141	117	1753	121	93	1796	115	80
1777	136	98	1758	128	130			
1778	153	130	1782	127	99			
1788	141	98	1797	122	115			
1793	151	177						

Provincial peaks:	London	Provinces
3-star (mean)	140	116 N=9
2-star (mean)	123	92 N=8
1-star (mean)	117	94 N=5

The pattern of crises in London and the rest of the country was
different. Hoppit's view is that, nationally, there were extreme fluctuations in bankruptcy between 1708 (when good data begins) and
1734, but from then until the 1770s things were more settled. After
1770 there were more violent short-term peaks.[29] However, in
London there was a three-star peak of bankruptcies in 1740, but there
was no such peak in the provinces, which had also escaped the slump
of 1726 to endure instead a three-star crisis in 1728. Thereafter, three-
star crises were absent until the 1770s, when economic life was
accelerating and major peaks in bankruptcy were accompanying that
acceleration. The middle years of the century were somewhat calmer
for all the country – calmer, that is, by comparison with what came
before and would come later. The underlying growth rate in London
may have been slow, but it was relatively stable. And the early 1760s
produced an exceptional crop of good years. Table 3.1 gives the details
of the crises, as well as showing that crises in London rarely coincided
with crises outside the capital.

An upsurge of bankruptcy in London did not necessarily infect the
rest of the country. Sometimes it might, but the links were by no

---

[29] Hoppit, *Risk and Failure*, p. 106.

Table 3.2. *Trade cycles in England, 1785–1855*

Peak	Trough	Amplitude
1785	1788	–
1792	1793	4.53
1796	1797	6.07
1800	1801	7.43
1802	1803	3.93
1805	1808	1.26
1811	1814	3.60
1815	1816	4.04
1818	1819	2.72
1825	1826	3.39
1828	1829	5.12
1830	1832	2.92
1836	1837	2.91
1839	1842	4.30
1845	1847	5.54
1853	1855	3.30

means systematic. The reverse was also the case: provincial peaks did not necessarily produce peaks in London.

Hoppit's data on bankruptcy is only available until the end of the eighteenth century; from then we have Aldcroft and Fearon's summary of trade cycles in the UK, while data specifically for London is in some respects sparser. Aldcroft and Fearon's summary for the years between 1785 and 1855 is shown in table 3.2.[30]

London followed this pattern, but not always precisely. As argued earlier, the depression in building that followed the boom of 1825 was particularly severe, with little recovery until 1836 and in some respects not until the late 1840s. The volume of imports also stagnated between 1825 and 1836. The recovery in building was relatively steady, although unexciting, until the late 1840s; imports, however, were climbing steadily, except for a hiatus – not really a slump – in the early 1840s. The previous section showed London to have been out of step for a good decade from 1826; otherwise it followed the trend.

There is no reason to believe that nineteenth-century crises were any worse than those of the eighteenth century: it would indeed have been difficult to have exceeded the severity of eighteenth-century crises, with the interruptions of war so often combining with interruptions to the flow of credit. But wars also had obvious and serious

[30] D. H. Aldcroft and P. Fearon, *British Economic Fluctuations, 1790–1939* (1972), p. 12.

effects on the labour market, both in the short and the medium term, and the next section will consider these. A slump in wartime was a serious matter, but the demands of the armed forces for manpower made it less serious than in peacetime. The next section examines this in more detail.

Wars and recruitment

Recruitment for a major war tightened the labour market enormously. When war coincided with a boom, there was the nearest approach to full employment that the age knew. But if there was a slump – and the outbreak of a war usually brought about a slump – then recruitment eased the overall level of male unemployment, but did not prevent it. Even if all the unemployed had been willing to join the armed forces – and it was notorious that many were deeply reluctant to do so – they had to meet the minimum requirements for health and height. After a while economic conditions improved, and recruitment then became more difficult. Finally, when a war ended, the survivors were unceremoniously dumped on to the labour market and caused a crime wave. Magistrates and parish constables, glad to rid themselves of their more unwelcome parishioners on the outbreak of a war, dreaded the outbreak of peace, regarding this as an evil only a little less fearful than a French invasion. In the capital, the crime wave was usually impressive: 'not only pickpockets but street-robbers and highwaymen, are grown to a great pitch of insolence at this time, robbing in gang, defying authority, and often rescuing their companions and carrying them off in triumph', as was lamented in 1748 and would be lamented again and again.[31] Some 157,000 men were discharged in 1713 and 1714, 79,000 in 1749 and 1750, 155,000 in 1764–5, 160,000 in 1784–5 and 350,000 after 1815. As a proportion of the adult male population of England and Wales this varied from between 4 to 5 per cent in the mid eighteenth century, to 10 per cent after the Peace of Utrecht and some 12 per cent after the battle of Waterloo.[32]

The statistics of the strength of the armed forces during this period are however of little value for historians seeking to consider the pressures that recruitment put on the labour market. Parliament voted for a military establishment of a certain size, and the army and navy then sought to recruit up to this level. Usually they failed, and sometimes they failed badly. For some years there are figures of the

[31] J. M. Beattie, *Crime and the Courts in England 1660–1800* (Oxford, 1986), pp. 213–35.
[32] *Ibid.*, p. 226n; D. Hay, 'War, dearth and theft in the eighteenth century: the records of the English courts', *Past and Present*, 95 (1982), p. 138.

number of men raised for the Regular Army, but these omit para-
military forces such as the militia or, during the Napoleonic Wars, the
Army of Reserve. Even with these limitations, they show the gap
between what was permitted and what was achieved. This gap was
not usually as enormous as in 1708, when the army was permitted to
recruit 18,657 men but only got hold of 868.[33] In 1777, a year of
'moderate prosperity', the army wanted 15,000 recruits and got 6,000.
The economic climate then took a turn for the worse[34] and 24,000 men
were picked up in 1778, the number then falling to 16,000 a year
during the succeeding two years, leaving the army short of 27,000
men in 1780.[35] The figures for the navy are just as deceptive, perhaps
more so, since the navy needed to be more selective with the recruits
that it could accept. Turnover was not always as drastic as it was after
the outbreak of war in 1739 when, in the course of sixteen months, the
navy received 26,521 men, discharged 19,354 for one reason or
another, had another 2,360 die and 2,143 desert – a total of nine-tenths
of those who initially joined.[36]

To make matters worse, even the official figures conflict. The latest
figures, compiled by Floud, Wachter and Gregory, are frequently
different from the data given from other, supposedly impeccable,
sources, although the trend is usually very similar. The bureaucracy
of the War Office is familiar to historians. For these reasons, table 3.3,
which gives the available statistics for manpower raised during the
wars, must be viewed with considerable caution.

When wartime coincided with a boom, the difficulties of recruitment were manifest:

The five hundred and Twenty Four Men that were sent from the Nore ... to
Man Mr. Vernon's Squadron, are distributed on board them, but surely there
never was such Wretches, many of them Boys of fourteen or fifteen years of
Age, ... and some upwards of Sixty or Seventy, but that is not the worst, for I
believe there are above one Hundred of them that must be Turned away,
being Bursten, full of the Pox, Itch, Lame, King's Evil, and all other Distem-
pers, from the Hospitals in London, and will serve only to breed an Infection
in the Ships; for the rest, most of them are Thieves, House breakers, Newgate
Birds, and the very filth of London ... In all the former Warrs I never saw a
parcell of Turn'd over Men half so bad, in short they are so very bad, that I
don't know how to describe it.[37]

[33] Scouller, *The Armies of Queen Anne*, pp. 111–15.
[34] Ashton, *Economic Fluctuations*, pp. 161–2.
[35] P. Mackesy, *The War for America, 1775–1783* (1964), pp. 110, 526. The figures exclude
militia and fencibles.
[36] D. A. Baugh, *British Naval Administration in the Age of Walpole* (Princeton, 1965),
p. 186.
[37] Admiral Cavendish to Admiralty, 20 July 1739, quoted in Baugh, *British Naval
Administration*, p. 165.

Table 3.3. *Recruitment for wartime, 1701–1815*

	Army establishment	Army effectives	Army recruits	Navy borne
1701	22,725	–		20,916
1702	52,396	30,369	–	38,874
1703	63,396	35,659	–	43,397
1704	70,475	36,256	–	38,873
1705	71,411	36,994	–	45,807
1706	77,345	41,429	–	48,346
1707	94,130	40,556	–	44,508
1708	91,188	40,274	–	47,138
1709	102,642	42,851	–	48,344
1710	113,268	42,236	–	48,072
1711	138,882	–	–	–
1712	144,650	–	–	–
1713	24,400	–	–	–
1714	16,347	–	–	49,860
1715	18,851	–	–	13,475
1716	–	–	–	13,827
1717	–	–	–	13,806
1718	16,347	–	–	15,268
1719	17,886	–	–	19,611
1720	19,500	–	–	21,118
1721	19,840	–	–	15,070
1722	19,840	–	–	10,122
1723	23,840	–	–	8,078
1724	23,810	–	–	7,037
1725	23,810	–	–	6,298
1726	23,772	–	–	16,872
1727	32,058	–	–	20,697
1728	28,501	–	–	14,917
1729	28,882	–	–	14,859
1730	23,836	–	–	9,687
1731	23,756	–	–	11,133
1732	23,756	–	–	8,360
1733	23,756	–	–	9,684
1734	25,634	–	–	–
1735	34,354	–	–	–
1736	26,314	–	–	–
1737	26,314	–	–	–
1738	26,896	–	–	17,668
1739	26,896	–	–	23,604
1740	40,859	–	–	37,181
1741	53,395	–	–	43,329
1742	51,044	–	–	40,479
1743	51,696	–	–	44,342
1744	53,538	–	–	47,202
1745	53,128	–	–	46,766
1746	77,664	–	–	59,750

Table 3.3. (*cont.*)

	Army establishment	Army effectives	Army recruits	Navy borne
1747	61,471	–	–	51,191
1748	64,966	–	–	44,861
1749	28,399	–	–	–
1750	29,194	–	–	–
1751	29,132	–	–	–
1752	29,132	–	–	–
1753	29,132	–	–	–
1754	29,132	–	–	10,149
1755	31,422	–	–	33,612
1756	47,488	–	–	52,809
1757	68,791	–	–	63,259
1758	88,370	–	–	70,518
1759	91,446	–	–	84,464
1760	99,044	–	–	85,658
1761	105,221	–	–	80,675
1762	120,633	–	–	84,797
1763	120,419	–	–	75,988
1764	31,773	–	–	17,424
1765	31,654	–	–	15,863
1766	31,752	–	–	15,863
1767	31,701	–	–	13,513
1768	31,700	–	–	13,424
1769	31,589	–	–	13,738
1770	30,949	–	–	14,744
1771	43,546	–	–	26,416
1772	30,641	–	–	27,165
1773	30,641	–	–	22,018
1774	30,641	20,443	–	18,372
1775	30,641	33,190	3,575	15,230
1776	50,234	33,897	11,863	23,914
1777	80,669	48,242	6,082	46,231
1778	82,995	53,302	23,978	62,719
1779	115,863	81,086	16,165	80,275
1780	122,677	88,034	15,233	91,566
1781	128,459	90,867	–	98,269
1782	131,989	89,336	–	93,168
1783	124,254	90,395	–	107,446
1784	30,680	–	–	39,268
1785	29,557	25,767	–	22,826
1786	33,544	26,465	–	13,737
1787	35,544	26,842	–	14,514
1788	32,117	29,174	–	15,964
1789	38,592	33,682	–	18,397
1790	38,784	34,207	–	20,025
1791	59,772	38,171	–	38,801
1792	56,859	36,557	–	16,613

Table 3.3. (*cont.*)

	Army establishment	Army effectives	Army recruits	Navy borne
1793	157,396	38,945	17,033	69,868
1794	211,893	85,097	38,563	87,331
1795	337,189	124,262	40,463	96,001
1796	251,316	111,996	16,336	114,365
1797	259,985	104,862	16,096	118,788
1798	269,582	102,563	21,457	122,687
1799	273,117	115,252	41,316	128,930
1800	245,811	169,428	17,829	126,192
1801	218,504	184,274	10,698	125,061
1802	208,668	196,156	7,403	129,340
1803	211,216	126,673	11,253	49,340
1804	308,085	185,127	11,088	84,431
1805	304,848	200,320	33,545	109,205
1806	326,744	213,314	20,677	111,237
1807	335,132	229,470	30,592	119,855
1808	359,315	258,062	30,592	140,822
1809	366,343	266,371	22,350	141,989
1810	368,346	269,631	22,350	142,098
1811	369,355	266,247	22,925	130,866
1812	371,527	278,307	24,359	131,087
1813	385,558	291,783	19,980	130,127
1814	394,351	301,730	13,564	–
1815	275,392	247,113	15,279	–

Source: Army establishment, R. Floud, K. Wachter, A. Gregory, *Height, Health and History. Nutritional Status in the United Kingdom, 1750–1980* (Cambridge, 1990), pp. 44–9. There are certain differences from hitherto standard sources, such as that of the army establishment, 1701–14 (R. E. Scouller, *The Armies of Queen Anne* (Oxford, 1966), pp. 344–9) and the army establishment from 1720 in C. M. Clode, *The Military Forces of the Crown* (1869), I, pp. 398–400. For men mustered 1702–10: J. Hattendorf, *England in the War of the Spanish Succession* (1987), p. 141. Men raised for army, 1794–1806: Clode, *Military Forces*, II, p. 593. Regular Army recruitment 1774–80: P. Mackesy, *The War for America, 1775–1783* (1964), p. 526; during the period 1775–83 the figures actually run from September to August; they have been ascribed to the year in which January falls. Navy, men borne: C. Lloyd, *The British Seaman* (1968), pp. 261–3.

But as there were slumps as well as booms, historians now tend to play down these more extreme assertions. Not all magistrates were like Falstaff and Shallow, otherwise the ships would never have taken to sea and the armies would never have fought. Scotland and Ireland provided helpful reservoirs of manpower, but many men still came from England, and their recruitment helped to tighten up the labour market everywhere, including London.

Although the military effort for the War of the Spanish Succession and the Seven Years War may have been comparable with that for the Revolutionary and Napoleonic Wars – in 1714 some 155,000 men were discharged, compared with 350,000 in 1815, but the population had doubled during the intervening century – it is the latter war that is best documented. The labour shortage caused by a combination of heavy recruitment and an economic boom quite justified Malthus' surprise in 1797, after four years of war, that his *Essay on Population* should be taken seriously: the book 'came before the public . . . at a time when there would be an extraordinary demand for men, and very little disposition to suppose the possibility of any evil arising from the redundancy of population', as he was to admit in 1817.[38] A few months earlier, at the end of 1796, recruits to the militia in London were given £21 on joining:[39] about eight months' income for a fully-employed labourer in 1790 and still some seven months' income in 1796.[40] This was the year when the government sought to raise another 60,000 men for the supplementary militia but could not get them. In 1799 the Lord Lieutenant of Middlesex refused to disband the Middlesex militia, despite the expense of keeping them under arms, because once disbanded it would be impossible to recall them later.[41] June 1800, supposed to be a depressed period for building, saw complaints of labour shortage at the building of the docks and canal at Blackwall and Limehouse. 'Years may pass', said the correspondent,

before this trifling number can complete the job. It may be said that war has made hands scarce: this is true, but I think an easy arrangement might make war favourable to rapid execution. Our numerous militia, who are sauntering about the kingdom in listless idleness (at all times, except harvest) might here be usefully employed.[42]

1804 saw renewed complaints of a shortage of labour for building the docks,[43] while the London Dock Company, in a desperate hurry to complete its works, tried to make the builders work not only in December, which was expensive and not very productive, but also on Sundays, which led the Bishop of London to threaten prosecution.[44]

---

[38] T. R. Malthus, *An Essay on the Principles of Population* (5th ed., 1817), p. xi.
[39] This figure is based on 553 returns and certificates of recruitment in the G.L.R.O.: MA/MN 196, 197, 198.
[40] For wage rates, see below, p. 170.
[41] J. R. Western, *The English Militia in the Eighteenth Century* (1965), p. 284.
[42] Anonymous correspondent in *Commercial and Agricultural Magazine*, 2, 10 June 1800, pp. 388–9.
[43] *Annual Register*, 1804, p. 353.
[44] London Dock Company, *Minutes*, I, pp. 387–8.

The price of substitutes in Middlesex for the Army of Reserve, a body intended only for home defence, varied in that year between £30 and £60.[45]

The memory of the 1808–9 recruitment campaign, when bounties climbed ever higher as the economic boom progressed, to reach forty guineas in Gloucestershire and £50–£60 in Forfar in Scotland, lingered for long enough to be embodied in subsequent legend, so that an Irish shoemaker could write, many years later, that the high bounties produced among London shoemakers

what was commonly called 'pair-making', which was to come into all parts of the country where the highest bounties were offered for substitutes, receive the bounty and then decamp with the spoil, to re-enact the same glorious feat in some distant locality. To such an extent was this practice become a terror in every part of the country that the pair-making tramps were in the end obliged to resort to the expedient of disguising their persons as farm-labourers, in smock-frocks and hobnailed boots.[46]

But this all came to an end by 1811. Recruitment in a boom produced a labour shortage; when there was a serious slump, recruitment was not enough to prevent unemployment.[47] Recovery after 1812 did not see a return to earlier levels of employment, and in 1815 some 350,000 men were demobilised, mostly on to the unskilled and semi-skilled labour market. Recruitment did not by itself produce a labour shortage unless there was a boom, although a boom in peacetime was unlikely to produce a labour shortage. It did not override the trend or the cycle, but it was a most crucial influence on the labour market.

The rest of the country and London

London was at the peak of its influence during the first half of the seventeenth century. From then, until around the middle of the nineteenth century if not later, its influence was declining. Other towns and regions were growing more quickly, industries left London, other ports expanded more quickly. The pace of provincial

---

[45] J. W. Fortescue, *The County Lieutenancies and the Army, 1803–1814* (1909), p. 70.

[46] O'Neill, 'Fifty years' experience', I, 295–26.

[47] A. D. Gayer, W. W. Rostow and A. J. Schwarz, *The Growth and Fluctuation of the British Economy, 1790–1850* (1953), I, pp. 8, 109; 'There had been some unemployment in 1793, 1797, 1803 and 1807–8; but that of 1811 was, so far as one can judge from the qualitative evidence available, on a much larger scale than on previous occasions within our period.' Floud, Wachter and Gregory, *Height, Health and History*, pp. 72–3, 77 suggest that the most serious recruitment problems for the army were between 1807 and 1814. This may have been partly a function of the sheer size of the armed forces. It is also not easy to reconcile with the larger gap between establishment and effectives during the 1790s, when the army was smaller: *ibid.*, p. 50.

life was quickening; London continued to dominate, but less absolutely than hitherto. The relative decline was not an even process, and it took a particularly large step during the early eighteenth century. The 'great depression' of eighteenth-century London began abruptly in 1726 and did not lift fully for some thirty years or even more. The rest of England saw uneven economic progress, but as a whole its progress was considerably faster than was the case in London. To a certain extent the divergence of provincial England was bound to occur – the capital's dominance during the early seventeenth century was too great to be sustained for ever. But the chronology of this divergence was not inevitable. London's population growth slowed down during the second half of the seventeenth century, but so did that of the rest of the country, and the capital's dominance was not seriously affected until the slower growth that appears to have begun there during the second quarter of the eighteenth century. Whatever depression there may have been in England during that quarter of a century, London appears to have felt it at least as badly and, what is more, felt it for longer. Net imports to the Port of London were not really on a rising trend until the late 1750s, its building not until the 1760s, while beer production took until the 1770s to be rising safely.

By the last quarter of the eighteenth century, London's economy seems to have been expanding healthily enough, although not as healthily as the industrialising regions. Wherever there is data for this period, the suggestion is of increases in production – though, since population was increasing rapidly, there may not necessarily have been an increase in per capita production, a conclusion not incompatible with what is known of real wage rates, at least up to 1815, or with the macro-economic suggestions of McCloskey and Crafts.

The second great divergence of London took place during the 1820s and 1830s, especially after 1826. There was growth, but it was less than the national average, and it took until the 1840s for this slower growth to end. Trade cycles in the capital were co-ordinated with what was happening in the rest of the country, but the trend was not. The slower growth may have begun rather earlier. That London's growth rate was slower between 1800 and 1840 than during the second half of the eighteenth century, which is the implication of the data, is difficult to accept, but that the capital's economy was growing more slowly than the national average is more acceptable.

But the trend and the cycle co-existed with very marked seasonal fluctuations. The importance of the latter is such that they merit a separate chapter.

4

Seasonal fluctuations

The pattern of seasonality

The long-term trend – even the cycle – was of far less importance to the daily lives of Londoners than were seasonal fluctuations in employment. Such fluctuations were inevitable. A mass market was insufficiently developed; the means of production and of transport were geared closely to the weather. Ships depended on the winds, while their cargoes might depend on the harvests of other countries; the food processing industries awaited the harvests, the sugar refineries awaited the West India fleet, the luxury trade and a host of services awaited the London Season.[1]

The effects of these fluctuations, although less widely felt in towns than in the countryside, were more marked than in the late nineteenth century, when a mass market was more developed, and production and transport depended less on the weather or the vagaries of upper-class demand. However, as late as 1909 the maximum difference between the numbers employed in the building trades during the busiest and slackest months was 20 per cent, even though in the winter the men were only working a 44-hour week instead of the 50-hour week of summer.[2] Stedman Jones has found variations of a similar extent in the 1880s.[3] In the eighteenth century, fluctuations were much more severe. House painters, according to Campbell in 1747, were idle for four or five months in the year, though they were an extreme case as 'there is not Bread for one Third of them'.[4] Tailors, he thought, were out of business for three or four months in the year,

[1] The question is discusssed on a national level by Ashton, *Economic Fluctuations*, chapter one, but very little work has been done on a local level.
[2] W. Beveridge, *Unemployment: a Problem of Industry* (1909), pp. 32–4.
[3] Stedman Jones, *Outcast London*, p. 380.
[4] Campbell, *London Tradesman*, p. 104.

unless they were exceptionally good,[5] and eighty years later Place confirmed that the slack season for tailors still lasted about four months.[6] Servants in the West End were in danger of being unemployed for six months in the year after the aristocracy had left the town. In all trades, people would be laid off during a slack period, and earnings for all the others would be less. Even the standard rate of pay might be less. Builders were paid more during the six warmer months, tailors charged more from March to July.

The extent of these fluctuations was increased by the nature of manufacturing in London, where factory production was minimal, where skilled labour was abundant, as were small producers with little fixed capital and hence little incentive and less means of stretching production over the year. An employer would retain a nucleus of his most skilled workmen during the slack season, but most of the others would be laid off. The capital requirements of an employer were further reduced by the fact that in many trades his employees would own their own tools. Builders, carpenters, shoemakers and silkweavers are obvious examples. An accurate assessment of the precise impact of seasonal fluctuations during this period cannot be made, such data not being assembled before the late nineteenth century. Different parts of the town were affected in different ways. Southwark, claimed a well-informed writer in 1809, was exceptional as most of its local manufacturers,

> being in a great measure independent of the fluctuations of trade, partly from the nature of the articles manufactured, and partly from the constant and regular demand created in London . . . the workmen are not only seldom out of employ, but their wages and employment are regular and constant, so that poverty and idleness, which results from the stoppage of vent, or from great extremes in the price of wages, are not nearly so frequent here as in other manufacturing districts.[7]

But a general survey can nevertheless be presented. There were three principal factors behind the fluctuations in London: 'tourism', then known as the London Season, the irregular arrival and departure of shipping in the Port and the weather.

The most obvious fluctuations in demand were caused by the Season. Those involved in the West End luxury trades – jewellers, goldsmiths and silversmiths, coachmakers, printers, furniture makers and so forth – were directly affected, as were the providers of local

---

[5] *Ibid.*, p. 193.

[6] Ashton, *Economic Fluctuations*, p. 7; F. W. Galton (ed.), *Select Documents Illustrating the History of Trades Unionism: The Tailoring Trade* (1896), p. 118.

[7] W. Stevenson, *General View of the Agriculture of the County of Surrey* (1809), p. 566.

services – servants, chairmen, grooms, porters, laundresses, pimps, prostitutes and criminals. Moll Flanders' chosen occupation (theft) suffered severely when the Season was over – so much so that she joined a gang that at that time of year usually left London for Stourbridge Fair.[8] Don Manoel Gonzalez, the Englishman posing as a Portuguese traveller encountered earlier in this book, considered that the West End in 1730 depended entirely on the aristocracy:

Towards autumn, when the town is thin, many of the citizens who deal in a wholesale way, visit distant parts of the kingdom to get in their debts, or procure orders for fresh parcels of goods; and much about the same time the lawyers are either employed in their several circuits, or retired to their country-seats; so that the court, the nobility and gentry, the lawyers and many of the citizens being gone into the country, the town resumes another face. The west End of it appears perfectly deserted; in other parts their trade falls off; but still in the streets about the Royal Exchange we seldom fail to meet with crowds of people, and in an air of business in the hottest season.[9]

The London Season existed in a clearly defined form at the beginning of the seventeenth century, when it began in the autumn, reached its climax at Christmas, and was over by June.[10] In the early eighteenth century the Season extended over very much the same period of time. Drury Lane and Covent Garden theatres were closed from mid May to mid September, and then only played on alternate nights until early October.[11] During the summer, all those who could afford it left the dust and stench of London behind them.

Gradually, as communications improved, the Season began later. The slack time for those doing odd jobs in West End houses, said Campbell in 1747, was 'from January to May. That is when the families are in town.'[12] By then it was possible to travel to London without excessive discomfort in December or January and the aristocracy and gentry took advantage of this for an extended stay in the country. Walpole managed to survive defeat in Parliament at the end of 1742, but fell in the spring of 1743 when the gentry had come up to town.[13] At the end of 1788 the Regency crisis brought many M.P.s up to London prematurely, but they did not bring their wives. 'Not many of the larger houses in the squares are as yet inhabited', said the *Public Advertiser* on 20 December 1788. In the mid eighteenth century, tailors

---

[8] D. Defoe, *Moll Flanders* (Everyman ed., 1930), p. 226.

[9] 'The voyage of Don Manoel Gonzalez', II, p. 95. See above, p. 44.

[10] F. J. Fisher, 'The development of London as a centre of conspicuous consumption in the sixteenth and seventeenth centuries', *Transactions of the Royal Historical Society*, 4th ser., 30 (1948), pp. 37–50.

[11] D. Marshall, *Dr Johnson's London* (New York, 1968), p. 177.

[12] Campbell, *London Tradesman*, p. 104.

[13] J. B. Owen, *The Rise of the Pelhams* (1957), pp. 27–8.

were paid more from March to July to compensate them for lack of employment at other times of the year;[14] the time of the Season continued to move forward and in 1811 Place described February and March as slack months for tailors.[15] By the 1830s the 'true' Season was said not to begin until April, although M.P.s and those connected with Parliament had to come to London in February. Everyone then remained in London until the end of July, when the racing began.[16]

Any assumption that the relative importance of the Season declined during the eighteenth century with the growth of a more stable London-based demand must be treated with caution. First of all, this would assume that the purchasing power of wealthy Londoners rose in the same proportion as that of the 'tourists'. After the mid eighteenth century, any such rise would be counterbalanced not only by rising landed revenues, but also by the increased number of wealthy families frequenting the capital for the Season. It has been suggested that it was only after 1815 that an increasing number of 'middling' gentry came to London for the Season,[17] but there is no reason why 1815 should be such an important turning point, and the increase in the numbers of wealthy tourists is likely to have been a gradual and steady affair. The development of the railway network must have made its impact, but the improvement of road transport during the previous century was more important.

Secondly, the demands of wealthy Londoners were not constant over the year: they themselves were, in many respects, geared to the Season. Daughters had to be taken to balls and married off; the Season was the time for conspicuous expenditure. When the Season was over, demand might well slacken, to increase again as Christmas began to approach. Summer was a dead time of year for the finishing trades: silkweavers had little work in July and August, tailors earned little from July to October.[18] By October, business was starting to revive, partly in belated response to the generally higher level of national economic activity during the summer, partly because the new harvest had been collected, so the price of bread might – with luck – fall and the purchases of the poor could rise accordingly; but principally because of preparations for the Christmas consumer boom. Preparing for Christmas was a gamble when so much work was completed to individual specifications, or was in danger of being

14 Galton, *Select Documents*, p. 18.   15 *Ibid.*, p. 118.
16 W. Howitt, *The Rural Life of England* (2 vols., 1838), I, p. 25.
17 E. W. Bovill, *English Country Life, 1780–1830* (Oxford, 1962), pp. 118–19.
18 Galton, *Select Documents*, p. 118.

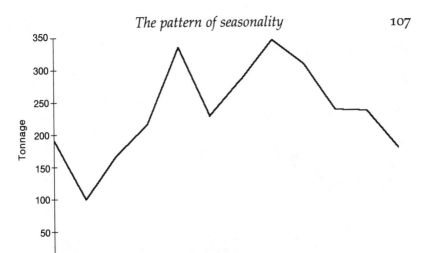

Figure 4.1 Monthly tonnage of ships entering the Port of London, 1835

out of fashion. The Southwark hatters had no such fears, and their production picked up as early as September.[19]

The seasonal pattern in London at the beginning of the nineteenth century was rather similar to that at the end of the century. During the previous two centuries, with the Season beginning earlier, autumn production for Christmas might well have run uninterrupted into spring production for the Season, though even then, as the case of the tailors indicates, it was liable to pick up around March. For the London finishing trades as a whole the gradual advance of the Season into the new year was a serious matter because of the slack period that was involved at the height of winter, when there was so little alternative work available. The gap between these two classes of demand, 'tourist' and London-based, and the instability of both, produced a margin of severely under-employed labour, the size of which depended to a large extent on the balance between these two classes, as well as on its willingness to move into alternative occupations at other times of the year.

The Season was the cause of the major fluctuation in demand; the Port caused the major fluctuation in supply. The broad lines of activity in the Port were predictable. Although eighteenth-century London's foreign trade markets were comparatively diversified, they were still sufficiently concentrated to show seasonal peaks. The conjunction caused by the trade winds and the harvesting of raw materials caused

19 *Select Committee on Artisans and Machinery*: P.P. 1824, 5, pp. 73–100, 148–54.

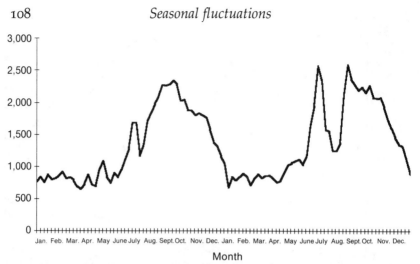

Figure 4.2 Weekly wage bills of the West India Docks, 1811–12 (in pounds)

such a peak in late spring when the American ships arrived. There
was a second, more important peak around September and October,
when the second arrival of the American and European ships was
supplemented by the West Indiamen. At the end of the year, or early
in January, there was a slight rise caused by the East India ships.[20] The
first year for which published monthly statistics are conveniently
available is 1835, which is before steamships were coming in numbers
sufficiently large to disrupt the pattern that was already well established in the eighteenth century. It is shown on figure 4.1.

War increased the concentration by making convoys necessary; it
increased the congestion in the Port, it increased the intensity of
fluctuations, and it made arrival times less predictable. 'Wars', said
William Vaughan, the principal campaigner for the West India Docks,
increased the hindrances to unloading,

by throwing commerce into fleets, which crowd the river so much, as not only
to clash with each other, as to landing and markets, but to occasion additional
delays, accidents and losses.[21]

Figure 4.2 shows what he meant.

Graphs of the arrival of ships in port are, however, misleading
when considering total employment, as they give no indication of

[20] The overall pattern of trade, and its seasonality is described in C. N. Parkinson (ed.),
The Trade Winds. A Study of British Overseas Trade during the French Wars, 1793–1815
(1948), especially chapters two, seven, eight, nine.
[21] W. Vaughan, *On Wet Dock, Quays and Warehouses for the Port of London* (December
1793), p. 4.

shipping departures. This topic is best discussed in conjunction with the major 'tourist' industry of the Port of London – seamen – as important to East London as the aristocracy was to Westminster,[22] filling the lodging houses and pubs, spending their money freely, and drawing down on their heads the denunciation of moralists and the gratitude of shopkeepers, publicans and pimps. By definition, most of the seamen arrived when riverside employment was at its height, and if they came in the autumn, as most of them did, they were likely to remain until at least the succeeding January. As their pay became exhausted more and more of them would be prepared to work on the river, and the work for which they were best suited was that of loading ships, where their specialised skills were useful. They could also compete with other labour and do so precisely at that time of the year when there was so little work available. However, if the weather permitted, they left just when the employment situation was at its worst. West Indiamen departed at the end of the year, American ships in January, European ships in January or February – thus relieving the waterfront and bringing a slack period to the local retailers.

The predominance of outdoor trades in so many parts of London, as well as throughout the country, underlines the importance of the weather, one of the most important influences in the lives of working families. In the age of sail, it dominated the life of the Port, not only in its yearly fluctuations as described above, but also in more unpredictable ways. Mayhew would estimate that an easterly wind put 20,000 men on the riverside out of work.[23] In other spheres the weather was also of central importance. A heavy shower would bring building and outdoor work to a halt and force costermongers to take shelter: Mayhew believed that in the country as a whole, between 100,000 and 200,000 people would be unemployed if it rained heavily.[24] Good weather, on the other hand, adversely affected coachmen and chairmen. Longer-run changes in the weather were more serious still. Many Londoners left town to gather the harvest: between 1830 and 1865 the minimum time for gathering the harvest was twenty-two days and the maximum seventy-one days; it generally varied between twenty-seven and forty days.[25] Some crops, such as hops, which were picked wholesale by the London poor on a kind of annual outing, were even less stable. The earnings a labourer could make by the harvest were of course liable to be in inverse proportion to its yield, and thus to its price.

22 Schwarz, 'Occupations and incomes', p. 93.
23 Mayhew, *London Labour*, II, p. 298.
24 *Ibid.*, p. 298.   25 E. L. Jones, *Seasons and Prices* (1964), pp. 62–3.

Winter always saw a fall in outdoor activity. It was bad for builders because daylight hours were shorter and the weather particularly unpredictable; shipbuilding appears to have come to a virtual halt, but repairs continued. Unfortunately, winter was also a time of reduced activity for most of the other major employers of labour in London. The Port had rather little shipping to handle; the luxury trades, dependent on the Season, suffered as the Season was pushed further into the new year. Winter was also a bad time for women's trades – dressmaking was an activity for the spring, attending markets and hawking goods outdoors depended very much on the weather and hours of daylight, the demand for servants and laundresses in the West End was lower than in the spring. Even if the labour force knew of alternative employment opportunities – an assumption that, to say the least, is dubious – there were nevertheless far fewer jobs available while more had to be spent on fuel, which might itself cost more during the winter months;[26] in a bad winter the supply of food to London might also be interrupted and its price would rise.

The poor relief records make clear the importance of winter. The overseers of the workhouse of Christ Church Spitalfields told the Poor Law Commissioners in 1834 that their workhouse normally had some 356 inhabitants, but as winter approached the total number 'generally increases to near five hundred'.[27] At the end of 1788 there were 408 inmates in Shoreditch workhouse, on 10 January 1789 there were 567, the total then gradually falling to 479 at the end of May and 358 by September, when it began to rise again.[28] There was the same trend during the winter of 1825–6.[29] In Poplar workhouse, for which there are monthly figures from July 1770 to August 1776, there were regular increases during November, December and January.[30] The Parliamentary enquiry of 1777,[31] which was supposed to give the total number of the poor in each parish workhouse in the country on Christmas Day and Midsummer Day in the years 1772, 1773 and 1774 but which is of use for only eleven London parishes, fortunately all of them populous, shows an average increase of 15 per cent for able-

[26] J. U. Nef, *The Rise of the British Coal Industry* (2 vols., 1932), II, p. 389. However, by the end of the eighteenth century a large number of colliers were employed in winter: S. Ville, 'Total factor productivity in the English shipping industry: the north-east coal trade, 1700–1850', *Econ. Hist. Rev.*, 2nd ser., 39 (1986), p. 361.

[27] *R.C. on the Poor Laws. Answers to Town Queries*, P.P. 1834, 35, 87g.

[28] G.L.R.O., P/91/1335: *Register of the Workhouse, St. Leonard Shoreditch*.

[29] Shoreditch Library collection, P/L/P/4: *Abstract of Accounts of the Poor 1825–26*.

[30] Mile End Library, local collection: *Register of the Workhouse, Poplar and Blackwall*.

[31] Second Report from the Committee appointed to enquire how far the orders of the last session respecting the Poor ... had been complied with. *Eighteenth-Century Reports*, 9, pp. 260–5.

bodied inmates in winter and of 19.8 per cent for the 'infirm'.[32] In St Saviour Southwark, mentioned earlier as having little seasonal fluctuation in production, the increase in able-bodied inmates was only 1.4 per cent, but in Bethnal Green it was 25 per cent and in Hanover Square in Westminster it was as high as 41 per cent.

A bad winter accentuated this. An exceptionally bad winter, such as that of 1813–14, the worst winter of the nineteenth century, evoked comparisons with 1740, caused a major crisis, and brought almost everything to a halt.[33] Masses of snow piled up, and by mid January the streets of London were becoming impassable. The mail arrived too late, so there was a royal proclamation to clear the roads to let it reach London, but this had no success. By the end of January the Thames had frozen solid; coal prices were already soaring as the Tyne had frozen before then, and the easterly winds had for some time previously been strong enough to bring the Port of London to a standstill. A correspondent in the *Morning Post* advised readers to pay tradesmen's bills promptly, as their business 'is rendered almost at a standstill' and prompt payment was a matter 'on which their present comfort and future success may depend'.[34] 'Never since the establishment of mail coaches', remarked *The Times* on 24 January, 'had correspondence met with such general interruption as at present. Internal communication must, of course, remain at a stand until the roads are in some degree cleared; for besides the drifts by which they are rendered impassable, the whole face of the country is presenting one uniform face of snow, no trace of road is discoverable, and travellers have had to make their paths at the risk of being every moment overwhelmed.' The danger was not only to travellers: in London the weight of snow on the roofs of houses was threatening to bring them down, so it was shovelled into the streets, to add to the confusion. With an average January temperature of −1.7°C (29°F)[35] tailors, silkweavers and shoemakers could not work – the silk deteriorated, the wax and glue needed by tailors and shoemakers froze. The East London Water Company congratulated itself, in *The Times* for having kept up the supply of water to sugar refineries, but other industries were presumably less fortunate, among them tanneries,

[32] There is evidence from Bethnal Green, Whitechapel, Shadwell, St Saviour Southwark, St George Hanover Square, St Giles and St George Bloomsbury, St James Westminster, St Margaret and St John Westminster, St Marylebone, St Martin-in-the-Fields, and St Andrew Holborn.

[33] This account is taken from *Gentlemen's Magazine*, *Annual Register*, *Morning Post* and *The Times*.

[34] *Morning Post*, 22 January, 1814.

[35] A. J. Drummond, 'Cold winters in Kew observatory', *Quarterly Journal of the Royal Meteorological Society*, 69 (1943), p. 23.

which needed large amounts of running water, or any establishment that depended upon regular deliveries of coal. One of the few activities that did flourish was that of clearing away snow, but it did not flourish sufficiently to employ all the poor. Upwards of 6,000 labourers in St Giles were out of work and their families were starving, according to the schoolmaster of its Catholic school, who for good measure also mentioned that of the seventy children in his school sixty had not eaten any food that day until he gave then some at noon.[36] At last, on the fifth of February the ice above London Bridge began to give way; a day later the ice in the Tyne, which had been twenty inches thick, broke up, letting the colliers escape,[37] and conditions then began to improve.

The winters of 1709 and 1716 may have been as bad, and the winter of 1740 was quite as bad, 'so that many who had lived Years at Hudson's-Bay declared they never felt it colder in those Parts' – a graphic, if somewhat absurd statement. Nevertheless, the Thames was frozen throughout January and February of that year, not breaking up until 27 February; the ice in St James' Park was ten and a half inches thick, the price of coal was treble that of January 1739, George II gave £150 to his own parish for coals and £100 to each of the other parishes in Westminster, and Sir Robert Walpole gave £1,000 to be distributed across Westminster.[38] But such winters were exceptional. What is more important is that the same effects appeared to a lesser extent during other bad, but not catastrophically bad, winters of the period, such as 1776, 1783–4, 1789 and 1796. Easterly winds prevented ships from arriving at the Port, or at least from having space to unload. Such winds usually coincided with bad winters, but they did not always do so. The winters of 1802–3 and 1804–5 were not particularly cold, despite an easterly wind, and even the summer of 1801 saw a predominantly easterly wind.[39] Until the old London Bridge was removed, the free flow of the Thames was impeded and consequently it froze more easily: in 1695, 1709, 1716, 1740, 1768, 1776, 1785, 1795 and 1814.[40] Work on the riverside, at a standstill when the river was frozen, was of course very spasmodic when the wind was predominantly easterly. However, except when the winter was

---

[36] *The Times*, 28 January 1814.   [37] *Annual Register*, 1814, p. 52.

[38] *Gentlemen's Magazine*, 10 (1740), p. 35 for the allegations about Hudson's Bay. See also G. Manley, 'The great winter of 1740', *Weather*, 13 (1958), pp. 11–17 and J. D. Post, *Food Shortage, Climatic Variability and Epidemic Disease in Pre-Industrial Europe. The Mortality Peak in the Early 1740s* (Ithaca, N.Y., 1985), pp. 61, 71, 187.

[39] C. E. P. Brooks and T. H. Hunt, 'Variation of wind direction since 1341', *Quarterly Journal of the Royal Meteorological Society*, 59 (1933), p. 377.

[40] J. H. Brazzel, *The London Weather* (1968), pp. 9, 15.

particularly bad the crisis did not spread inland with full force, and thus escaped journalistic notice. Except for 1740 or 1814 the worst distresses among Londoners would not appear to be caused by a bad winter alone, but by a bad winter coinciding with high bread prices, with economic depression or – worst of all – with both. Should either of these conditions apply then it was the winter, even when it was not particularly harsh, that was the critical season. The winter of 1800–1 was comparatively warm, but the Spitalfields soup society was distributing soup at 1d. a quart for fully 222 days, from 18 November until 27 June, selling a total of 542,000 quarts. The average temperature during the winter of 1811–12 remained above 4.4°C (40°F), but a combination of high bread prices and trade depression led to the distibution of more than 540,000 quarts between December 1811 and the end of June 1812. This was quite exceptional: soup societies were normally in a position to cease distributing their soup well before the new harvest had been collected: in 1813 they were at work from the beginning of January until 17 February, in 1818 from January until 27 February.[41]

So, unless the weather was quite especially bad, a cold winter was not enough in itself to cause a crisis. High bread prices, or a decline in demand were more serious, as either of these compelled the marginal groups in their trades to turn to casual labour, and brought out many wives and children in an effort to supplement the family income. In all these cases the crisis came in winter, however much hardship might be felt over the rest of the year.

Nevertheless, the weather did not behave in an entirely arbitrary fashion over the years, and while its vagaries were not, on the whole, likely to produce a crisis of exceptional proportions, its longer-term fluctuations had a considerable effect on employment and on living standards. Wind directions have been recorded for London from 1667 to 1685, 1713 to 1747 and from 1787 to the present day, and they have been predominantly westerly or south-westerly with the exception of the years from 1740 to 1747 and 1794 to 1810. In the latter period easterlies dominated thirteen out of seventeen years – summer as well as winter – as well as an additional two summers, leaving only 1802 and 1807 as years when the wind direction for at least half the year was not predominantly easterly. For well over a century after 1810 there were no years when the direction of the wind was predomin-

---

41 G.L.R.O., P/93/CTC/1/55: *Minute Book of the Spitalfields Soup Society*. The minute book is blank for 1814.

Figure 4.3 Wet seasons in London, 1690–1850

antly easterly, although there were such seasons.[42] The importance of easterly winds in bringing activity on the Thames to a halt has been pointed out. The period under review was, of course, one of expanding trade in the Port of London, notwithstanding inconvenient easterly winds, but the easterlies, in conjunction with the convoy system, must have exacerbated greatly the irregularity of the arrival of shipping in the Port, and therefore the extent of fluctuations in employment and living standards on the riverside. As will be shown later, it also played its part in increasing the pool of casual labour.

After the wind, there was the rain, affecting most of all the trades further inland. There do not appear to be any conveniently accessible figures of the number of days in each year during which it rained heavily, but there are annual figures of rainfall collected in centres near London from 1696 onwards. A survey of this material found that 'the outstanding points are the high frequency of wet years during the period 1815–44, and the absence of wet years during the period 1785–1814.'[43] Easterlies, so frequent between 1794 and 1810, were not,

[42] Brooks and Hunt, 'Variation', pp. 377, 383. There were none until 1933, when this article appeared.

[43] B. G. Wales-Smith, 'Monthly and annual totals of rainfall representative of Kew, Surrey, from 1697–1970', *Meteorological Magazine*, 100 (1971), pp. 345–62. The comment on the frequency of wet years is from Brazzel, *London Weather*, p. 126 and is based on a less complete survey, but figure 4.3 also makes the point.

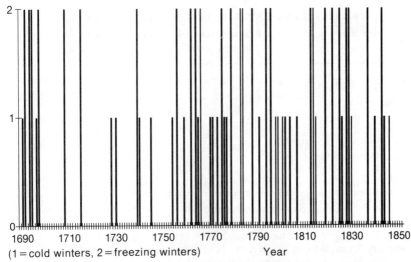

1690   1710   1730   1750   1770   1790   1810   1830   1850
(1 = cold winters, 2 = freezing winters)   Year

Figure 4.4 Cold and freezing winters in England, 1690–1850

it appears, conducive to rain, but once they stopped the rain returned and 1816 and 1817 were particularly wet years.[44] Years when rainfall was significantly below the average occurred in 1780, 1781, 1788, 1795, 1796, 1802 and 1807, after which there were no such years until 1840.[45] The rain tended to affect different employments than did the east wind, but its effects were very widespread, and were beneficial to employment and to living standards from 1785 to 1814, but had the opposite effect from 1815 to 1844.

The periodicity of cold winters was definitely marked. Figure 4.4 shows this diagrammatically: each vertical line shows a winter when the average temperature over three months of December, January and February was less than 3°C; a higher line shows when the monthly mean temperature for any of these months was at or below freezing point – a level defined by meteorologists as 0.5°C.[46]

It will come as no surprise to agricultural historians to see that there was a clustering of bad winters during the 1690s, and then extremely few until the mid century, after which cold winters were spaced out more evenly. Table 4.1 shows this in another fashion.[47]

[44] Brazzel, *London Weather*, pp. 128–9.
[45] *Ibid.*, p. 128. 'Significantly' means when annual rainfall is 20 per cent or more below the 1916–50 average: *ibid.*, p. 126.
[46] Drummond, 'Cold winters', p. 23.
[47] Lamb, *Climate*, II, pp. 569–70; G. Manley, 'Central England temperatures: monthly means 1659–1973', *Journal of the Royal Meteorological Society*, 100 (1974), pp. 393–6.

Table 4.1. *Cold and freezing winters in England, 1690–1850*

	Cold winters	Freezing winters
1690s	6	4
1700–25	2	2
1726–50	5	1
1751–75	10	4
1776–1800	12	7
1801–25	8	4
1826–50	7	6
Total	50	28

The right-hand column includes the winters of 1815 (average temperature 3.7°C, January temperature 0.3°C), 1826 (average temperature 3.8°C, average January temperature 0.4°C) and 1829 (average temperature 4°C, average January temperature 0.3°C), none of which rank as 'cold' winters, but which do appear in the column for freezing winters.

Sources: H. H. Lamb, *Climate: Present, Past and Future* (2 vols., 1972 and 1977), II, pp. 569–70; G. Manley, 'Central England temperatures: monthly means 1659–1973', *Journal of the Royal Meteorological Society*, 100 (1974), pp. 393–6.

The years between 1811 and 1820 were worse than the figures suggest: average monthly temperatures fell to 2°C (36°F) or below in the January of 1813, 1814, 1815 and 1820, as well as in February 1814. A cold winter from 1812 to 1813 was followed by the coldest winter of the century from 1813 to 1814; particularly heavy rainfall during 1816, 1817 and 1819, and a cold winter from 1819 to 1820. Even had the decade been prosperous the effects of the weather would have been serious. And of course the decade was far from prosperous. But the 1770s were as bad, with seven cold winters, two of them freezing, and four wet years.

There were hard years and hard decades. Nevertheless, when considering the general nature of seasonal fluctuations, one must conclude that, apart from the weather, there was no major factor that would affect the severity of such fluctuations, and even the weather did not alter their severity in the long run. For such a change to take place would require considerable technological and social changes, among which the development of a stable mass demand for manufactured goods would be the most important. This did not happen during the period under review in this study. The critical question is therefore whether the intensity of cyclical fluctuations showed any signs of changing, and the previous chapter has established that they did not.

Seasonality, casual labour and houses of call

The effects of seasonal fluctuations on the labour force depended of course on the nature of the economy and its labour force. Employers had adapted themselves to fluctuations, this being one of the main reasons for the multiplicity of small firms and domestic production in London, where short runs of production in factories with plenty of fixed capital would so often have entailed diseconomies. The labour force adapted itself to seasonal fluctuations, but it was also moulded by them, and this, in turn, moulded the character of the surplus of labour that existed in London for most of the year. The casual labourer, as understood in the present meaning of the word, was at the far end of a wide spectrum of 'casual' labour, stretching from the most skilled trades down to the totally unskilled. The casual labour market was by no means caused by the large number of small employers and the small extent of local labour markets, but it was exacerbated by these factors. The domestic system lent itself admirably to large supplies of semi-skilled, underemployed workmen and women. As Beveridge was to point out in his seminal study of 1909, a large number of small employers, each with their own supplies of marginal labour, increased the size of the casual labour pool in almost all industries, although in those industries where wage rates were fixed – either in practice (as with tailoring) or in law (as with silkweaving) – there was obviously a limit to the numbers that could be employed at short-time during the slack season.[48] The tailors, consequently, made allowance for this with a lower rate of pay during the slack season, as did bricklayers and their labourers. However, even if all the employers in a particular trade were to use all their marginal labour at any one time or other, there was nevertheless no guarantee they would all be doing so simultaneously, so the more employers in a trade, the larger the fringe of marginal labour. The second factor increasing the size of the casual labour fringe was, as Beveridge showed, chance; if an employer required 100 men each day, selected on a completely random basis, and the men themselves needed to work for three days a week to obtain enough to live on, the number of men applying for work each day would settle down at 200.[49]

Beveridge's analysis applies, of course, to a situation of general labour surplus. If labour is difficult to obtain, or if marginal labour is too inefficient to be worth employing, employers will not permit such fluctuations, or will, at least, attempt to lessen their effects. Consequently, the higher one ascends in the scale of skilled trades, the

[48] Beveridge, *Unemployment*, pp. 77–81.   [49] *Ibid.*, p. 78.

less his analysis applies. Adam Smith's belief that some trades were paid more to enable the men to survive the slack season[50] applied less to the bricklayers and masons whom he mentioned as examples, than it did to the coachmakers and goldsmiths whom he did not mention. In the latter trades, where labour was scarce, the employer needed to be sure of having suitable men available whenever he might need them.

Because of the deficiency of eighteenth-century sources, it is not easy to find many examples of truly marginal labour – those men 'trapped' at one particular employer, receiving just sufficient work to subsist, but not sufficient to earn enough to subsist in their main trade, and needing to exercise others as well. Those examples that have survived refer to men, but of course women were more likely to be trapped, being paid worse than men and kept to the same area by their husbands' jobs. Campbell mentions tailors and painters; later in the century we hear of coalheavers, masons and, of course, in the country, agricultural labourers in the Speenhamland counties. The coalheavers and the tailors do, however, provide good examples of the effects of fluctuations. In fact, they are both particularly interesting not only because of their 'casual' fringe, but also because the constant possibility of work appears to have prevented a large part of this fringe from moving into alternative occupations at different times of the year, thus greatly increasing the effects of seasonality.

The coalheavers' trade was very fluctuating, often changing from hour to hour because of the contrary winds, as well as changing at different seasons of the year. Sir John Fielding said in 1786 that if colliers were able to sail regularly and arrive according to plan, the number of coalheavers would be excessive. Nominally their earnings were high – some 10s. a day in 1770, and from 17s. to 18s. in 1800.[51] But the publicans who employed them compelled them to spend most of their earnings on drink and, according to Colquhoun, they did not take more than 15s. a week back home. The drinking, he said, was

not always from choice, but necessity; since, if the liquor which is sent them is refused, which is generally to the amount of 12s. per man for each ship, they lose the favour of their employer, and the preference which he has it in his power to give them; and also, the subsistence money of 5s. a week, advanced them as a temporary loan, for maintenance when out of employment.[52]

---

[50] A. Smith, *Wealth of Nations*, ed. E. Cannan, 6th ed. (2 vols., 1961), I, pp. 115–16.
[51] M. D. George, 'The London coalheavers', *Economic History*, 1 (1927).
[52] Colquhoun, *A Treatise on the Commerce and Police*, pp. 144–5.

The 5s. a week subsistence money is particularly interesting in this context, as it kept the coalheavers in the trade, even when it was slack. Even before the inflation of the 1790s it was less than three days' pay for an unskilled labourer; at the time Colquhoun was writing it was less than two days' pay. Fifty years later Mayhew found the same system of work among publicans and others directly employing dock labour:

There are parties living in the neighbourhood of Wapping and Ratcliffe who undertake, for a certain sum per score of tons, to have the requisite quantity of ballast put aboard the ship. These parties are generally either publicans, grocers, butchers, lodging-house keepers ... and they only employ those parties who are customers at their houses ... The reason of the publicans, grocers, butchers, or lodging-house keepers undertaking the job is to increase the custom at their shops, for they make it a rule to employ no heavers but those who purchase their goods from them ... Before the establishment of the Coal-whippers' Office, the contractors for ballast were solely publicans ... The butchers and grocers generally pay the men 6d. and some 1s. in the score less than they themselves get; but, like the publican, their chief profit is made out of the goods they supply ... The constant men are the first gang working out of the public house, or butchers' or grocers' shops. The constant men with the publicans are those that are the best customers. 'If they didn't drink,' said my informant, 'they'd be thought of very little use.' These constant men make three times as much as the casualty men, or, in other words, they have three times as much to drink ... Generally, one-fifth part of what the publicans' constant men earn is spent in drink. The casualty men are those belonging to no regular houses: but these, if taken on by a publican, are expected to spend the same amount in drink as the constant men.[53]

The public house was at the centre of the labour market, even without the crude intimidation practised on the coalheavers. It was the natural centre of information in the locality.[54] As it was a natural meeting place, outdoor employments such as building often paid their men in a public house, and employers might subcontract all responsibility for wage payment to a particular publican. From this arrangement the publican got rid of excess small change – which, with a shortage of coins of small denominations, the employer might find difficulty in having in sufficient quantity – and acquired customers; the employer had a place where his men could be paid, had less cause for worry, could arrange for food and drink to be served on duty, and had a centre for recruiting his men.[55] A public house also gave credit: according to *Low Life*, in 1764, on a Saturday morning between midnight and 1 a.m. the passer-by could see in the streets of London

53 Mayhew, *London Labour*, III, pp. 272–3.
54 B. Harrison, *Drink and the Victorians* (1971), pp. 53–4.
55 *Ibid.*, p. 57; G. W. Hilton, *The Truck System* (Cambridge, 1960), p. 81.

Victuallers carrying the Scores of Tradesmen, such as Coachmakers, Carpenters, Smiths, Plaisters, Plumbers and others in the Building Branch of Business to the Pay-Tables, in order to clear their last Week's Reckoning, and if possible to get a Trifle paid off from an old score.[56]

Some publicans made a regular practice of providing East Indiamen with crews, by getting sturdy men into their debt, and then giving them the alternatives of a voyage to India, or the Fleet prison.[57] According to Campbell, credit from the publicans was as regular a system for the tailors as it was for the coalheavers:

Custom has established it into a Kind of Law, that the House of call gives them [tailors] Credit for Victuals and Drink, while they are unemployed; this obliges the Journeymen on the other Hand to spend all the Money they earn at his House alone. The Landlord, when once he has got them in his Debt is sure to keep them so, and by that Means bind the poor Wretch to his House, who slaves only to enrich the Publican.[58]

But Campbell exaggerated. Francis Place described how the journeymen tailors used public houses for their own benefit, and the system was of long standing. Employers wanting men could send to certain public houses, known as 'houses of call', and they would get them, but in order of seniority. The house of call formed the nucleus of the tailors' trade union,[59] and as the publican did not employ any of the tailors himself, there was a limit to the exactions he could make upon them: although he could put pressure on individual tailors, who got into debt, he was unlikely to risk losing the patronage of the entire trade union branch. Houses of call – whose very name testifies to their function as labour exchanges for particular trades – were very common in London in the eighteenth century. There was the keeper of a public house in 1732 'where journeymen often resort to him in order to get work in the hat-making trade', and by 1750 we know of houses of call for peruke makers, printers, carpenters, joiners, silk-weavers and tailors as well as hatters. When campaigning for the repeal of the Combination Acts in 1824, Place mentioned that he had written to the houses of call for 'hatters, smiths, carpenters, weavers, boot and shoemakers . . . metal workers . . . bakers, tailors, plumbers, painters, and glaziers, bricklayers and bookbinders'.[60]

When considering casual labour, the important question is the size of the individual house of call's catchment area. In view of the

---

[56] Anonymous, *Low Life* (1764), pp. 2–3.
[57] Marshall, *Dr Johnson's London*, p. 222. No reference is given.
[58] Campbell, *London Tradesman*, p. 193.   [59] See below, p. 189–91.
[60] P. Clark, *The English Alehouse, 1200–1800* (1983), p. 230; G. Wallas, *The Life of Francis Place, 1771–1854* (1898), p. 211.

tendency of trades to concentrate in particular areas,[61] it is probable that for many trades the houses of call functioned quite effectively as a labour exchange. Tailors were spread over all of London but thanks to their strong organisation, appear to have limited themselves to a few houses of call in the City and the West End. The Fieldings attempted to set up a central registry for servants, but the best servants never came to it, so it failed.[62] Unskilled trades, especially outdoor trades, could not, however, recruit their labour on a plan as centralised as the tailors' purported to be. In diffused trades, the recruitment centres would be similarly diffused, and the margin of underemployed labour correspondingly greater. Place mentioned a house of call for brick-layers, but he did not refer to one for their labourers. Because of the large numbers of public houses, centres of recruitment might be quite numerous, but the area covered by each of them might be very limited, and the overall reserve of labour proportionately larger. The local publican was thus likely to be giving more credit to the men in these trades, and the men were likely to be unable to leave a particular district because of the credit facilities available to them.

The peculiarities of the London labour market with its fluctuations, its fragmentation, and the multitude of small employers with little fixed capital intensified the casual labour problem, but did not create it. Had it been possible to unify the disparate labour markets, the size of the casual labour fringe could have been reduced to the smallest size necessary to meet the maximum variations in the demand for labour; if fluctuations had been avoidable it could have been reduced yet further. But the result would have been employment for some, and no employment at all for a large number of those who obtained at least a precarious living on the margins of their trades. The funda-mental cause of the casual labour market was the relative oversupply of unskilled labour, caused not so much by the seasonal demand for it, but by more underlying reasons connected with its supply. These would include inadequate training, difficulties of adaptation and, most fundamentally of all, the system of production itself, which involved a comparatively highly paid but relatively small nucleus of workers, forming about 15 per cent of the total population, or perhaps some 30–40 per cent of the labour force, while the remaining 50–70 per cent of the working population were outside this well-protected pale, mostly in trades easily learnt and often poorly paid.

Seasonality did not cause casual labour: the very term is anachronis-tic for this period. That a large town should have an 'overstocked'

---

[61] See above, pp. 32–3.
[62] M. D. George, 'The early history of registry offices', *Economic History*, 1 (1927).

labour market was no surprise to contemporaries. Periodic surges of demand, whether through the tourism of the London Season or the shipping of the Port, provided a welcome demand for poorly paid and not very skilled labour. But seasonality would strengthen the hold of the local labour markets on their labour and, together with the differential availability of work for women and children, it contributed greatly towards creating localised pockets of the very poor. It was by no means the only factor causing such localities, but it was an important factor. Seasonal fluctuations were predictable, and the wages paid reflected this. People expected them and took precautions. Except when there was a particularly severe winter, cyclical fluctuations were the critical factor: during a boom there was more employment during the peak season and less fall during the subsequent slack season; during a slump there was the opposite effect. But for all their predictability, the effects of seasonality on the labour market, on the geography of poverty, and on the meaning of the term 'employment' were by no means negligible.

Because of the lack of statistics, any attempt to estimate the extent of these fluctuations cannot claim very much precision. Nevertheless, it is useful to form a minimal notion of the extent of the upheaval that was caused each year. In the 1850s Mayhew believed that there were about 30 per cent fewer persons employed in the building trades in winter than in summer, and also that a quarter of the workers employed by the London Season were laid off at the end of it.[63] More reliable figures for the 1880s indicate a 30–35 per cent fluctuation among bricklayers between busy and slack weeks; among the trades dependent on the Season, the change could be as great as 60 or even 90 per cent.[64] There are no figures for employment in the entire Port dating from the period of sail, as opposed to figures for the arrival of shipping, but figure 4.2, showing the weekly wage bill paid at the West India Docks in 1811 and 1812, indicates an immense swing. On the whole, therefore, it seems quite probable that it would be conservative to suggest that 20 per cent of those in the most skilled trades were marginal, and needed to spend some part of the year doing semi-skilled jobs. As for the semi-skilled, a figure of 25 per cent seems reasonable. In a bad year, these figures would almost certainly be too low.

Seasonality was at the heart of the experience of the capital's labour force. It affected a large proportion directly each year, and affected more during a cyclical slump or a particularly severe winter. It contri-

---

[63] Mayhew, *London Labour*, II, p. 299.
[64] Stedman Jones, *Outcast London*, pp. 41, 380–3.

buted considerably to the casual labour problem in the capital, trap-
ping many in their trades or their localities, with just enough work to
keep them where they were. It influenced the structure of the labour
market and the house of call, it underlay the vital importance of credit
and pawnbrokers, without which so many household budgets could
not have been kept together. No study of the labour market is complete without it.

5

The population of London: the ending of the old regime

There is no need to apologise for including a chapter on population in a study of London during the eighteenth and nineteenth centuries; there is, however, a need to apologise for its unashamedly old-fashioned methodology. London was fortunate in having its Bills of Mortality – 'official' but highly inaccurate statistics of births and deaths in the central area of the metropolis. Attempts to use them systematically have usually foundered and future work will be based on much more reliable family reconstitution studies. But such work is slow to emerge, while little has been published on the subject since Dorothy George's uncharacteristically uninformative chapter in *London Life*. The Bills provide some information on the death rate; they provide much more information on causes of death and on the relationship between the death rate, harvests and living standards, and it is these that will be examined in this chapter. The chapter is divided into five parts. The first part examines the various estimates for London's population between 1600 and 1850. The second part considers what can be deduced from the Bills about the death rate. The third part examines the changing causes of death in the capital. The fourth part examines what connection – if any – existed between bad harvests and mortality, while the final parts seek to draw conclusions about mortality and economic growth.

The growth of London

It has become customary to take the figures suggested by Wrigley in 1967 as reasonable estimates for the capital's population.[1] These figures were designed to give approximate orders of magnitude, and were never intended to bear the weight that appears to have been

[1] Wrigley, 'A simple model', p. 44.

Table 5.1. *London's population, 1550–1851*

	Wrigley	Finlay/Shearer
1550	70,000	120,000
1600	200,000	200,000
1650	400,000	375,000
1700	575,000	490,000
1750	675,000	–
1801	900,000	–
1811	1,050,000	–
1821	1,274,000	–
1831	1,595,000	–
1841	1,948,000	–
1851	2,362,000	–

placed on them. Finlay and Shearer have recently constructed a new series for 1550–1700, based on new demographic data:[2] in table 5.1 it is given alongside Wrigley's figures.

Despite all the work that has gone into these figures, it must be stressed that, until the 1801 census, most of them are 'best guesses'. The Finlay/Shearer figures are themselves in danger of being supplanted in the course of time. As an example of the range that is embodied in 'guesstimates' of this nature, Sutherland, writing before the Finlay/Shearer research, estimated that the population of the capital in 1665 – before the Plague and the Fire – was between 512,000 and 597,000 depending on the multiplier used for baptisms.[3] Gregory King, with whom it always seems unsafe to disagree, made an estimate of 527,000 for London's population in 1688.[4] The 1750 figure of 675,000 – frequently repeated – has gained acceptance through such repetition: it was quoted by Dorothy George who derived it from Rickman's manipulation of the parish register abstracts.[5] In fact, Rickman produced an estimate of London's population as being 674,000 in 1700 and 676,000 in 1750, figures that Dorothy George was inclined to accept since she doubted that there had been much increase in the population between these years, despite asserting that 'the population had certainly increased between 1700 and 1720'.[6] She presumably assumed that it declined thereafter.

The population of the capital may not have declined, but it is

[2] Finlay and Shearer, 'Population growth', pp. 37–57.
[3] I. Sutherland, 'When was the Great Plague? Mortality in London 1563 to 1665', in D. V. Glass and R. Revelle (eds.), *Population and Social Change* (1972), p. 310.
[4] Wrigley, 'A simple model', p. 44.   [5] *London Life*, p. 319.   [6] *Ibid.*, p. 38.

Table 5.2. *Percentage natural increase in population of England required for different estimates of London's growth*

(1) Percentage increase required to fill the natural decrease in London's population.
(2) Percentage increase required for the capital to grow at rate suggested by Wrigley.
(3) Percentage increase required to grow at rate suggested by Finlay/Shearer.

	(1)	(2)	(3)
1550–99	4.7	14.4	10.7
1600–50	7.5	22.0	20.2
1650–99	192.0	274.1	245.9
1700–49	43.7	56.7	67.7
1750–1801	9.0	19.3	19.3

nevertheless likely that the new set of statistics exaggerate its growth between 1650 and 1750. Wrigley and Schofield provide 'corrected' versions of the Bills of Mortality, by quarter century.[7] Until 1775 they show a surplus of deaths. Merely to balance births and deaths in London would have required the percentage of the natural increase in the population of England and Wales as given in the first column of table 5.2; for the population to increase according to Wrigley would have required the percentage in the second column; for Finlay/Shearer the third column.

During the second half of the seventeenth century population growth at the rate suggested by Finlay and Shearer would have involved London taking two and a half times the natural population increase of the whole of England, while Wrigley's figure would have involved even more – and that at a time when the catchment area for migrants to London is supposed to have become much narrower than previously.[8] There is therefore little doubt that growth slowed down after 1650; in fact, if we are to accept Sutherland's estimates of the capital's population in 1665 then growth between the Plague and the Fire and the end of the century may have been minimal. Even minimal growth would have required a migration rate to London nearly double the natural rate of population increase for the country. We do

---

[7] Wrigley and Schofield, *Population History*, p. 168.
[8] P. Clark, 'Migration in England during the late seventeenth and early eighteenth centuries', *Past and Present*, 83 (1979), pp. 73–4; M. J. Kitch, 'Capital and kingdom: migration to later Stuart London', in A. L. Beier and R. A. P. Finlay (eds.), *London 1500–1700: The Making of the Metropolis* (1986), pp. 224–51.

know that the damage caused by the Fire was not rapidly repaired, despite the inscription on the Monument in 1669 which declared otherwise.[9]

However, Dorothy George was probably correct in her conviction that London's population grew between 1700 and 1720. At any rate, there was a very strong building boom in London after 1715, coal imports to the capital were rising steadily by the advent of regular data in 1713. There is certainly much evidence of a boom during the decade after the Peace of Utrecht. From the mid 1720s there is evidence for stagnation, as is argued in chapter three. Beer production fell, coal imports to London stagnated, retained imports to London showed no significant growth between 1725 and 1740 and then fell.

To summarise this discussion, it is likely that London's population grew very rapidly from the middle of the sixteenth century until the 1660s. By the end of the century growth was perhaps beginning to accelerate again, and it definitely accelerated between 1715 and 1725. Then there was stagnation – for all we know there may even have been decline – until the 1750s (when the trade figures suggest a revival) or the 1760s (when foreign trade, coal imports and the building index revived). Thereafter, growth was rapid, with the population growing by some 50 per cent by the end of the century. This was far slower than the growth between 1550 and 1650, or than growth would be between 1801 and 1851, but it was a great change from the years between 1666 and 1750.

The rise and decline of the death rate

Irrespective of how much the Bills of Mortality have been tortured by successive demographers from the early nineteenth century onwards, they have consistently shown that the crude death rate (CDR) in eighteenth-century London was declining. 'The mortality of London was at the rate of 80 per 1,000 in the latter half of the seventeenth century, 50 in the eighteenth, against 24 in the present day' declared Farr in 1885,[10] making bold assumptions about the size of London's population. The early demographers were also clear that there had been a time when the capital's death rate was very much higher than the rest of the country; by the time of civil registration in the 1830s they agreed that it was not much higher, the national CDR at the end

---

[9] T. F. Reddaway, *The Rebuilding of London after the Great Fire* (1940), pp. 244–9, 278–83.

[10] W. Farr, *Vital Statistics* (1885), p. 131.

of the decade being about twenty-two per thousand and in London twenty-three per thousand.[11]

Specifying the causes for this decline created some difficulty, mainly because of the simultaneous decline of gin drinking on the one hand and infantile mortality on the other.[12] However satisfying it was to attribute the decline in overall mortality to a decline in gin drinking, it was not easy to see how this was responsible for a decline in infant mortality. Neither was it compatible with a closer scrutiny of the Bills themselves. Dorothy George, who was happy to fit into the tradition, mentioned a wide range of causes, mainly related to Hanway's reforms and to hospitals.[13] Naturally she was driven to be sympathetic to the argument that the children born to gin-drinking mothers must have been rather sickly.[14] This meant that – most unusually for someone so meticulous with her sources – a detailed examination of the Bills was not necessary. The end of plague, followed – eventually – by the decline of gin drinking on the one hand, and the growth of smallpox inoculation on the other, seemed to provide sufficient explanation.

The fundamental and long-recognised problem that faced all the early demographers was, of course, that the Bills of Mortality were so inaccurate. 'One of the most defective of its kind' said Maitland in 1756,[15] since it omitted all dissenters' burial grounds, and a fair number of Anglican burial grounds as well as all those who lived within the area of the Bills but chose to be buried outside that area. Maitland himself toured the cemeteries that were not included – some of them within the area of the Bills – adding more than a tenth to the total number of burials.[16] To compound matters, the London burial grounds were becoming very overcrowded and it became increasingly undesirable to be buried there. The overcrowding was made worse by the popularity of coffins: during the sixteenth century the poor were mostly buried in shrouds so their bodies decomposed quickly and when more space was required their remains were flung unceremoniously into a bone yard. One thinks of poor Yorick. Cheap wooden coffins made decomposition take much longer. Recent work would suggest that coffins had become widespread by the late seventeenth

11 J. Brownlee, 'The health of London in the eighteenth century', *Proceedings of the Royal Society of Medicine*, 18 (1924–5), epidemiology section, p. 74. Brownlee was unusual in disagreeing with this, but he had the population within the area of the Bills fluctuating between 726,000 and 732,000 over the course of the century: *ibid.*, p. 74.

12 The classic statement for this is in *London Life*, pp. 40–55. Also M. C. Buer, *Health, Wealth and Population in the Early Days of the Industrial Revolution* (1926), p. 33.

13 *London Life*, pp. 55ff.   14 *Ibid.*, p. 41.

15 W. Maitland, *The History and Survey of London* (1756), II, p. 740.

16 *Ibid.*, pp. 740–2.

century, if not earlier, while a century later Eden noticed a burial club which provided all its members with 'a strong elm coffin ... close drove, with best black jappaned nails'. That would crowd out a cemetery very rapidly.[17]

However, the earlier demographers were not wrong in their belief that London's death rate was falling. Throughout most of the seventeenth century the CDR in London is considered to have been around forty per thousand, and more when there was a plague.[18] The national CDR – and this would include London – was between twenty-five and thirty per thousand. In 1841 the civil registration statistics for London showed a CDR of twenty-three per thousand,[19] while the national CDR was twenty-two per thousand.[20] The CDR in the capital had fallen by some 40 per cent from a level far higher than the national average (itself higher than the provincial average) to a level nearly identical with a lower national average. Where the early demographers were wrong, however, was in their belief that the CDR in London was constantly falling.

A more precise view of mortality in London requires a number of family reconstitution exercises. So far, there is only one, of London Quaker families, whose life expectancy at birth was distinctly declining during the late seventeenth century, and was worse during the first half of the eighteenth century than during the last quarter of the seventeenth century. The CDR among the Quakers finally fell during the third quarter of the eighteenth century, but it was not really until the last quarter of the century that it fell decisively below seventeenth-century levels.[21] There was nothing very exceptional about the Quakers: even a simple exercise that takes Wrigley and Schofield's re-working of the Bills by quarter century and subjects them to the assumptions that London had 11 per cent of England's population and that it had 10 per cent of the population (bounds which contain most of the estimates for the capital's population) shows a similar pattern (table 5.3).[22]

[17] C. Gittings, *Death, Burial and the Individual in Early Modern England* (1984), pp. 114, 240.

[18] R. A. P. Finlay, *Population and Metropolis. The Demography of London, 1580–1650* (Cambridge, 1981), p. 112. Sutherland calculated that a plausible, non-plague CDR for London between 1632 and 1635 would be 42.2 per thousand, 'When was the Great Plague?', p. 308.

[19] The mean for the annual reports of the Registrar General, 1840–2 puts the figure at 23.34 per thousand of the 1841 population.

[20] Wrigley and Schofield, *Population History*, pp. 534–5.

[21] J. Landers, 'Mortality and metropolis: the case of London, 1675–1825', *Population Studies*, 41 (1987), p. 64; J. Landers, 'Some problems in the historical demography of London, 1675–1825', Cambridge University, Ph.D. thesis, 1984, pp. 206–7.

[22] It had 10.4 per cent in 1801 and 10.6 per cent in 1811.

Table 5.3. *London's crude death rate under different assumptions*[a]

(1) London has 10% of England's population.
(2) London has 11% of England's population.
   (Average figure for quarter century)[b]

	(1)	(2)
1675–99	44.2	40.3
1700–24	45.5	41.4
1725–49	49.7	45.2
1750–74	39.9	36.3
1775–99	32.5	29.6
1800–24	22.8	

Notes: [a] The London mortality statistics are the 'corrected' versions of the Bills of Mortality in Wrigley and Schofield, *Population History*, p. 167.
[b] The figures for London's population have been calculated as follows:

	10% of England's population	11% of England's population
1675–99	494,000	543,000
1700–24	522,000	574,000
1725–49	547,000	602,000
1750–74	613,000	674,000
1775–99	740,000	814,000
1800–24	1,050,000 (1811 census)	

There is no escaping the increase in the CDR during the first quarter of the eighteenth century, and it is only on the assumption that during the second quarter of the eighteenth century London suddenly had a larger proportion of the nation's population than during the first quarter of the century – a singularly unlikely event – that it is possible to escape the conclusion that the CDR was rising during the first half of the eighteenth century. Landers and Mouzas suggest a rise from 47.2 per thousand between 1670 and 1699 to 51.8 per thousand between 1724 and 1759,[23] while Wrigley and Schofield suggest a significant rise in infant mortality during the first half of the eighteenth century.[24]

But why did the death rate rise? A crude assimilation of rapid urban growth, a deteriorating environment, and a higher death rate is rendered suspect – to say no more – by the stagnation in the capital's

[23] J. Landers and A. Mouzas, 'Burial seasonality and causes of death in London 1670–1819', *Population Studies*, 42 (1988), p. 69.
[24] E. A. Wrigley and R. S. Schofield, 'English population history from family reconstitution: summary results, 1600–1799', *Population Studies*, 37 (1983), p. 161.

Table 5.4. *Convulsions and infant mortality*

(1) Deaths from convulsions as percentage of all deaths.
(2) Deaths 0–1 as percentage of all deaths.
(3) Correlation coefficient of number of deaths from convulsions with number of deaths 0–1.
(4) Correlation coefficient of column (1) with column (2).

	(1)	(2)	(3)	(4)
1675–99	17.5	–	–	–
1700–24	27.8	–	–	–
1725–49	28.1	35.4[a]	0.982	0.964
1750–74	27.4	34.9	0.840	0.707
1775–99	23.8	33.3	0.845	0.587
1800–24	18.2	28.3	0.395	0.439

Note: [a] 1728–49

population during the second quarter of the eighteenth century, and by the continuing decline in the CDR during the rapid population growth of the nineteenth century. An equally crude assimilation of the death rate with earnings is also suspicious: as chapter six will show, earnings showed a tendency to fall from the mid century and were certainly lower for many years of the Revolutionary and Napoleonic Wars than previously. A more detailed analysis is required. Logically this should start with infant and child mortality.

Convulsions were the major cause of infant deaths and, as expected, table 5.4 shows that, over the long run, the proportion of deaths from convulsions peaked during the first half of the eighteenth century and then declined fairly steadily. This is roughly parallel to the decline in the proportion that deaths from ages 0–1 formed of all deaths.

Between 1675 and 1699 17.5 per cent of deaths were caused by convulsions; during the next seventy-five years the figure was well over a quarter. The peak quarter century was 1725–49, when there were 25 per cent more deaths on average than 1675–99. This is consistent with an increased population, but 71 per cent of the rise in mortality was caused by the number of deaths from convulsions doubling. A further 4 per cent of the rise in mortality was caused by an increase in deaths from 'teething'. The years between 1725 and 1750 saw a relatively low rate of immigration to the capital, so the proportion of children in the population might well have been higher than fifty years earlier. However, this alone would not account for the full increase in deaths from convulsions. The death rate for infants rose a great deal: for Quaker infants – and there is no reason to believe that Quaker infants were unrepresentative – it had been 260 per thousand during the second half of the seventeenth century and it rose by a third to 342 per thousand between 1700 and 1750, falling to 276 per thousand during the next fifty years and falling further to 185 per thousand between 1800 and 1849.[25] It also rose for Quaker children aged 1–4 from 244 per thousand during the late seventeenth century to 298 per thousand during the first half and 253 per thousand during the second half of the eighteenth century, before falling to new depths of 165 per thousand between 1800 and 1849.[26] As a result, half the Quaker children were surviving to the age of fifteen during the late seventeenth century, 39 per cent between 1700 and 1749, 49 per cent during the next half century and 60 per cent during the first half of the nineteenth century.[27]

Statistics on the age of death become available from 1728, so, starting with the CDR of 51.8 per thousand that Landers suggests for the 1730s and ending with a figure of 23 per thousand for 1838–44, the main components in the fall in mortality can be isolated. Nearly half of the fall – 46.4 per cent to be precise – was concentrated among those aged under two. Another two per thousand – or 7 per cent of the total fall – were in the age group 2–4. Then there was little change until a decline of some 2–3 per thousand for each decade of those in their twenties and over. The actual profile of age of death in table 5.5 did not change very much: 51.5 per cent of deaths were under the age of ten in the 1730s, 45.6 per cent between 1838 and 1844 – but the likelihood of dying fell drastically. Infants and children under two were almost three times less likely to die in the 1840s than in the 1730s, those aged 2–4 were about 1.8 times less likely, those aged 5–9 some 1.6 times less likely to die.

The causes of the decline in mortality are less clear. Convulsions disappeared during the nineteenth century, a relic of a medically barbarous age, to be replaced by a diagnosis that was more precise, if no more curable. Table 5.6 shows how the decline in the major diseases other than convulsions – consumption, smallpox and fevers – accounted for nearly half the decline in mortality between the 1730s and 1838/44. However, table 5.6 must be handled carefully. The Bills would have brought together consumption and pneumonia. Small-

---

[25] Landers, 'Some problems', p. 156.   [26] *Ibid.*, p. 156.
[27] Calculated from Landers, 'Some problems', p. 156. See also Wrigley and Schofield, 'English population history from family reconstitution', p. 160 n. 13, where the proportion of Londoners surviving to the age of 15 is calculated at 450, 400, 400 and 500 per thousand for each of these half centuries.

Table 5.5. *Fall in mortality by age, 1730s–1838/44*[28]

	Mortality per 1,000			
	1730–9	1838–44	Change	% of decline
Under 2	20.2	6.8	−13.4	46.4
2–4	4.7	2.6	−2.1	7.3
5–9	1.8	1.1	−0.7	2.4
Total under 10	26.7	10.5	−16.2	56.1
10–19	1.6	0.9	−0.7	2.4
20–29	3.8	1.6	−2.2	7.6
30–39	4.7	1.8	−2.9	10.0
40–49	4.6	1.9	−2.7	9.3
50–59	3.8	1.8	−2.0	6.9
60+	6.7	4.5	−2.2	7.6
Total	51.8	23.0	−28.9	100

Note: Totals may not add up precisely because of rounding.

pox would have been correctly diagnosed (although not fulminating smallpox, which caused convulsions, usually in infants, before the spots appeared). The term 'fever' covers an enormous range of diseases. 'Fever' was by no means confined to typhus, but typhus was an important component, and by 1838/44 typhus was killing at the rate of 0.9 per thousand, whereas a century previously fever had been killing 8.2 per thousand. If typhus is assimilated to fevers, then 42 per cent of the fall in mortality can be 'explained'; omitting fever, falls in consumption, pneumonia and smallpox 'explain' 21.2 per cent.

If all those who died under the age of two died from convulsions, or in any case did not die from a disease in table 5.6, then it would be possible to say that a little under half the fall in mortality came from a fall in infant mortality, and almost all the rest of the fall was caused by a decline in consumption and pneumonia, smallpox and fevers. This would not explain the nature of the convulsions or fevers, but it would be a considerable advance in our knowledge. The question, therefore, is whether convulsions can be isolated.

Convulsions were not fevers. Over the long run, deaths from fevers and deaths from consumption went very closely together: r for a 25-year moving average of the deaths from convulsions and deaths from fever between 1670 and 1830 is 0.949. But this simply means that

[28] Naturally the ages may well be imprecise at the margins, but they are indicative in a general sort of way.

Table 5.6. *Principal components of the fall in mortality, 1730s–1838/44*

	Mortality per 1,000			
	1730–9	1838/44	Change	% of decline
Consumption and pneumonia	8.2	5.4	−2.8	9.7
Smallpox	3.9	0.6	−3.3	11.5
Fever	6.9			
Typhus		0.9	−6.0	20.8
Total	19.0	6.9	−12.1	42.0

they both followed the same long-run trend. Examined by quarter century their interaction is much less straightforward. There are two elementary methods of comparing the data on fevers and convulsions: by comparing fluctuations in the number of deaths from these causes, and by comparing fluctuations in the proportion that each of them formed of the total number of deaths. The drawback of the first method is that it takes no account of the changing size of the population, which could dominate the movement in the figures for individual diseases; the drawback of the second method is that if other causes of death should decline then consumption and fevers will be given sudden and unwarranted importance. To be sure, the correlations reached by both methods should be significant and point in the same direction. Table 5.7 shows that they fail to do so.

It was only during the last quarter of the seventeenth century that both the coefficients were significant at the 95 per cent confidence level and comparatively high, at 0.641 for numbers and at 0.552 for proportions. For the next half century the signs conflicted, but there was a tendency for fevers and convulsions to be opposed to each other: the correlations from numbers are insignificant but the correlation from proportions is −0.513 for the first quarter of the eighteenth century and −0.587 for the second quarter. Of course the latter period saw both fevers and convulsions running at a particularly high level. For the second half of the eighteenth century the correlations from proportions are insignificant, while those from numbers are both positive and significant – but both fevers and convulsions were declining during these years.

There is some ambiguity on whether convulsions were related strongly to smallpox. Convulsions were related rather strongly to smallpox for children aged between two and four, and quite strongly for children aged between five and nine. But they were not related to

Table 5.7. *Convulsions and fever: correlation coefficients*

(1) Correlation of number of deaths from fever with number of deaths from convulsions.
(2) Correlation of percentage of deaths from fever with percentage of deaths from convulsions.

	(1)	(2)
1675–99	0.641	0.552
1700–24	0.240 (not significant)	−0.513
1725–49	0.289 (not significant)	−0.587
1750–74	0.470	−0.33 (not significant)
1775–99	0.525	0.263 (not significant)
1800–24	0.267 (not significant)	0.118 (not significant)

infant deaths (table 5.8). Smallpox can cause convulsive behaviour in infants and lead to death before the spots appear, but the correlation with infant deaths in table 5.8 is not very strong. Landers' more sophisticated tests have also failed to find such a connection,[29] and one is forced to conclude that there is no obvious explanation for the decline in infant mortality.[30] Smallpox must have made a contri-

[29] Landers, 'Mortality and metropolis', p. 71.

[30] M. K. Matossian, 'Mold poisoning and population growth in England and France 1750–1850', *J. Econ. Hist.*, 44 (1984), p. 680, suggests that a major cause of the decline in convulsions was a decline in ergot poisoning caused by a fall in the consumption of rye bread, which is less subject to mould poisoning. The switch to potatoes was better still, for the same reason. The same argument is put forward by Matossian in 'Death in London, 1750–1909', *Journal of Interdisciplinary History*, 16 (1985), pp. 183–97. This is an interesting argument, but one would like to see the author deal with the more obvious objections: (i) Londoners did change to wheaten bread during the course of the eighteenth century, but mortality from consumption became worse; (ii) mortality was particularly high 1806–14 at 24.9 per cent of all deaths, when bread was expensive, and fell, usually to not more than 18 per cent for the succeeding fifteen years, when bread was cheaper; (iii) it takes an adult a few years to die from consumption; (iv) children may indeed die more quickly, but there were many other hazards to their health, smallpox for one: P. Razzell, *The Conquest of Smallpox* (1977), p. 104, points out that infantile deaths from smallpox would be a major cause of convulsions, the child often dying before the appearance of other symptoms. In 1779 Lettsom believed that largely because of this, smallpox mortality in London was double the level given in the Bills: *ibid.*, pp. 106–7. There were of course other infantile diseases, such as whooping cough (not reliable in the Bills, but which caused 3 per cent of all deaths during the 1840s, and a very much higher proportion of infantile deaths) and measles. The searchers were inclined to use the term 'convulsions' to describe all infant deaths; (v) the diagnosis of pneumonia in the Bills; (vi) the proportion of people actually dying from the disease: see below; (vii) tubercular milk. In addition, Matossian's argument has been carefully investigated by Anne Hardy, 'Diagnosis, death and diet: the case of London, 1750–1909', *Journal of Interdisciplinary History*, 18 (1988), pp. 387–401.

Table 5.8. *Convulsions and smallpox: correlation coefficients by age*

	Deaths 0–1		Deaths 2–4		Deaths 5–9	
	Number	%	Number	%	Number	%
1728–49	0.355	−0.031	0.579	0.412	0.602	0.456
1750–74	−0.179	−0.036	0.183	0.836	0.201	0.688
1775–99	0.192	0.502	0.288	0.780	0.322	0.596
1800–24	0.511	0.529	0.695	0.603	0.074	−0.166

bution, as must fevers, but the contribution appears to have been limited. The obvious factor for investigation is weaning. By the late eighteenth century breast feeding may perhaps have continued for longer into a child's life, and it may also have begun earlier. Medical attitudes to colostrum, which particularly protects an infant in the first six weeks of life, also changed. Before 1673 all medical writers condemned it; after 1748 they all praised it.[31] The timing of this change in medical opinion is less than ideal, but one must allow for a time lag.

The fall in the age-specific death rate for those aged between two and nine accounted for less than a tenth of the total fall in the CDR between the 1730s and the 1840s, but it was more significant than these figures alone might suggest. The correlations in table 5.8 between deaths from convulsions and deaths from smallpox produced relatively insignificant results for infants, but tended to be significant for ages 2–4 and sometimes 5–9. Landers gives smallpox considerably more responsibility for the rise and fall of the death rate in the eighteenth century than would be suggested from the Bills. Furthermore, a decline in the mortality of these age groups would not only show directly in the statistics, but would – as with a decline in infant mortality – also suggest a fall in morbidity, and thus a smaller proportion of the population weakened by having experienced smallpox or fever and surviving that experience. To demographers, however, the significance of changes in mortality of this age group extends further. The death rate in London had always been high. London more or less followed the national trend as revealed by family reconstitution studies for English parishes, which show a higher death rate for infants during the first half of the eighteenth century than was the case during the preceding half century or would be the

[31] V. Fildes, *Breasts, Bottles and Babies: A History of Infant Feeding* (Edinburgh, 1986), pp. 81–97, 199.

Table 5.9. *Expectation of life of London Quakers at birth and at age 30*[32]

	At birth	(1700–49 = 100)	At age 30	(1700–49 = 100)
1665–99	28.75	135	28.65	108
1700–49	21.75	100	26.35	100
1750–99	29.8	140	31.75	120
1800–49	35.45	167	31.9	121

case thereafter. What was different was that children aged between two and four in provincial parishes tended to enjoy a relatively stable mortality rate between 1650 and 1800, whereas in London the age-specific mortality rate for this age group rose from 244 per thousand during the second half of the seventeenth century to 298 per thousand during the next half century, then fell to 253 per thousand.[33] Smallpox was not the sole reason for this, but it was probably the major reason. It also became more deadly after the first decade of the eighteenth century[34] and was killing people at a rate four times that of the previous half century. During the second half of the century it declined – maybe its toxicity was less, maybe inoculation helped – but it did not fall to its seventeenth-century levels until the nineteenth century. A great part of the rise in mortality in the eighteenth century, as well as of its decline thereafter, can be attributed to smallpox. But not all of it. Among the Quakers, smallpox was responsible for 8.8 per cent of infant deaths between 1700 and 1749 and 8.6 per cent during the succeeding half century; for ages 1–4 the proportion fell from 8.6 per cent to 7.6 per cent and for ages 5–9 it fell from 9.7 per cent to 6.5 per cent.[35] This does not account for much of the fall in infant and child mortality. In London as a whole, the fall in recorded smallpox mortality could have accounted directly for only 11.4 per cent of the decline in the CDR between the 1730s and 1838/44. The indirect effects could, of course, have been greater.

The fall in infant and child mortality accounted for over half the fall in mortality between the 1730s and the 1840s; that of infants and children under two accounted for nearly 47 per cent of the fall. There was of course a fairly substantial fall in adult mortality as well. The

---

[32] Landers, 'some problems', p. 157. I have taken the midpoint of the range and the mean for the two sexes. Earle, *Making*, pp. 307–10, has a decline in mortality for middle-class London adults during the early eighteenth century, which is interesting, but needs more support.

[33] Landers, 'Mortality and metropolis', p. 64; Wrigley and Schofield, 'English population history from family reconstitution', p. 157.

[34] Landers, 'Some problems', p. 200.   [35] *Ibid.*, pp. 156, 200.

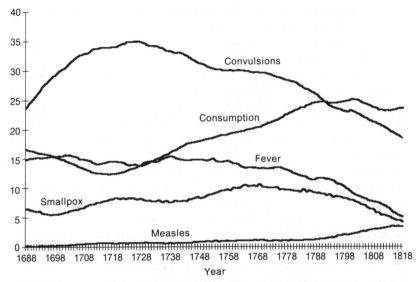

Figure 5.1 Percentage of deaths from various causes, London, 1688–1818
(25-year moving averages)

expectation of life of London's Quakers aged thirty fell during the first half of the eighteenth century, but then rose. However, as table 5.9 shows, it changed a great deal less than expectation of life at birth.

People's chances of dying altered, but so did the diseases from which they might die. The next section examines the changing causes of death.

The changing face of mortality in London

Figure 5.1 shows, on 25-year moving averages, the proportion of recorded deaths caused by five of the major killing diseases in the capital – consumption, smallpox, measles, fever and convulsions. There are five major conclusions to be drawn. First, the enormous dominance of convulsions for most of the period, moving as expected along with infant mortality, so rising from 20 per cent of all deaths during the late seventeenth century to just under 30 per cent by the 1720s, falling slowly until the early 1780s and falling more rapidly thereafter. Secondly, there is the rise and subsequent fall of smallpox mortality; thirdly, the slow rise of measles; fourthly, the considerable increase in the proportion of deaths from consumption – overtaking convulsions by the late 1780s as the major single cause of death in the capital; and, fifthly, the decline of fever.

Convulsions and smallpox have already been discussed. The apparent increase in deaths from consumption is deceptive. Since the death rate was falling, the proportion of the population being killed by consumption was also falling, from some 8.3 per thousand in the 1730s to 5.4 per thousand between 1838 and 1844. The apparent increase in consumption in figure 5.1 – which would also have included pneumonia in the eighteenth century – was a direct consequence of the decline in other causes of death. If nothing else got you first, consumption or pneumonia was rather likely to get you in the end. So when infant mortality increased during the early eighteenth century the proportion of total deaths from consumption duly fell from 15 per cent during the 1690s to 12.5 per cent during the succeeding two decades, going as low as 8.3 per cent in the 1730s. Subsequently, as infant mortality declined the proportion of deaths from consumption duly increased, reaching a quarter of all deaths in the 1780s and 1790s. Assuming that all those who died from consumption were over the age of ten[36] then consumption, measured on 25-year moving averages, caused the deaths of a third of all those aged ten and over during the 1740s, and 45 per cent at its peak during the 1780s. What is surprising is that it then showed a tendency to fall. It was still causing 30 per cent of adult deaths during the 1820s, but it was less important as a cause of death than it had been earlier. Between 1838 and 1846 consumption and pneumonia together caused 23 per cent of all deaths, falling to 17.5 per cent of deaths between 1847 and 1850. Much of this fall may be deceptive, a result of changes in diagnosis and terminology, the desire by the poor to avoid the intrusion of doctors (as opposed to 'searchers') into their homes, and a variety of other reasons. Anne Hardy is suspicious of the apparent sharp fall in consumption between 1831 and 1838, with a further sharp fall in 1841, but a much slower fall thereafter, when registration procedures had been tightened.[37] Indeed, why tuberculosis should have declined at all during this period is unclear. Living standards may have been improving somewhat, but there was still plenty of squalor, while atmospheric pollution in the capital was increasing.[38] Matossian's argument that a switch to potatoes from wheaten bread would have reduced vulnerability to infection is strongly disputed by

---

[36] Landers, 'Mortality and metropolis', p. 71, found the highest z scores from the age of twenty upwards; they were significant for ages 0–4, but far lower than those of adults. Z scores are sophisticated coefficients that take account of the internal autocorrelation within each series.

[37] Hardy, 'Diagnosis', pp. 395–7.   [38] See below, pp. 235–6.

Anne Hardy and at the very least remains to be proved.[39] Like smallpox in the eighteenth century, tuberculosis was a universal infection – early in the twentieth century more than 90 per cent of the British population were infected with it.[40]

The apparent rise of consumption during the eighteenth century is, therefore, primarily a statistical illusion caused by falling infant mortality. In addition, it was partly 'caused' by a fall in child and adult mortality from fevers and smallpox. It is not at all clear why fevers declined. Indeed, it is not clear what these fevers were. At the very least a seasonal analysis is essential. Fevers were at a high level during the first sixty years of the eighteenth century, causing some 15 per cent of all deaths. Since the early eighteenth-century CDR was higher than that of the late seventeenth century, fevers had obviously become more lethal. From the 1760s fevers were declining as a cause of death, and declined continuously thereafter, to be down to 3.6 per cent of deaths during the 1820s. The extent of this fall may be deceptive: typhus alone caused 3.9 per cent of all deaths between 1838 and 1844 according to the civil registration statistics, so it would be rash to draw many conclusions until more detailed investigations have been carried out. The dirt, poor water supply and general overcrowding that was the background to so many fevers did not significantly improve during this period – the price of bread was lower before the decline in the 1760s than subsequently, and the prolonged warfare of the late eighteenth and early nineteenth centuries discouraged house building. Hospitals may have had some limited responsibility for the decline. The point is not whether hospitals cured anyone or not – they may have done harm, and patients with infectious diseases were not usually segregated from other patients – but that they removed infectious patients from their neighbourhoods. The critical factor would be the extent to which the patient was infectious before entry to hospital.[41] But the effect of hospitals would obviously be limited.

The previous section showed that fevers were not convulsions, neither were they particularly a disease of infants.[42] The significant correlations of fevers were not with infancy but with childhood, and they are only to be found in the second half of the eighteenth century

---

39 Matossian, 'Death in London', pp. 193–7; Hardy, 'Diagnosis', pp. 397–401. See above, n. 30.
40 Hardy, 'Diagnosis', p. 398.
41 This counters T. McKeown and R. G. Brown, 'Medical evidence relating to English population change in the eighteenth century', *Population Studies*, 9 (1955), pp. 119–41 and McKeown, *The Modern Rise of Population* (1976), pp. 149–50.
42 Matossian, 'Death in London', p. 191, seeks to link peaks in deaths from fevers with peaks in births; the nature of a birth peak is not clear.

Table 5.10. *Deaths from convulsions and fever: correlation coefficients*

(1) Correlation of number of deaths from fever with total number of deaths in given age group.
(2) Correlation of percentage of deaths from fever with percentage of deaths from fever in given age group.

	Deaths 0–1		Deaths 2–4		Deaths 5–9	
	(1)	(2)	(1)	(2)	(1)	(2)
1728–49	0.242	−0.62	0.373	−0.067	0.452	0.047
1750–74	0.494	−0.455	0.906	−0.452	0.769	−0.123
1775–99	0.526	0.060	0.785	−0.463	0.639	−0.067
1800–24	0.198	−0.035	0.478	0.339	0.311	0.171

(see table 5.10). Using the method of tables 5.7 and 5.8 and comparing not only the numbers but also the proportion of deaths, fevers are really significant only between 1750 and 1800 for the age group 2–4. As pointed out earlier, this is the age group whose mortality in London during the first half of the eighteenth century had been so different from trends elsewhere in the country. Otherwise fevers related to adults, and they declined for some reason.

Measles was one of the few diseases that was killing more people in the 1840s than earlier. Obviously a childhood disease, deaths from measles were rising steadily as a proportion of deaths from the 1790s, until by the 1820s the disease was rivalling smallpox – admittedly a much reduced smallpox – as a killer. At present, measles has the capacity to kill in less developed countries and to do so fairly quickly, and it is considered particularly responsive to the nutritional state of the host,[43] so it is curious to see it rise during the prosperous 1780s, though less curious to see it continue to rise thereafter, peaking at 7 per cent of all deaths in 1812. However, it was at 5 per cent during the boom year of 1825, while during the succeeding two years of depression it fell. Heberden's incredulity at the number of deaths from measles towards the end of the eighteenth century – 'the scarlet fever and malignant sore throat. . .may easily be mistaken for measles by better judges than mothers and nurses'[44] – should be tempered by the fact that the civil registration statistics had measles causing 4.8 per

[43] R. I. Rotberg and T. K. Rabb (eds.), *Hunger and History* (Cambridge, 1985), report of the conferees: 'The relationship of nutrition, disease and social conditions: a graphical presentation', p. 308.
[44] Quoted by McKeown, *The Modern Rise of Population*, p. 10.

Table 5.11. *Deaths from measles: average difference from the mean by quarter century, 1750–1824*

	%
1750–74	66.2
1775–99	51.8
1800–24	34.4

cent of all deaths in 1848. In view of the fall of other infectious diseases in London it is difficult to see why measles should have become more of a killer.[45] It is possible – it is no more than a suggestion – that we are dealing with a relatively new disease. There had of course been previous epidemics of measles, but the disease had not lingered.[46] It has been suggested that a population of about one million is required to support measles as an endemic infection: interestingly, this is the size that London was approaching at this time.[47] An infectious disease became endemic in London when London achieved the minimum size for this to occur. Immunity to that infection gradually spread within London and then moved out from London into a larger catchment area. That this applies to measles is supported strongly by table 5.11, which shows the progress of mean annual deviations from a 25-year mean. A new infectious disease would deviate strongly from the 25-year mean, but as the disease became established the deviations would become less pronounced.

Long-term trends can give misleading impressions. Life was full of

[45] Floud, Wachter and Gregory produce interesting data suggesting that the average height of the poorest London street children, recruited by the Marine Society, increased during the Napoleonic Wars, and then stabilised, with children born in the 1820s being smaller (*Height, Health and History*, pp. 197, 289, 304–5). As the authors say, the evidence of heights is difficult to reconcile with the wage-rate data, unless it is argued that 'if there were significant gains in real incomes for the working class between the 1820s and the 1850s they were bought at a very high price' (*ibid.*, pp. 287–91, 304–6). Height indicates the totality of environmental pressures, but the fact that the height of the Marine Society recruits did not fall to eighteenth-century levels is at least enough to rule out immiseration as a cause of the increase in deaths from measles.

[46] A Dyer, 'Epidemics of measles in a seventeenth-century English town', *Local Population Studies*, 34 (1985), pp. 35–45, for an example. In this case – Bolton in 1635–6 – at least 31 per cent of infants aged between six and eleven months died.

[47] McKeown, *The Modern Rise of Population*, pp. 79–80. 'While the disease was known for centuries it is probable that the aggregation of populations which occurred in the nineteenth century created optimum conditions for the survival and spread of the virus. It is therefore possible that industrialisation led to increased mortality from measles.'

irregularities and crises. The most obvious irregularity that may have affected mortality was the price of bread, which therefore needs to be examined more carefully.

Crisis years

Wrigley and Schofield have examined years of particularly high mortality – defined as mortality being 10 per cent or more above a 25-year moving average – and concluded that crisis mortality showed no particular tendency to be caused by high bread prices. Sometimes the two coincided, often they did not. A combination of harvest crises and surges in mortality did not occur on a *national* scale in the eighteenth century, although such combinations might well be found locally.[48] But that is not to say that mortality was not responsive to the price of bread: in the same volume Lee demonstrates that about 16 per cent of the fluctuations in mortality can be explained by movements in the price of bread. The response of mortality to bread prices came less during the year of higher prices than during the succeeding two years. However, four and five years after the price rise deaths showed a tendency to fall, so 'the net cumulative effect over five years was essentially zero, except when prices were extremely high (more than 44 per cent above average). This suggests that most price variations merely altered by a couple of years the timing of deaths which would in any case soon have occurred.'[49] Furthermore, after 1746 the relationship was yet weaker.[50]

Such a relationship makes cruder forms of analysis suspect, in particular Appleby's failure to find much relationship between bread prices and deaths in London between 1550 and 1750.[51] Lee's methodology has been applied to eighteenth-century London by Galloway.[52] An increase in grain prices, he concludes, 'is clearly associated with an increase in deaths among Londoners in the middle and older age groups'. But the statistical association is not very strong, although this is masked by a multiple correlation coefficient which includes variations in temperature, rainfall and births, and which thereby achieves a high and significant figure. Furthermore, Galloway's beta coefficients for wheat prices with mortality tend to be low and not to follow any obvious pattern. Most of them are statistically insignificant, and

---

[48] Wrigley and Schofield, *Population History*, pp. 328, 331. 'Thus while very high food prices appear to have had some effect on death rates in the following year, very high death rates were not significantly associated with above-average food prices.'

[49] *Ibid.*, pp. 371–2, 399.   [50] *Ibid.*, pp. 375–6.   [51] See below, n. 70.

[52] P. R. Galloway, 'Annual variations in deaths by age, deaths by cause, prices and weather in London 1670 to 1830', *Population Studies*, 39 (1985), pp. 487–505.

the sign is confusing, having a weak tendency to be positive during the same year as the increase in grain prices, to be negative during the subsequent year, positive the year after and negative during the two subsequent years.[53] The effect of the weather on the survival of airborne infections and vectors is likely to have been more significant.[54] Landers' analysis of the connection of bread prices and mortality is not inconsistent with this.[55] There is a statistically significant correlation of bread prices with deaths from smallpox and deaths from consumption between 1675 and 1750, but not between 1750 and 1825. How this connection would have functioned during the earlier years is as mysterious as why it would not have functioned during the later years. The ratio of infant deaths to bread prices is not meaningfully connected – its most meaningful correlation is with the temperature in July and August – suggesting intestinal infections – and to a certain extent with rainfall. Smallpox, too, was affected more by the weather than by bread prices (although in this case the connection with bread prices was significant). Landers speculates that bad weather might have encouraged more migration to the city and hence more deaths.

The relevant demographic, harvest and climatic data can, of course, be manipulated with increasing degrees of refinement. There is probably little point in carrying this very much further than has been done until the Bills themselves are disaggregated into monthly totals and more medical evidence comes to light about the nature of particular epidemics, especially fevers.[56] Nevertheless, an elementary exercise may not be out of place, if only to highlight some of the principal factors involved.

Wrigley and Schofield have produced a typology for crisis years, of one-star, two-star and three-star crises, the one-star crisis having deaths 10 per cent or more above their 25-year moving average, the two-star crisis having deaths 20 per cent or more above this average, while the three-star crisis designates 30 per cent and upwards.[57] The methodology has been used to examine bankruptcy in chapter two.

[53] *Ibid.*, pp. 501–2.   [54] *Ibid.*, pp. 498–9, 503–5.

[55] Landers, 'Mortality, weather and prices in London, 1675–1825: a study of short-term fluctuations', *Journal of Historical Geography*, 12 (1986), pp. 356–9.

[56] Despite an earlier disagreement with Matossian (see above, n. 30) I must acknowledge her work on mould poisoning as a valuable example of the kind of research of which one would like to see more. Many fevers must have been caused by poisonous fungi in the wheat and one should take contemporary descriptions of disease seriously. My disagreement is with the 'Growth of mold poisoning, 1981–1985' from the original 'Mold poisoning: an unrecognized English health problem, 1500–1800', to the article discussed above in n. 30.

[57] Wrigley and Schofield, *Population History*, pp. 332–3.

F

Table 5.12. *Mortality crises in London, 1690–1830*[58]

	%		%
1694	113	1746	116
1714	112	1762/3	119
1719	113	1772	120
1723	114	1777	111
1726	112	1793	113
1729	110	1795	110
1740/1	123	1800	121

Table 5.13. *Increases of mortality in crisis years: proportion of increased mortality caused by smallpox, fever, consumption and bread prices*[59]

Year	Increase in mortality (compared with adjacent years)	% of increase caused by:				Bread prices as % adjacent years
		Smallpox	Fever	Consumption	Total	
1694	4,097	17.3	46.9	8.2	72.4	72
1714	4,924	29.9	26.7	4.8	61.4	83
1719	2,358	66.4	4.7	5.3	76.5	130
1723	3,346	47	4.4	3.4	54.8	95
1726	2,676	−45.3	24.8	17.7	−2.9	82
1729	2,436	34.4	35.8	−2.7	67.5	125
1740/1	5,505	12.1	31.3	9.0	52.4	108
1746	4,762	40.8	9.1	12.6	62.5	101
1762/3	4,402	23.0	10.5	20.2	53.2	101
1772	4,335	60.9	6.1	8.4	75.4	106
1777	3,610	27.4	13.6	12.2	53.2	107
1793	2,022	31.7	16.8	22.6	71.1	105
1795	1,914	−88.2	10.8	63.2	−14.3	115
1800	4,314	26.0	8.5	22.1	56.6	161

[58] If one-year peaks (i.e. deviations from adjacent years) are taken there are two more years that should be included – 1710 (109 per cent of a 25-year average, 118 per cent of a three-year average) and 1733 where the figures are identical to 1710. Landers, 'Mortality, weather and prices', pp. 353–5, uses 11-year moving averages to produce slightly different years.

[59] Bread prices were ranked by their percentage deviation from the average of the two adjacent years (four adjacent years for 1740/1 and 1762/3). For 1800, 1797/9 and 1801/2 were taken.

Taking the London Bills of Mortality between 1690 and 1830 there were three two-star crises – the combined years 1740–1 (producing an average of 123 per cent), 1772 (120 per cent) and 1800 (121 per cent) – and eleven one-star crises. Table 5.12 illustrates them. Examination of these years leads to some interesting conclusions, as is shown in the more detailed analysis of table 5.13.

Table 5.13 shows clearly that the connection of high mortality with high bread prices is by no means obvious. High bread prices might coincide with a high death rate, as in 1795 or 1800, but there was no system in it. For four of the fourteen years bread prices were actually lower than the average of the two adjacent years; for another seven they were 8 per cent or less higher and even if 1740/1 is disaggregated it does not change the basic picture.[60] A systematic connection between high mortality and high bread prices might have been apparent had it not been for the prevalence of epidemic diseases which were not particularly responsive to nutrition, such as smallpox, or not *immediately* responsive, such as consumption. It takes about two years to die from consumption: the statistics on the age of deaths show, for instance, that 1795 – when a one-star crisis coincided with high bread prices – saw in fact a fall in infant and child mortality (ages 0–4) of a third from the average of the adjacent years, while deaths from consumption increased by nearly two-thirds; two-thirds of the total increase in deaths were among those aged sixty and over. At other times, the overall increase in mortality was caused by an increase in infant and child mortality that had little to do with bread prices. Bread prices were not particularly high in 1772 and 1777, but during the former year infant and child deaths (ages 0–4) were nearly 60 per cent higher than their level of the adjacent years, while in 1777 they were 71 per cent higher. The year 1746 saw stable and rather low bread prices, but an increase in mortality of 16 per cent from the adjacent years, over two-fifths of which were caused by a rise in infant deaths.

The reason for this was smallpox. Two of the fiercest outbreaks of smallpox came in 1719 and in 1723, before the age-specific mortality figures are available. But the third greatest outbreak was in 1772, when it accounted for 60.9 per cent of the increase in overall mortality, while 70.7 per cent of the increase in deaths were in the age group 0–4. In 1746 smallpox caused a 40.8 per cent increase in mortality; deaths of those aged 0–4 caused 42.8 per cent of this increase. At the other extreme, in 1795, deaths from smallpox fell by 88 per cent from the

---

[60] Rank order correlation coefficient with crisis years (based on a 25-year mean) was insignificant at 0.044.

level of the adjacent years, while infant and child mortality fell by over a third.

But, as smallpox was not always the major cause of crisis years, its fluctuations did not dominate the movement in the proportion that infant deaths caused of the total. The rank order correlation of smallpox with deaths of those aged 0–4 taken for the fourteen crisis years is statistically significant, but at 0.517 not very high, not 'explaining' more than 27 per cent of deaths,[61] despite our knowledge that smallpox affected mainly young children. For this there were two reasons: consumption and – more importantly – that group of diseases the Bills chose to call 'fevers'.

Since consumption took time to kill, its rank order correlation with bread prices, taken for the fourteen crisis years, is naturally insignificant.[62] It affected the statistics in table 5.13 erratically, not usually by very much except 1762–3, 1793 and 1800, when it caused a fifth of the increase in mortality and 1795, when it caused a quite exceptional 63 per cent of the increase. Appleby failed to find much connection between grain prices and deaths from consumption during the seventeenth and early eighteenth centuries, nor does table 5.13. The increase in 1800 may be explained by the difficult times of the 1790s, but not the increase of 1793 or even 1795. The long-term upward trend in the proportion of deaths from consumption peaked during the 1790s, so the high contribution of consumption to the increase in mortality may simply be a reflection of this.

Finally there is fever. Creighton was insistent that great outbreaks of fever – sometimes, but not always, typhoid – coincided with years of distress.[63] It was not difficult for him to find such examples – 1714, 1741, 1798, 1816–19 – but he also omitted those years of high prices without particular epidemics, such as 1795. The rank order correlation of bread prices with fever, although higher than with smallpox, remains statistically insignificant and extremely low.[64] Appleby found the general correlation between the incidence of fever and the price of bread to be weak during the seventeenth century: it is also weak during the eighteenth century. The difficulty is that some types of fever are quite responsive to the host's nutritional state, others less so. Some fevers may have declined in virulence, but McKeown is in-

---

[61] This is the rank order correlation for the proportion of the increase in mortality caused by the rise in infant mortality with the proportion of the mortality increase caused by the increase in smallpox mortality.

[62] $r = .231$.

[63] C. Creighton, *A History of Epidemics in Britain* (2 vols., 1894), II, pp. 59–60, 78–80, 139–40, 167–70.

[64] $r = .097$.

clined to limit this to scarlet fever.[65] Certainly the connection with nutrition is not obvious. Fever did less harm during the second half of the eighteenth century, when bread prices were rising, than between 1720 and 1750 when they were low, while the slump in building activity in the capital and its slow growth for many of these years does not suggest overcrowding overwhelmingly worse than later in the century.[66]

This general survey of mortality provides a general support for Wrigley and Schofield, as well as for the suggestion that there is a 'threshold of nutrition'. Below this threshold a person is very vulnerable, once safely above it, changes in food availability would not have had an immediate – or even noticeable – effect.[67] In fact, as far as many diseases are concerned, this level would appear to have been reached in England by the early eighteenth century, explaining why the years of crisis mortality bore no particular relation to changes in the level of nutrition.

Mortality, migration and 'improvement'

It is now possible to put some of this evidence together. The major reason for the rise in the death rate from the late seventeenth century until the middle of the eighteenth century was the effect of a more virulent smallpox as well as some other diseases on the death rate of infants and children, and of fevers on adult mortality. The decline of smallpox may have had something to do with inoculation, although McKeown and Brown dispute this – and, indeed, if only the direct (as opposed to the secondary) effects of smallpox inoculation are considered it could only have accounted for 11.4 per cent of the fall in the CDR between 1730 and 1838/44. McKeown and Brown were therefore thrown back on to Sherlock Holmes' principle that when the impossible has been eliminated whatever remains, however improbable, must be the truth[68] and duly pointed to improved nutrition. However, McKeown himself admits that the toxicity of smallpox is

---

65 T. McKeown, 'Food, infection and population', in R. I. Rotberg and T. K. Rabb (eds.), *Hunger and History*, p. 33.

66 See above, pp. 79–84.

67 See M. Livi-Bacci, 'The nutrition–mortality link in past times: a comment', in R. I. Rotberg and T. K. Rabb (eds.), *Hunger and History*, pp. 95–100; S. C. Watkins and E. van de Walle, 'Nutrition, mortality, and population size: Malthus' court of last resort', in R. I. Rotberg and T. K. Rabb (eds.), *Hunger and History*, pp. 26–8.

68 McKeown, 'Food, infection and population', pp. 29, 31–3; McKeown, *The Modern Rise of Population*, pp. 161–3.

little affected by the host's nutrition,[69] Appleby failed to find a statistical correlation between deaths from smallpox and bread prices between 1629 and 1750,[70] this chapter has likewise failed to find such a connection, nor is a connection necessarily to be expected in subsequent years, with the spread of inoculation. Smallpox deaths happened to be at an all time numerical high in 1796, when bread prices were high, but they were much lower in 1801, when bread prices were higher, low during the difficult decade of 1811–20, but rising a little during the boom of 1820–5. Smallpox was affected by two things – the spread of inoculation and then vaccination during the second half of the eighteenth century, and by the potency of the disease itself. It happened to be more potent during the period of low bread prices in the early eighteenth century than later. Consumption would seem to be a better candidate for McKeown and Brown: but it is difficult to reconcile a steady increase in deaths from consumption during the relatively prosperous decade of the 1780s with a precipitate fall in deaths from consumption during the difficult years between 1811 and 1820, and a steady rise during the rapidly improving years 1821–5.

There was a considerable fall in the death rate from at least the last quarter of the eighteenth century, if not from the 1750s; by the end of the eighteenth century it was falling to a level below that of nonplague years in the seventeenth century and it continued to fall. But it would be a bold man who could claim unhesitatingly that the years between 1750 and 1810 saw an improvement in living standards in London. As part three of this book will show, real wage rates for artisans and labourers show a downward trend: they declined slowly from the 1760s, more rapidly during the 1790s. The wage rate, of course, makes no allowance for unemployment or underemployment, the distribution of skills within the workforce, and the various factors that make it theoretically possible for declining real wage rates to be combined with increased welfare. An ever declining real wage rate for artisans could also mask a tendency for the proportion of artisans in the total population to be increasing, and thus for the overall level of welfare to be greater – but this is rendered doubtful by the fact that differentials between artisans and labourers in the building trades show little sign of moving, over the medium or long runs. Rather conclusively, the poor boys who were measured by the Marine Society during the eighteenth century were remarkably short in

---

[69] Rotberg and Rabb (eds.), *Hunger and History*, p. 308; A. J. Mercer, 'Smallpox and epidemiological change in Europe; the role of vaccination', *Population Studies*, 39 (1985), p. 294.

[70] A. B. Appleby, 'Nutrition and disease: the case of London, 1550–1750', *Journal of Interdisciplinary History*, 6 (1975), pp. 1–22.

stature – 'so short that only two of the 81 ethnic groups for which modern height data are available record lower adolescent heights. These are the Lumi and Bundi of New Guinea – two exceedingly impoverished populations.'[71] The Marine Society boys did not become much taller between 1775 and 1790, and their average height actually fell for the next two decades.[72] One must profess some surprise at being told that this group was above the nutritional threshold referred to earlier. Colquhoun, ever inclined towards exaggeration but not, when he was referring to his own direct experience, creating wholly fictitious statements, claimed that in 1795 some twenty-five out of thirty of those balloted for the militia in the Tower Division were found to be below the minimum height required.[73] In view of the heavy recruitment for the armed forces that had taken place previously, the sample would hardly be representative, but it is nevertheless indicative. The evidence of improved diet is, to say the least, not forthcoming before about 1810, and allowing for the hardships of the decade, not unambiguous until later.[74]

There is, however, a certain amount of evidence that from the mid eighteenth century London was becoming cleaner. The Fleet Ditch was filled in 1747, Westminster received a Paving Act in 1762 and other parts of the town followed suit, providing for gutters and regular scavenging and cleansing. Manure acquired a commercial value by the 1760s and was regularly shipped out of town.[75] Furthermore,

The streets are also better and more regularly cleansed; and by the addition of several new works, water is becoming much more plentiful than it was heretofore: and this has been a gret means of contributing, not only to greater cleanliness in our houses, but also towards purifying the air by washing the filth out of the kennels and common shoars.[76]

71 R. W. Fogel, S. Engerman, R. Floud et al.,'Secular changes in American and British stature and nutrition', in R. I. Rotberg and T. K. Rabb (eds.), *Hunger and History*, p. 270.
72 See above, n. 45. Floud, Wachter and Gregory, *Height, Health and History*, pp. 197, 167–9.
73 Colquhoun, *A Treatise on Indigence*, p. 159.
74 'Synergy' may be a helpful concept here – meaning that 'the behaviour of most diseases is shaped by the nutritional state of the host' (Ann C. Carmichael, 'Infection, hidden hunger and history', in R. I. Rotberg and T. K, Rabb (eds.), *Hunger and History*, p. 51). Diseases can combine, to have more severe effects than any individual disease would warrant. It offers intriguing possibilities.
75 *London Life*, pp. 107–8; Rudé, *Hanoverian London*, p. 136; W. S. Lewis, *Three Tours through London in the Years 1748, 1776, 1797* (New Haven, 1941), p. 51; Buer, *Health, Wealth and Population*, pp. 82–3; J. Middleton, *View of the Agriculture of Middlesex* (1798), p. 301, who added that 99 per cent of the night soil ended up in the Thames.
76 W. Wales, *An Inquiry into the Present State of Population in England and Wales* (1781), pp. 18–19.

How widespread the improvements were is another matter: a disproportionate number were limited to Westminster, and usually only to parts of Westminster. In 1774 there were complaints about the custom of making paupers' graves large enough to accommodate three or four coffins abreast piled seven high, and not closing them until they were full;[77] many dunghills and smells lasted well into the nineteenth century, new horrors were always being reported on with suitable indignation, and Londoners would not have found it easy to avoid intestinal diseases. The improvements were patchy, as will be argued in the conclusion to this book.[78] In a town which, by the late eighteenth century, was expanding so rapidly, it was not likely to be otherwise.

However, what is beyond dispute is that during the course of the eighteenth and nineteenth centuries London moved from being a town where mortality was very much higher than in the country as a whole to one where mortality was comparable. We know that seventeenth- and eighteenth-century London, in common with many other towns of the period, was a reservoir of infections which were not so endemic in the countryside.[79] By the nineteenth century, vulnerability to infection in both town and country in southern England appears to have become reasonably similar, and London was no longer a national reservoir of lethal infections. To a certain extent this is self-evident, but there is a need for supporting evidence that describes the process whereby the capital's catchment area developed a pattern of immunities similar to that of the capital. The area must have been wide: the unprecedentedly large armed forces of the Revolutionary and Napoleonic Wars would have had a tendency to pass through London, but the death rate in southern England did not, to the best of our knowledge, increase. This regional immunity was certainly not the case during the late seventeenth century, when there was a strong increase in the CDR in south-east England *outside* London, the CDR being higher than at any other time between 1600

---

[77] *London Life*, p. 345. Another problem was reported from St George's-in-the-East in 1772 where the Paving Commissioners had raised the level of Old Gravel Lane by 2 ft 5 ins so that the front doors were unusable: G.L.R.O. MJ/SP/ITR/Oct./99.

[78] This is clearly demonstrated in Landers, 'Mortality and metropolis'.

[79] A recent and very relevant discussion of this, to which my discussion is much indebted, is J. Walter and R. Schofield, 'Famine, disease and crisis mortality in early modern society', in J. Walter and R. Schofield (eds.), *Famine, Disease and the Social Order in Early Modern Society* (Cambridge, 1989), pp. 1–73. For deaths from smallpox and fevers, Galloway, 'Annual variations', pp. 498–500; for the analysis of the age variations, Landers, 'Mortality and metropolis', pp. 72–5 and 'Mortality, weather and prices', pp. 356–61.

and 1800.[80] It has been argued recently that this was directly due to a quicker pace of economic life – a combination of more crowded housing and hence more dirt, and greater contact with a lethal metropolis. On the other hand, increases in the death rate could also be caused by distress. The relatively simple analyses of fever and smallpox earlier in this chapter did not reveal much connection with prices, and when the overall picture is considered this is indeed so. But a more detailed analysis reveals some interesting patterns. There were statistically significant responses of typhus, smallpox and some fevers to price fluctuations within the same or the succeeding year; there is also a statistically significant match between these diseases and deaths from adults in their twenties. Malnutrition had very little to do with it, overcrowding was a great deal more important. Increases in prices produced stress in the countryside and stimulated a migration towards London; new arrivals would be particularly likely to be living in poor conditions and less likely to have immunities against some of the infections endemic in the capital.[81] However, in the longer term, greater intensity of movement between the capital and southern England would have spread the degree of immunity to the capital's infections. In the short run, the provincial death rate would have increased, but in the long run it would have fallen. Such a process may well have taken place in south-east England between the late seventeenth and the late eighteenth centuries. Wrigley and Schofield's national statistics cover too broad an area for our purposes, but Landers has shown that between 1675 and 1750 instability in the national CDR was greater than in London.[82] The capital's death rates were higher, but were also more stable than those in the rest of the country. This was not the case after 1750, when the national CDR varied less than that of the capital, as well as varying less than it did during the late seventeenth century. This is suggestive, although not conclusive. We need more detailed local studies of diseases, as well as of migration patterns. The decline in the death rate took place; historians are not sure why.

Mortality and economic growth

The cities of pre-industrial Europe absorbed resources on an enormous scale. The larger the cities were, the more resources they

---

[80] Mary J. Dobson, 'The last hiccup of the old demographic regime: population stagnation and decline in late seventeenth- and early eighteenth-century south-east England', *Continuity and Change*, 4 (3), December 1989, p. 413.
[81] Landers, 'Mortality and metropolis', p. 67.   [82] *Ibid., passim.*

consumed, but when they passed a certain threshold their consumption of conspicuous goods and services increased disproportionately. A large capital city had a large and highly specialised service sector as well as an aristocracy resident for some of the year. Such a city – or rather, the luxurious part of such a city – was much more the epitome of luxury than a small country town, no matter how hard the latter might work to close that gap by developing its attractions as a tourist centre. Even with the wealthiest provincial cities there was a qualitative as well as a quantitative difference. Westminster had 1.8 per cent of the population of England and Wales in 1801 but had 7.8 per cent of the employers of manservants in England and Wales in 1780, a total of 1,939, compared with Bath's 335 and York's 145.

At the same time, such a city generated disproportionately large quantities of dirt, squalor and disease. Some of the diseases came through the dirt and the squalor, others through the number of people, there being a sufficiently large population for certain infections to remain endemic. The towns devoured people and, until late in the eighteenth century, London devoured more people than virtually all the other towns of England put together.

The towns made their due and often underestimated contribution to economic growth, playing a key role in welding the grid of a market economy on to so many disparate regions and creating an increasingly integrated national economy. They grew because the national economy grew and they gave their own stimulus to this growth. They benefited from agrarian booms, they benefited from trading booms, but above all the large towns benefited from population growth, and this involved immigration. With a death rate so much higher than the birth rate, the towns sought to drain the countryside. If they could not do so, then their own economy was likely to cease growing. It would not necessarily decline, wage rates might be relatively high, but building would stagnate, imports to the town would stagnate, many types of investment would not take place. In the absence of countervailing forces, the effect throughout the region would be considerable.

The need for a continuous stream of immigrants was one of the dangers of the pre-industrial urban system: an increasing population contributed towards an economic upswing which, in turn, increased the levels of migration, urbanisation and thus mortality, which would – if the birth rate failed to respond in time – dampen the upswing. This happened in London, during the thirty years or so from the mid 1720s. Those who denounced the capital for parasitism may have been saying more than they realised. The very existence of established patterns of immigration to a lethal town would dampen population growth in the surrounding region and if such growth were in any case low – as it was during the late seventeenth and early eighteenth centuries – then the stimulus for local economic growth may itself have been lacking. More contact with London led to significantly higher death rates in the country; a lower level of rural immigration contributed towards slower economic growth in London and threatened to undermine it.

By the late eighteenth century this pattern was changing. London's death rate was falling and falling for many reasons, but one significant reason was that London's catchment area had developed a pattern of immunities similar to that of the metropolis. The increased economic activity that spread disease and increased the hinterland's death rate eventually balanced out. Mortality among new arrivals was no longer a major hazard to longer-term economic growth. At the same time, for different reasons, infant death rates were declining, and the capital expanded rapidly. The next period of relatively slow growth rates after 1825 was not caused by slow population growth. Structures had not changed fundamentally, seasonal and cyclical fluctuations continued unabated but mortality, one of the underlying forces that had traditionally controlled the growth if not also the decline of great cities, was no longer a constraint. At the same time, even without great increases in productivity, rapid population growth was no longer a sure guarantee of a decline in real wages.

PART III

The standard of living and the London trades

One of the most common methods used by historians when discussing living standards is to produce a series of wage rates and a series of prices, divide the two and emerge with a real wage rate series. This method makes no pretence of examining the quality of life, problems of urbanisation, sanitation, health and so forth, but it is of some help for those examining material living standards. There are obvious drawbacks to this approach, such as whether the trades for which data happens to have survived were representative, as well as the inevitable drawback that the data by its very nature makes no allowance for unemployment, and tends to refer to adult men. Prices are also problematic: most of the surviving information is about wholesale prices. Since we know little about consumption patterns in the past, there are problems of constructing suitable weights for an index.

These are all problems that can be more or less overcome – at least if one is not interested in the short run – and an index, with all its strengths and weaknesses, is duly presented in chapter six. The suggestion is that real wage rates (and to a considerable extent real wages) were comparatively high during the second third of the eighteenth century, falling thereafter, and rising again after the Napoleonic Wars. The decline of the second half of the eighteenth century is a pattern common to southern England, while the nineteenth-century rise appears to be part of a national pattern.

Taken uncritically, such an index and such conclusions can conceal more than they reveal. In the first place, an index of wage rates only applies to a wage-earning labour force, and the extent of such a labour force is by no means obvious for much of this period. While it is probable that most people were dependent on somebody else for a livelihood, that is not to say that they expected to receive a daily or weekly money wage and nothing more. Apprentices obviously did not, nor did many government employees, who regularly received letters of credit. In the armed forces, men might be lucky even to receive that. Furthermore, the concept of remuneration by a reasonably predictable money wage, and only a money wage, was by no means universal for much of this period. Civil servants expected commissions, the more senior in rank the larger the commission. Workmen expected perquisites as much as did politicians. The problem of perquisites is difficult for historians. Might perquisites have been so valuable as to have eroded the value of the monetary wage? It is because of these two problems – the problem of the creation of a waged labour force, and the problem of the extent of the wage – that chapter six begins by discussing the nature of the wage, in order to establish more precisely the limitations of an index of real wages.

Secondly, there is the problem of averages. Many trades would have been above the average and many below, and during periods of rapid structural change, such as the industrial revolution of the eighteenth and nineteenth centuries – or the deindustrialisation of the late twentieth century – there is no particular likelihood that wages in the various trades would have followed the same trends, up or down. As has been repeatedly argued, the economy of the capital did not undergo fundamental changes between 1700 and 1850. This diminishes the problem to a certain extent. But during the first half of the nineteenth century, especially after 1820, there is a definite dichotomy between the pattern of improvement revealed by the real wage rate data and the complaints of a large number of London trades. For tailors, shoemakers, for cabinet makers, this was a period of crisis when their unions collapsed, their skills were diluted and their earnings fell. It was a period of Owenism, of desperate attacks on 'sweaters', of Chartism. What is more, what was happening in London was not unique. In France and Germany grain prices fell less than in England after the Napoleonic Wars, so indications of general improvement are harder to find, but neither are there many indications in the French and German statistics that conditions overall were steadily deteriorating.[1] However, an influential group of commentators felt strongly that, whatever the statistics might say, things had become worse and would, in the absence of suitable action, become worse still. France and Germany had problems that England did not have – for a start they had to cope with English competition in many of their major industries. They also had problems of over-

---

[1] See the references in L. D. Schwarz, 'The standard of living in the long run: London 1800–1860', *Econ. Hist. Rev.*, 2nd ser., 38 (1985), n.69.

population on the land, something possibly experienced in England in the Speenhamland counties, but not elsewhere. But their pessimists shared with the pessimists in England a concern at what was happening to the semi-skilled trades. Everywhere these were under attack from unskilled labour. This applied especially to those ubiquitous urban crafts, tailoring and shoemaking. In the middle of the century the London tailors looked back to a golden age that had ended when they lost a strike in 1834.[2] The tailors of Paris underwent the same process, complaining loudly in 1848 of *confection* – ready-to-wear clothing being produced in the home, often by wives and children and sold to an anonymous general public, rather than being produced to individual order in the workshop.[3] The same complaints were emerging, during the same decade, from towns as diverse as Düsseldorf[4] and New York.[5] When the same process seemed to be taking place, at the same time, in towns that appeared to be in such different stages of economic development, one is entitled to ask whether these towns had in fact more in common than was apparent at first. One may also ask what economic processes were at work, since new 'machinery' was not one of them.[6]

London offers an excellent example of these various processes at work. The histories of living standards, as given by the indices of real wages, give one story; the histories of trades often give quite different stories. Frequently the two fail to coincide. John Breuilly has suggested that historians should distinguish between five types of craft production during the nineteenth century. There were the occupations transformed or even created by industrial growth, such as engineering. Secondly, there were those crafts that maintained their earlier skills and occupational identity but shifted into large-scale units of production, such as printing. These kept their labour aristo-

---

[2] See below, p. 179.
[3] C. H. Johnson, 'Economic change and artisan discontent: the tailors' history, 1800–1848', in R. Price (ed.), *Revolution and Reaction* (1975), pp. 87–114; J. W. Scott, 'Men and women in the Parisian garment trades: discussions of family and work in the 1830s and 1840s', in P. Thane, R. Floud and G. Crossick (eds.), *The Power of the Past* (1984), pp. 67–93.
[4] H. Lenger, 'Polarisierung und Verlag: Schuhmacher, Schneider und Schreiner in Düsseldorf, 1816–1861', in U. Engelhardt (ed.), *Handwerker in der Industrialisierung* (Stuttgart, 1984), pp. 127–45.
[5] Jane Rendell, *The Origins of Modern Feminism* (1985), pp. 166–7.
[6] See, for instance, B. H. Moss, 'Parisian producers' associations (1800–1851): the socialism of skilled workers', in R. Price (ed.), *Revolution and Reaction*, pp. 77ff: between 1800 and 1848 few trades were completely transformed by machinery, but 'they suffered from the competition of less skilled and unapprenticed labour producing cheaper and ready-made goods in domestic piece work, sweated workshops, subcontracted gangs and prisons and convents'.

cracies, high earnings and occupational exclusiveness. A third category, such as weavers, was destroyed by industrialisation. Fourthly,
there were trades such as jewellery on the one hand, or barbering on
the other, that hardly changed at all. And fifthly, there were those
trades mentioned in the preceding paragraph, trades that Breuilly
considers to have been basic to the artisanal labour movement of the
nineteenth century. They supplied the basic demands of the domestic
population. There was a large stable market for their products. Production and distribution could be separated. There was scope for
de-skilling, not through new machinery but through more complex
divisions of labour. Breuilly's examples are shoemaking, tailoring,
furniture-making and the rather special case of building.[7] They could
be considered, in large part, as semi-skilled. Chapter seven of this
book examines three such trades that were of particular significance in
the capital: tailoring, shoemaking and furniture-making. It also examines one of the doomed trades – silk weaving – a large-scale activity of
particular importance within the capital. For the first three of these
trades production units remained small and start-up costs were not
high but the workers saw – or claimed to see – a great growth of
large-scale capitalist control over distribution. In the middle of the
century all four trades were complaining loudly to Mayhew that
during the preceding generation their conditions of work had taken a
drastic turn for the worse. It is a story that has often been told; what
has been told less often is why this process had not occurred a century
earlier. There was nothing new about sweated labour in the capital;
many trades lived in danger of the degradation that overtook these
four trades during the first half of the nineteenth century. Chapter
eight draws some conclusions from this analysis and examines some
of the institutions, processes, acts of God and governments that
helped the London trade to defend themselves: in particular raw
material costs, the law, the use of apprentices and the periodic labour
shortages caused by war.

[7] J. Breuilly, 'Artisan economy, artisan politics, artisan ideology: the artisan contribution to the nineteenth-century European labour movement', in C. Emsley and
J. Walvin (eds.), *Artisans, Peasants and Proletarians 1760–1860* (1985), pp. 198–200.

6

The making of a wage rate

The wage: concept and reality

When examining the higher ranks of the professions, especially government service, during the seventeenth and most of the eighteenth centuries, one looks in vain for the concept of a regular salary that was supposed to reflect the hours of work and was *all* that a person received by way of remuneration. 'It was not the salary of any place that did make a man rich but the opportunity of getting money while he is in the place' was the advice that persuaded Pepys to become secretary of the Navy Board,[1] while until the end of the eighteenth century it was customary for persons in the Crown's employment who paid out money to be given a commission of about 1 per cent by the receiver of the payment, a practice quite different from bribery.[2] In 1788 the Head Clerk of the office of the Navy Comptroller had a salary of only £240 but fees of £1,737; in 1781 he had received as much as £2,510 in fees.[3] There was also a wide range of ad hoc payments: during the 1730s the Doorkeeper of the Court of Chancery was paid 10s. for every case heard, but 2s. of this went to the Usher of the Rolls, 2s. 6d. to the Cryer, 1s. to the Lord Chancellor's Tipt-Staff and the Registrar's Bagbearer, while the Master of the Rolls' Tipt-Staff and the Court Keeper each received 6d.[4]

This was paid in cash; eighteenth-century workmen had a reputation for not being paid entirely in cash. Sometimes the government might be slow in paying them; during the seventeenth century arrears of a year had been very common and they were not unknown during the early eighteenth century, with a group of tradesmen petitioning in

---

[1] B. Pool, *Navy Board Contracts 1660–1832* (1966), p. 3.   [2] *Ibid.*, pp. 37, 144.
[3] *Ibid.*, pp. 112–13.
[4] Earle, *Making*, p. 62.

1719 for £54,910 owed to them from the reign of William III.[5] As late as 1762 wages at Chatham dockyard were fifteen months in arrears.[6] Such arrears were common enough for the armed forces and for those working in the royal dockyards, but in the building trades long arrears were probably more common for building contractors than for their workmen. Nevertheless, even when the workmen were paid in cash, they did their best to ensure that it was not only cash that they received. The coal hewers of the North and the coal-meters of the Thames had fuel allowances. Ironworks and other establishments using coal often gave some to their workers at little or no cost. Mates of West Indiamen had rights to the sweepings of sugar and coffee from the hold of the ship, coopers to the produce of broken barrels on the ship, everybody to the produce of a barrel broken on the quay. Gangsmen and coopers had a claim to the drainings of molasses and spilt sugar on the floor of the warehouse, the labourers in the corn ships believed themselves entitled to the grain that had been removed as samples. As Ashton wrote,

In each case the workers saw to it that the crumbs from the master's table were ample. Casks were handled not too gently; sacks were liable to burst open; shipwrights took care that their wives did not go short of firewood. The line of demarcation between the extension of established rights and barefaced robbery is difficult to draw ... Yarn returned to the warehouse might be light weight ... Wool pickers, spinners and weavers had ample opportunities of purloining material and of disposing of it by sale.[7]

Workers at powder mills had 'liberty at their leisure' to split deal and dip it into the brimstone prepared for the making of the gunpowder, thus making matches. The scraps tailors left behind from cutting out cloth – 'cabbage' – were their customary right.[8] Shipwrights in the Admiralty yards had the right to take home 'chips' – such wood as remained after they had finished cutting out the shapes for the ships – and they made profitable use of the practice throughout the seventeenth and eighteenth centuries. Chips came to be defined as pieces of wood less than 3 feet long, which turned out to be the width of staircases in many dockyard towns.[9] It was a practice that had been opposed – fruitlessly – since at least the seventeenth century: in 1783

[5] *Ibid.*, pp. 361–2, n. 16.
[6] J. Rule, *The Experience of Labour in Eighteenth-Century Industry* (1981), p. 130; R. A. Morriss, *The Royal Dockyards during the Revolution and Napoleonic Wars* (Leicester, 1983), pp. 102, 104.
[7] T. S. Ashton, *An Economic History of England: The Eighteenth Century* (1955), p. 208.
[8] Rule, *Experience of Labour*, p. 126.
[9] H. E. Richardson, 'Wages of shipwrights in H. M. dockyards, 1496–1788', *Mariners' Mirror*, 33 (1947), pp. 265–74.

dockyard gatekeepers were instructed 'to suffer no person to pass out of the dock gates with Great Coats, large Trousers or any other Dress that can conceal stores of any kind ... No trousers are to be used by the labourers employed in the storehouses and if anyone persists in such a custom, he is to be discharged the Yard.'[10] But it was not until the beginning of the nineteenth century that the Admiralty finally bought out the practice at the cost of 6d. a day.[11] The traditionalist and terrorising Lord St Vincent was First Lord, and for St Vincent to make such a concession was rare indeed. Chips, however, were merely one example of a widespread practice. Servants expected to receive 'vails': visitors to the houses of the great were confronted by a row of servants on their departure and were expected to reward them suitably – those visitors who wished to return found it advisable to pay up.[12] Vails were quite different in principle from practices such as taking commissions from shopkeepers or selling worn-out clothing and other things that the employer no longer needed: the latter depended on the acquiescence or ignorance of the individual employer, which might or might not exist, and is a common enough characteristic of the twentieth century, while vails were a particular feature of the period and were eventually stamped out. In fact, additions to wages appear to have been fairly universal:

Bugging to the hatter, cabbage to the tailors, blue-pigeon flying to plumbers and glaziers, chippings to shipwrights, sweepings to porters, red sailyard docking to navy yard workers, flints and thrums to weavers, vails to servants, privileges to west country clothiers, bontages to Scottish agricultural workers, scrappings and naxers to coopers, wastages to framework knitters, in all these the eighteenth-century labourer appropriated a part of his produce or a part of the materials of his labour.[13]

Does this make a mockery of the wage rate? It is arguable – and has been argued – that the eighteenth century saw a sustained attack on non-monetary remuneration, and that by the early nineteenth century the attack had been more or less successful. Peter Linebaugh has openly speculated on this. 'We can', he said, writing of the early nineteenth century,

make a division in the London working classes. One part of it, artisans primarily, forged historical definition and clarity by virtue of its organisational novelty and political initiative. This class vanguard was built upon a base that

[10] *Ibid.*, pp. 267–8. Exactly how the workmen got the wood out of the yards and the Admiralty tried to stop it is not clear.
[11] M. Oppenheim, 'The royal dockyards', *Victoria County History*, Kent (1926), II, pp. 368, 386.
[12] J. J. Hecht, *The Domestic Servant Class in Eighteenth-Century England* (1956), pp. 158–73; Earle, *Making*, pp. 219–20, 376, n. 26.
[13] P. Linebaugh, in *Bulletin of the Society for the Study of Labour History*, 25 (1972), p. 13.

was largely organised by money, the wage hierarchy particularly . . . Against the money economy must be set a still inchoate mass of traditions springing from a larger proletarian base and belonging to a profounder historical continuum. This was part of the 'labouring poor' that Patrick Colquhoun feared and studied . . . it was unalterably antipathetic to wage discipline.[14]

The problem with this argument is that there is no serious evidence that payments in kind were less extensive in the nineteenth century than they had been a century earlier. 'Pilfering' continued to exist on the London riverside because the conditions that were conducive to it did not change, just as weavers argued about thrums as long as the handloom survived. Linebaugh's argument is certainly striking, but unfortunately there is little evidence for his argument that the 'deserving poor' went for the wage while the 'undeserving poor' did not, and that this was a struggle that was taking place throughout the eighteenth century. That payments in kind were under attack from many sources during the course of the eighteenth century is not in question. What is in question is whether there was any system in it, or even whether such an attack was particularly unprecedented. Employers under pressure would cut back on perquisites, and when times improved they might relax. Prosecution Associations – associations of masters designed to stamp out 'abuses' in a trade – appear to have been active during depressions, but not afterwards. Their activities were cyclical, not long-term.[15] Particular conditions of work permitted particular kinds of appropriation, while the same conditions set the limits to such appropriation. But non-monetary appropriation did not take place in an economic vacuum. It was part of what has been called 'exchange entitlement': part of the entire package of goods that the employee received and that the employer had to disburse.[16] Workmen might perhaps not be paid entirely in cash if it was cheaper for the employer not to do so, if he could give them something else that either met their requirements directly – such as drink purchased wholesale – or other goods that might be exchanged by his employees without the medium of cash. In any case, for much of this period the national supply of cash was unsatisfactory and substitutes had to be

---

[14] P. Linebaugh, 'Labour history without the labour process: a note on John Gast and his time', *Social History*, 7 (1982), pp. 319–28.

[15] J. Styles, 'Embezzlement, industry and the law', in M. Berg, P. Hudson and M. Sonenscher (eds.), *Manufacture in Town and Country before the Factory* (Cambridge, 1983), pp. 186–7: 'It appears that the incidence and intensity of [employers'] controls often varied according to the fortunes of an industry, just like their manipulation of truck and false weights.' Also P. J. R. King, 'Crime, law and society in Essex, 1740–1820', Cambridge University, Ph.D. thesis, 1984, p. 132.

[16] A. Sen, 'Starvation and exchange entitlements: a general appraisal and its application to the great Bengal famine', *Cambridge Journal of Economics*, 1 (1977), pp. 33–59.

found. Business was highly seasonal, credit very widespread, payment of bills to retailers irregular. Employers would have welcomed a way of reducing their dependence on cash and of spacing out their payments. Employers everywhere were inclined to provide liberal allocations of beer; it is unclear to what extent they regarded these as part of their wage costs. In 1760, after thirty-eight years of stability, the price of beer in London rose, but neither the amount of beer distributed to building workers not the wages paid to them appears to have fallen in compensation.[17] Other employers might provide fuel. Institutions that had difficulty in raising wage rates without the permission of various committees must have needed to find ways round this difficulty at times. The cost of living increased enormously between 1795 and 1800; wage rates for builders employed by Greenwich Hospital did not increase so their remuneration must have been made up in some less direct way.[18] The keepers of the warehouses for the West Indian and American trades were not inclined to pay their labourers generously and, indeed, sometimes paid them nothing at all. But men worked there for the right to remove dirty sugar, spices and tobacco: the warehouse keeper had his goods moved and his warehouse cleaned at little or no cost to himself. So long as the goods that the men removed were genuinely dirty there was no problem and indeed when on trial for theft during the eighteenth century the common defence was to argue this. If juries believed it, then they found the defendant innocent.[19]

The precise economic context of exchange entitlements was crucial. There was nothing 'moral' about entitlements. Apprentices – in theory supposed to be outside the market system and who were certainly paid as though this was the case – were always liable to be used as cheap labour, and were increasingly boarded out, as were farm servants, a tendency that accelerated rapidly during periods of inflation, such as the Revolutionary and Napoleonic Wars.[20] All the exchanges, whether in cash or kind, were themselves subject to the trade cycle, and were afforded when times were good. The crucial variable was the monetary wage rate, and it was this that Englishmen of the eighteenth century took seriously. They complained when it was cut,

---

[17] Mathias, *Brewing Industry*, pp. 111–13.

[18] R. S. Tucker, 'Real wages of artisans in London, 1729–1935', *Journal of the American Statistical Society*, 31 (1936), pp. 73–84, who wrote of real wages falling to 'Asiatic standards'. He took the data from J. R. McCulloch, *A Dictionary of Commerce and Commercial Navigation* (1840), pp. 952–3.

[19] P. D'Sena, 'Perquisites and pilfering in the London docks, 1700–1795', Open University, M.Phil. thesis, 1986.

[20] Snell, *Annals*, pp. 67–103.

they went on strike to raise it,[21] they fought for Acts of Parliament to fix it,[22] they rioted when Irish labourers were undercutting it,[23] and they were very worried about the competition of foreigners.

> During the Ferment raised last Winter [1751], all over the Nation, by the proposal of a general Naturalization, few of either Side of the Question descended to the Examination of Particulars. All our Arguments ... turned to the increase of Numbers, the lowering of Wages, and other Advantages to the Nation ... In this Case the lower Class was most immoderately divided, on the subject of lowering Wages. This was a Consequence on all hands presumed to follow.[24]

At its most cautious, it can at least be said that the money wage rate was probably *the* major component in the income of many urban dwellers as well as being a good indicator of what was happening with non-monetary forms of remuneration. It is, however, more a barometer of changes in incomes than an accurate monitor.

The overall context for a discussion of living standards, as measured by the daily wage, is of course the creation of a labour force paid by such a wage or, at least, by piece rates tied to some notion of what a day's wage should be. And it is this question – which lies at the very core of the history of London's development during these years – about which we remain relatively ignorant. Answering this question involves studying two processes that were not quite identical and were certainly not simultaneous, namely the growing capital required to set up in trade, and the development of a waged labour force that was employed by the owners of this capital. The two are obviously linked, and intimately so, but when their development is viewed historically, as opposed to conceptually, it is obvious that the linkage is not straightforward. A closely related theme, that of the connection between the growth of a waged labour force and the disappearance of the handicrafts, has similarly been found to be a slow and complex process in all the countries where it has been examined.[25]

The level of capitalisation required to set up in a trade has been discussed in chapter two: it was at least £100, and usually rather a lot more, so no journeymen on some £40 a year in the mid eighteenth

---

[21] C. R. Dobson, *Masters and Journeymen: A Prehistory of Industrial Relations, 1717–1800* (1980), *passim*.

[22] See below, chapter seven, for tailors and silkweavers.

[23] G. Rudé, '"Mother Gin" and the London riots of 1736', in G. Rudé, *Paris and London in the Eighteenth Century* (1970), pp. 201–21.

[24] Richard Parrot, *Reflections on Various Subjects Relating to Arts and Commerce* (1752), pp. 52–3.

[25] L. D. Schwarz, 'The formation of the wage: some problems', in P. Scholliers (ed.), *Real Wages in Nineteenth- and Twentieth-Century Europe* (Berg, Oxford, 1989), pp. 21–39.

century could have afforded it without generous support or credit. This was already the case by the late seventeenth century[26] though there is some evidence that it had not been the case during the sixteenth century.[27] Chapter two has established that about 20–30 per cent of London's population were 'middle class', depending on the definition used, and that only about 5 per cent of London's 'plebeian' population were self-employed (outside building), but that does not mean that the remaining 95 per cent were regularly waged. Seventeenth-century wage earners had a reputation of being marginal persons in society. Woodward has argued that those who depended only on their wages for a livelihood were very much at the bottom of the social pyramid, and very much a minority within the plebeian population.[28] Many who earned a wage had additional sources of income – they frequently had some income from the land; many others were, in effect, small-scale contractors, supplying raw materials as well as labour, and being paid as such. Of course they were not averse to working for a wage when necessary, but only a minority would have been full-time wage earners, earning a wage and only a wage. Furthermore, this minority can be reduced yet further when one deducts servants, apprentices, professional people, shopkeepers, prostitutes and criminals from this number. In addition, many single people lived in their employer's house and had their board and lodging paid for – women as domestic servants, men as servants or apprentices, sometimes even as journeymen prior to setting up on their own. There was a large sink of underemployed labour, now known as the service sector, such as part-time servants, porters, carriers, dockers, hawkers, pedlars, washerwomen, all of whom worked erratically for piece rates. Finally, an unspecified proportion of those who remained, such as stevedores and dockers, worked in gangs, hiring themselves out for a lump sum for each job. There was a great deal of subcontracting, and thus a hierarchy of employers. Nicholas Barbon, the master builder of late seventeenth-century London, subcontracted to smaller builders, who themselves subcontracted in turn.[29] Quite a number of people may have earned wages for a part of the year, but not all that many would have been full-time wage earners.

Even in 1851 we must be on guard against careless use of the term 'waged labour force'. Dependent it may have been, but waged much

---

[26] Earle, *Making*, pp. 106–8.   [27] Rappaport, 'Social structure', pp. 115–23.
[28] D. Woodward, 'Wage rates and living standards in pre-industrial England', *Past and Present*, 91 (1981), pp. 28–45.
[29] Summerson, *Georgian London*, p. 45.

of it was not. In the capital, half the female workforce and 5 per cent of the male workforce consisted of domestic servants, subject to many constraints, and much subordination, but not receiving a weekly wage. The male labour force included many dependent on casual pay and casual work – 8 per cent of its members were engaged in non-railway land transport, and another 7 per cent in general labour. These were activities which might, with luck, produce a wage large enough to support its practitioners, but might well not do so. Another 14 per cent were in dealing – usually self-employed.[30] This reduces the potentially waged male workforce to 63 per cent of its original number; many of those who remain were only earning regular wages for a part of the year, as the chapter on seasonality showed. Others were apprentices. It would, therefore, be quite wrong, even in 1851, to assume that the overwhelming majority of London's workforce – even the male workforce – depended on a regular money wage, which was only interrupted at times of cyclical crisis. But the money wage rate provides an indication of what was happening to the workforce.

The money wage

The only long-term series of data on London wages available at present are daily wage rates for the building trades. Fortunately, the building trades were fairly representative of many other London trades. The summaries of typical wages published by Campbell in 1747[31] and Collyer in 1761[32] bear this out. In 1824, carpenters compared themselves with 'tailors, shoemakers and others in the building line'[33] and twenty years later the carpenter's daily wage of 5s. 'was the hallmark of the trade unionist in the Chartist period'.[34] Bricklayers and carpenters were, of course, paid less than highly skilled craftsmen such as jewellers, or the more skilled watch makers, but such men did not form a large proportion of the labour force.[35] Wage rates for the building trades therefore provide an indication of the general movement of male incomes. Unfortunately, such data as survives tends to come from institutions – institutions kept records – but institutional wage rates were relatively stable. There are some suggestions that private building contractors in London varied their

---

[30] See above, pp. 23–6.   [31] Campbell, *The London Tradesman, passim.*
[32] Collyer, *The Parents' and Guardians' Directory, passim.*
[33] *S.C. on Artisans and Machinery*, P.P. 1824, 5, p. 180.
[34] H. Goodway, *London Chartism* (Cambridge, 1982), p. 178.
[35] See above, p. 42.

wage rates more than the institutions;[36] there is some evidence that wage rates outside building, especially in trades more subject to international competition, may have fluctuated more than they did in the building trades.[37] The institutional figures should therefore be regarded as *indicators* of earnings in the private sector.

Accepting this, there remain the notorious technical drawbacks of wage-rate statistics. They make no allowance for unemployment or underemployment. Unemployment, for instance, fluctuated a great deal, but there is no reason to believe that the incidence of economic crises, when viewed over a century and a half, became significantly worse; indeed, in the course of the nineteenth century crises may have become rather less painful an experience, as chapter three has suggested. At least there were not so many wars to contend with. Wage-rate series are of limited help with assessing household income, since they refer to males, and to fit adult males at that. However, they are the best that we have. They are proxies of earnings, and *must* be viewed over a series of years. They are *not* reliable indicators for individual years, but indicators of trends. What these trends were is shown on figure 6.1. They show a familiar pattern of long periods of stability broken by the Revolutionary and Napoleonic Wars. There was a limited degree of flexibility – in both directions – during the first forty years of the eighteenth century, but it was small and, considering the drawbacks of the data, it would be wrong to draw strong conclusions from this. It is, however, interesting that carpenters had begun their rise during the 1770s, which at least suggests that the notion of a customary wage rate, whatever the cost of living, was not universal.

The cost of living

A rather large – though not quite fatal – snag that faces the compiler of cost-of-living indices for the eighteenth century is that we do not know how working people spent their money. There are some special groups that compiled cost of living indices as part of a pay claim, such as the tailors in 1752 and the saddlers in 1779,[38] but they did so very much in outline form, and they are open to charges of special plead-

---

[36] Dr Jeremy Boulton, personal intimation, based on his research into wage rates in seventeenth-century London.
[37] K. H. Burley, 'An Essex clothier of the eighteenth century', *Econ. Hist. Rev.*, 2nd ser., 11 (1958–9), pp. 293–4. Between 1747 and 1759 this particular clothier gave extensive discounts from the standard rate for his spinners, but did not give discounts to his weavers.
[38] *London Life*, p. 169.

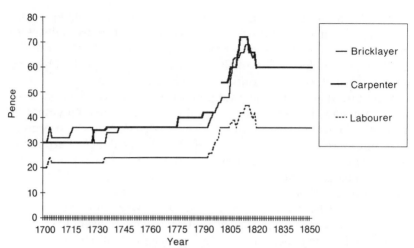

Figure 6.1 Money wage rates in London, 1700–1850
(For full data, see Schwarz, 'Standard of living', pp. 36–8)

ing. The compositors did it in more detail in 1810, but their standard of living has been described as reflecting an 'affluence approaching middle-class standards'.[39] There are budget that may be more reliable for shoemakers in 1825 and for carpenters in 1839, but the first attempt at an objective budget for Londoners was not made until 1841, by S. R. Bosanquet, who provided six budgets, all evidently biased towards the poorer section of the working class; none of his six families was headed by skilled workers, and they all tended to have more children than would have been likely fifty or eighty years previously. None of the children appears to have had any sort of employment; it is also doubtful whether the mother was earning.[40]

Fortunately, this ignorance is not a critical defect as, for most of the time, most of the cost of living indices, whatever their weights, tend to run more or less in harmony. There are large differences of detail between them, but the quality of the data is such that only large movements have much significance. Another snag that is at least as important as ignorance of weights, is that there is only occasional

[39] M. D. Burnett, *Plenty and Want: a Social History of Diet* (Harmondsworth, 1968), p. 62.
[40] S. R. Bosanquet, *The Rights of the Poor and Christian Almsgiving Vindicated* (1841), pp. 91–8. The shoemakers' budget is in *Trades Newspaper*, 28 August 1825; the carpenters in *Charter*, 14 April 1839. Earle, *Making*, pp. 271–2, analyses the estimate made in 1734 by Jacob Vanderlint of 'the necessary charge of a family in the middling station of life'.

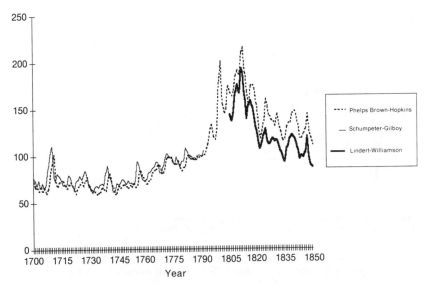

Figure 6.2 Cost-of-living indices, 1700–1850 (1790 = 100)

access to retail prices and one is forced to rely on wholesale prices instead. Even the reasonable assumption that over the long run wholesale and retail prices move in harmony is of little help in the short run.

Three different cost-of-living indices are involved: Schumpeter–Gilboy (SG), which runs from 1700 to 1792,[41] Lindert–Williamson (LW) as amended by Crafts, which begins in 1780[42] and Phelps Brown–Hopkins (PBH) which covers the entire period.[43] They are shown on figure 6.2. SG, which is only an eighteenth-century index, is very similar to PBH. The two indices correlate for this period at 0.9436, so it makes sense to use PBH, which covers a longer period. The LW index is another matter. Its general pattern is similar to PBH,

[41] E. W. Gilboy, 'The cost of living and real wages in eighteenth-century England', *Review of Economic Statistics*, 18 (1936), pp. 134–43 and subsequently republished in A. J. Taylor (ed.), *The Standard of Living in Britain in the Industrial Revolution* (1975), pp. 1–20.

[42] P. H. Lindert and J. G. Williamson, 'English workers' living standards during the industrial revolution: a new look', *Econ. Hist. Rev.*, 2nd ser., 36 (1983), p. 10; Lindert and Williamson, 'Reply to Michael Flinn', *Econ. Hist. Rev.*, 2nd ser., 37 (1984), p. 93; N.F.R. Crafts, 'Real wages, inequality and economic growth in Britain: a review of recent research', in P. Scholliers (ed.), *Real Wages in Nineteenth- and Twentieth-Century Europe: Historical and Comparative Perspectives* (Berg, Oxford, 1989), pp. 75–95.

[43] E. H. Phelps Brown and S. V. Hopkins, 'Seven centuries of the price of consumables compared with builders' wage rates', reprinted in E. M. Carus-Wilson (ed.), *Essays in Economic History*, ii, pp. 179–96.

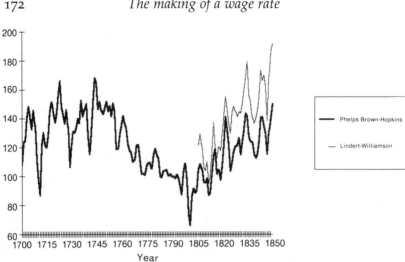

Figure 6.3 Real wage rates of London bricklayers, 1700–1850 (1790 = 100)
(For full data, see Schwarz, 'Standard of living', pp. 39–41)

but it is consistently lower.[44] There appear to be two reasons for this. The first reason is that LW allows for the cheaper clothing of the industrial revolution. The second, and more important reason, is that LW gives a greater weight to food, especially cereals. PBH gives cereals 20 per cent, meat 25 per cent and butter 12.5 per cent, which makes it an index for artisans. LW is probably a better index for the poorer workers.

Real wage rates

Figure 6.3 puts the evidence together. It is of interest in two respects. First, there is the improvement in real wage rates during the early nineteenth century – more precisely, for about a decade from 1814 – which will be familiar to historians since it is found in many parts of the country. Money wage rates fell rather little; prices fell a great deal. The process was repeated at the end of the 1840s, this time without money wage rates falling at all – a useful supplement to the forces of order gathered outside Kennington Common, and a suitable initiation to the High Victorian years.

The second striking aspect of figure 6.3 is the fall in real wage rates during the second half of the eighteenth century and it is this, rather

---

[44] There is also an apology for an index produced by Tucker, which is supposed to cover the entire period, but Tucker failed to specify his weights and his source only specified quinquennial prices until 1805. See above, n. 18.

Table 6.1. *Decennial changes in London bricklayers' real wage rates, 5-year moving averages, 1750–1800*

1750–59	− 9.5%
1760–69	−14.2%
1770–79	− 0.5%
1780–89	−11.1%
1790–1800	−14.6%

than the nineteenth-century rise, that is more remarkable. Table 6.1, which shows the changes in real wage rates in London, based on a five-year moving average, from their level of the previous decade, gives a more detailed picture.

The fall in real wage rates during the 1790s is undeniable, but there were two periods of sharp fall before then: the years between 1750 and 1770, and the 1780s. The 1780s saw a high level of economic activity, so there is room for doubt about the course of earnings as suggested in table 6.1, but the mid eighteenth century is another matter, and the evidence is national. Grain riots were beginning on quite a large scale from the later 1750s,[45] the Book of Orders was re-issued in 1758,[46] and the riots continued into the 1750s, especially 1766.[47] On the national level, Dobson has found a sharp increase in industrial disputes during the 1760s,[48] while in London there were the labour disputes associated with John Wilkes.[49] The detailed local evidence – such as it is – suggests that the decline in real wage rates was stopped in Yorkshire and Lancashire during the 1760s, and in large areas north of the Severn–Wash line it was made good during the 1770s, but south of that line the decline does not appear to have been decisively reversed, despite signs of recovery being evident in the 1770s in various places. By 1790 it is probable that many groups of workers north of the Severn–Wash line had higher wage rates (and also higher earnings) than their forebears had enjoyed in the mid century. South of this line such groups must have been few.[50] But wage rates were to fall again in the 1790s. Employment was high for most of the time, so for much of the country the worst hardship was confined to the famine years of

[45] R. B. Rose, 'Eighteenth-century price riots and public policy in England', *International Review of Social History*, 6 (1961), pp. 277–92.
[46] W. J. Shelton, *English Hunger and Industrial Disorders: A Study of Social Conflict During the First Decade of George III's Reign* (1973), p. 78.
[47] *Ibid., passim.*   [48] Dobson, *Masters and Journeymen*, pp. 22, 154–70.
[49] G. Rudé, *Wilkes and Liberty* (Oxford, 1962), chapter six.
[50] L. D. Schwarz, 'Trends in real wage rates, 1750–1790: a reply to Hunt and Botham', *Econ. Hist. Rev.*, 2nd ser., 43 (1990), pp. 90–8.

1795–6 and 1800–1. After 1815, and perhaps already after 1812–13, the situation was reversed: prices fell and employment decreased. Wages sometimes fell, but did not usually fall very much, so real wage rates rose, and rose extensively, particularly during the early 1820s and 1840s.

To what extent did the movement of wage rates reflect the movement of earnings? The dangers of drawing conclusions about the short term have been stressed throughout this chapter, but were there longer-term trends in employment and economic activity that would modify the U-shaped curve of figure 6.3?

First, there is the possibility that the decline in earnings during the 1750s and 1760s was not as great as the data suggests because the depression in the capital during the second quarter of the eighteenth century depressed earnings, however high real wage rates. The suggestion of chapter three was that the underlying cause of the depression was a low rate of population growth which held back the growth of demand for many items, especially for housing. This does not suggest that there was a particularly large surplus labour force in the capital, compared with later years. Even if it is believed that the wage-rate data provides an inflated picture of earnings during these years, it would not be a very inflated picture. The subsequent fall in real wage rates would be reduced by a little, but the picture would not be significantly changed. Economic activity during the second half of the eighteenth century was not at such a high level as to counteract the depressions of the early eighteenth century. The 1760s were troubled, wars naturally caused their own troubles; however, the years from 1784 were good.

The second qualification relates to the years of the Revolutionary and Napoleonic Wars and their aftermath: there is little doubt that over the war years as a whole falls in real income were less than the statistics suggest. The evidence for this has been presented in chapter three: although the mobilisation of such large numbers was possible without enormous disruption to the economy – no economy that can mobilise such a large proportion of its labour force without an enormous effect on the labour market or the economy could claim that its human resources had been used very effectively before then – nevertheless the mobilisation must have tightened the labour market considerably so that falls in earnings were not, on the whole, as great as falls in real wages. It is, in fact, not true that real wage rates were consistently below their pre-war level throughout the war years. They were so during the 1790s, but less so thereafter. On the PBH index, bricklayers were above their level of 1790 for eight years out of the twenty-three from 1793 to 1815; on LW they were ahead for eighteen years. The average wartime wage level for bricklayers, even on the pessimistic PBH, was 95 per cent of the level of 1790, and if the notorious years of 1795–6, 1800–1 and 1812–13 are excluded it was 99 per cent. But the downturn of 1811 and 1812 brought these conditions to an end. Prices were falling from 1814 but the depression was followed before long by the ending of recruitment and the demobilisation of some 350,000 men. At the same time, employment opportunities for women fell drastically, at least in London, since they could no longer be employed sewing uniforms for the army and navy,[51] and unemployment must have ensured that the number of jobs available for women and children would have fallen in any case. It was not until the 1820s, when employment had revived and the price level was declining, that the situation can really be said to have improved significantly.

Thirdly, there is the large and difficult question of rent. Rents and housing conditions merit a study of their own, but the comparatively small amount of work that has been done so far does not overthrow the conclusions of this chapter. A survey of the poor parish of St George's-in-the-East, made in 1848, found that the very poorest workers were paying about 20 per cent of their income in rent, while those slightly better off, such as tailors, coopers, or bricklayers, paid about 16 per cent.[52] Dorothy George claimed that up to the 1790s the London working man spent some one-eighth of his income in rent – assuming constant work.[53] That he had constant work is very unlikely, but assuming, for the sake of argument, that this was the case and that rents rose from an eighth to a fifth of a man's income, then real wage rates in the 1840s would need to be reduced by some 7.5 per cent. This by no means wipes out the entire increase in real wage rates after the Napoleonic Wars.

However, it is more useful to discuss the movement of rent in stages. The period of high wages in the early part of the eighteenth century was also a period when building was depressed, and therefore is unlikely to have been one of soaring rents. By the last third of the eighteenth century the population was growing more quickly, civic 'improvement' – meaning the demolition of cheap houses for open spaces and more expensive houses – accelerated, the Building Act of 1774 was passed and apparently enforced, and rents duly increased. A sample of forty-eight streets and courtyards in the Tower Division – one of the fastest growing areas – found a 13 per cent increase in real rateable values (deflated by PBH) as fixed for the land

[51] See below, p. 190–1.
[52] Statistical Society of London, 'An investigation into the state of the poorer classes in St George's-in-the-East', *Journal of the Statistical Society of London*, 11 (1848), pp. 200–1, 208–9; Stedman Jones, *Outcast London*, p. 216.
[53] *London Life*, p. 104.

tax between 1770 and 1790. Land tax assessments are highly dubious data, but in the poor Tower Division there is not likely to have been systematic under-recording of rateable values.[54]

However, the same sample revealed that real rateable values fell by a third between 1790 and 1815. A combination of slightly higher monetary values and falling prices raised them by 14 per cent between 1815 and 1820 but, nevertheless, the real rateable values of this sample were precisely identical in 1820 to their level of 1770 and had actually fallen by a quarter from the level of 1790. Unfortunately, the sample did not progress beyond 1820.

Rateable values were stickier than rents, especially rents for rooms; wartime conditions did not encourage building, and the extent of the fall after 1790 is not easy to accept, even on the argument that the money value of rates did increase, but prices increased more. But the existence of such a fall is also borne out by the data on Schedule A of the income tax between 1806 and 1814 (table 6.2). This was supposedly calculated on the basis of the rent that an owner could obtain for his property on the market.[55] From 1806 it is usually possible to distinguish 'housing' from other properties.

Table 6.2. *Assessment of rents under Schedule A, houses only, fixed prices (PBH index), 1806–14*[56]

City of London	91
Westminster	90
Middlesex, excluding City and Westminster	104
England and Wales (1808–14)	96

[54] The detailed examination is in Schwarz, 'Conditions of life', pp. 284–94. There are obvious problems with using the land tax registers but at any rate entry fines were disappearing by the 1760s and the land tax in the Tower Division is likely to have been at rack rent level. Rudé, who criticises the land tax registers (*Hanoverian London*, p. 16), is nevertheless prepared to use them, for want of anything better: *ibid.*, pp. 16–17, 42, 59; *Wilkes and Liberty*, pp. 85–9.

[55] A. Hope-Jones, *Income Tax in the Napoleonic Wars* (Cambridge, 1939), pp. 20–1; P. K. O'Brien, 'British incomes and property in the early nineteenth century', *Econ. Hist. Rev.*, 2nd ser., 12 (1959–60), p. 257. It was levied on all houses with annual rentals of £5 and above, which meant that few houses in London would have escaped it: Hope-Jones, *Income Tax*; Schwarz, 'Conditions of life', pp. 288–91. Mile End New Town was sufficiently poor to merit attention by the House of Commons Committee enquiring into the effects of high food prices in 1801: 529 out of 630 houses in the parish paid a yearly rent of 'only' £11 and under, while the average rent of the remaining 101 was 'only' £19: Fifth Report of the S.C. on the High Price of Provisions, *Eighteenth-Century Reports*, 9, p. 121.

[56] Figures for the years 1803–10 are in P.P. 1812–13, 12, pp. 235ff. Figures for 1812 are in P.P. 1814–15, 10, pp. 85ff. Figures for 1814 are in P.P. 1856, 4, appendix 62a, but these are national figures only.

According to the sample evidence, the Tower Division's assessment on houses fell by 10 per cent in real terms between 1807 and 1814, a fall comparable to the figures for the City and Westminster, but not typical of the rest of Middlesex, where rents remained roughly steady.[57] However, taking the overall picture, it is not implausible that rents were stickier than prices for many of the wartime years, perhaps because forecasts of inflation were too low. After the war, rents rose, but not sufficiently to counteract the increase in real incomes following the fall in other prices. Needless to say, the fall in real wage rates during the second half of the eighteenth century remained and quite probably deepened.

What does this suggest about the crucial figure in living standards – household incomes? As family size increased, women and children would be expected to earn more as compensation for a male wage that failed to rise in due measure, if at all. In some parts of the country – for instance, in areas where employment in textiles was expanding – they would have succeeded in doing this. In many of these regions male wage rates kept up with price rises for much of this period – at any rate until the 1790s – and are likely to have been in a good position to have withstood the inflation of the wartime years. It is very likely that subsequent research will show that it was precisely in those areas where male earnings rose the most that the earnings of women and children also rose considerably. Whether this was the case in London is much more doubtful. None of the evidence presented in chapter one gives any reason to believe that women's earnings would have shown any significant rise during the eighteenth century, while the fall in male wage rates during the second half of the eighteenth century does not suggest a tight labour market. There is no reason to believe that at any point women's earnings increased above their ·customary very low level. But during the Revolutionary and Napoleonic Wars women established themselves in many occupations traditionally regarded as male preserves. It could hardly be expected that they should leave them abruptly after more than twenty years. Their presence had a drastic effect on many of the old London trades: what was happening in many of these trades during the first half of the nineteenth century was in direct opposition to the pattern of improvement that figure 6.3 showed. The problem for tailors, for shoemakers,

---

[57] The detailed figures for individual parishes are in the relatively unused E182 series in the P.R.O.: those for the Tower Hamlets are E182/639, 641, 645, 648, 653. Hope-Jones prints graphs for various Middlesex parishes; some of them cover only the years between 1812 and 1815: *Income Tax*, pp. 93–8.

for furniture makers was not that the 'official' wage was too low; it was that it was not usually earned. The 'official' wage was a standard to which they aspired. The next two chapters explore this apparent contradiction.

7

The challenge of sweated labour: a tale of four trades

On the existence of sweated labour before Henry Mayhew

When Mayhew was doing his rounds for the *Morning Chronicle* during the year before the Great Exhibition, the sweated domestic workers whom he interviewed knew precisely when their plight had begun.

Of the 21,000 working tailors ... resident in London, I should add that there are not above 3,000 belonging to what is called the honourable portion of the trade. The remaining 18,000 are those who are engaged in the cheap, slop, or dishonourable trade ...

Up to the year 1834, the 8th of George III ('which,' I am told, 'regulated the time of labour for tailors at twelve hours per day, with the intent of compelling the masters to get their work done on the premises, as well as of equalising employment, and giving to each operative tailor the opportunity of earning a decent maintenance for himself and his family') was tolerably well adhered to; but at that period the masters gradually infringed the provisions of the act. Sweaters became numerous, and a general strike was the consequence. The strike acted antagonistically to the view of the journeymen tailors, and from that time up to the present, sweaters and underpaid workmen have increased, until the state of trade, as regards the operative tailors, appears to be approaching desperation.[1]

Shoemakers dated their decline earlier:

The next ... strike was more disastrous; this took place in 1812, and through it the West-end and City separated, and became two distinct bodies ... Several masters, not being able to get their work made in town, cut it out and sent it to Northampton and other parts of the country to be manufactured, resolving on a general reduction; while others had their export orders executed in the country, and the men left town and made the work at a far greater reduction of wages than were offered in the lowest-rated shops in town. Warehouses for the sale of country work were then opened in many parts of the metropolis,

---

[1] E. P. Thompson and E. Yeo (eds.), *The Unknown Mayhew. Selections from the Morning Chronicle 1849–1850* (1971), pp. 218, 220.

while merchants gave their export orders to Northampton, so that the trade was lost to both masters and men, and though nearly 45 years have passed since that period the trade has never recovered the blow it then struck against its own prosperity.[2]

For carpenters and cabinet makers it was a postwar phenomenon:

About three-fourths or four-fifths of the carpenters working in the metropolis, I am informed, are from the country, for it is only within the last fifteen or twenty years that the London masters have taken apprentices. Before that time apprentices were taken – with but a few exceptions – only in the City, and those who served their time did so solely with the view of 'taking up their freedom' afterwards. Large masters in London would not then be troubled with lads, though small jobbing masters generally took one or two. Now, however, there is scarcely a master in London but what has some youths in his employ, and many of the large builders have as many lads and 'improvers' as they have men, while some of them have even more. All these are used as a means of reducing the cost of men's labour. 'When I first came to town, twenty years ago' (said one of the carpenters whom I saw), 'I never knew a lad to be employed in any of the large firms in which I worked.' ... A great number of country carpenters are still attracted to London under the belief that the wages here maintain their former rate. When they arrive in the metropolis they find out to their cost that they can obtain employment only among the speculative builders and petty masters, where but two-thirds of the regular wages of the trade are given; and once they take to this kind of work, it becomes impossible for them, unless very prudent indeed, ever to get away from it.[3]

Little masters, both in the general and fancy cabinet trade ... work on speculation, carrying their goods, when made, to the 'slaughter houses' for sale. This mode of business was hardly known until about twenty years ago. Prior to that time a little master was a man of limited means, having a front shop for the display of his goods, and a contiguous workshop for their manufacture.[4]

Most historians of nineteenth-century labour have accepted this at its face value.[5] There seems good reason for them to have done so. The years between 1815 and 1850 were difficult for many trades, and not only in England. Similar forces seem to have been at work in many countries: there are many complaints of 'sweating', of poverty, of the dilution of craft standards, of women and children entering trades from which they had hitherto been excluded.[6] Yet that there had been much poverty in urban trades before the nineteenth century goes without saying. 'Low productivity, static techniques and labour as the main factor of production meant long hours of arduous toil to produce

---

[2] *Ibid.*, pp. 294–5.   [3] *Ibid.*, pp. 404–5.   [4] *Ibid.*, p. 469.
[5] E.g. J. A. Schmiechen, *Sweated Industries and Sweated Labour: the London Clothing Trades, 1860–1914* (Illinois, 1984), pp. 7–23.
[6] See above, pp. 158–9.

a small amount.'[7] Long hours of work for subsistence earnings or – which is pretty much the same thing – earnings equivalent to those of a labourer, were hardly new. One need go back no further than Campbell's 1747 account of the London trades.[8] House painters, for instance:

There is not Bread for one Third of them; and at all Times in the City of London and Suburbs, they are idle at least four or five Months in the Year . . . The Journeymen of this Branch are the dirtiest, laziest, and most debauched Set of Fellows that are of any Trade in and about London.

Bookbinders:

The Journeymen make but a mean Living; they seldom earn more than Ten Shillings a Week when employed, and are out of Business for Half the Year.

Silver and gold button makers:

The Silver and Gold Button-Maker is a pretty ingenious Business: He must have a Fancy and Genius for inventing new Fashions; a good Eye . . . and a clean dry Hand. It requires no great Strength, and is followed by Women as well as Men, which has reduced the Trade to small Profits, and a small Share of Reputation; the Women are generally Gin-Drinkers, and consequently, bad Wives; this makes them poor, and, to get something to keep Soul and Body together, work for a mere Trifle, and hawk their Work about to the Trade at an Under-Price, after they have cheated the Lace-Man of his Stuffs. This has reduced the Craft to a very low Ebb.

Upholsterers:

A Tradesman who is a good Hand in the Upholder's own Branch is paid Twelve or Fifteen Shillings a Week; and the Women, if good for anything, get a Shilling a Day.

Tailors:

They are as numerous as Locusts, are out of Business about three or four Months in the Year, and generally as poor as Rats.

Milliners:

They [the shopkeepers] have vast Profits on every Article they deal in; yet give but poor, mean Wages to every Person they employ under them: Though a young Woman can work neatly in all manner of Needle-Work, yet she cannot earn more than Five or Six Shillings a Week, out of which she is to find herself in Board and Lodging.

[7] D. C. Coleman, 'Labour in the English economy of the seventeenth century', in E. M. Carus-Wilson (ed.), *Essays in Economic History*, II, p. 299.
[8] Campbell, *London Tradesman*, pp. 135, 152, 170–1, 181, 192, 208, 225.

Stay makers:

A Women cannot earn above a Crown or Six Shillings a Week, let her sit as close as she pleases.

But during the second half of the nineteenth century, 'sweated labour' meant not only low pay: it meant the division of labour, the dilution of craft skills and, in particular, it meant outwork.[9] The final assembly might be carried out at the employer's premises; the rest of the work was carried out by the employee at his or her home. It meant a permanently overstocked labour market, where the workers were paid piece rates and paid so little that they had to work very long hours to keep body and soul together, thereby flooding the market with their goods even more. As Mayhew insisted, 'under-pay makes over-work'.[10]

Yet outwork was not new. 'Probably few of those who read the evidence given before the Lords' Committee on the sweating system', wrote Unwin,

can have been aware of how extensive and various were the industries still carried on in domestic workshops, and fewer still are likely to have realised that the evils then brought to light were the lingering traces of what constituted the great industrial problem of Tudor and Stuart times, just as the conflict between organised wage-earners and their employers constitutes the great industrial problem today.[11]

Before May Day [1517] poor handicraft people which were wont to keep shops and servants and had labour and living by making pins, points, girdles and gloves, and all such other things ... had thereof sale and profit daily, until about thirty years ago a sort began to occupy to buy and sell all such handicraft wares called haberdashers ... whereby many rich men is risen upon the destruction of the poor people, which poor people perceived themselves having no living and were bound prentices in London not able to keep no houses nor shops, but in alleys sitting in a poor chamber working all the week to sell their ware, on the Saturday brought it to the haberdasher to sell ... which would not give them so much winning for their wares to find them meat and drink saying they had no need thereof; their shops lay stored full of [wares from] beyond sea.[12]

As poverty in eighteenth-century London was, if anything, greater than in the nineteenth century and many had a desperate need to earn some money somehow, it would not be surprising if widespread

---

[9] D. Bythell, *The Sweated Trades. Outwork in Nineteenth-Century Britain* (1978). Note the title of the book, but see also pp. 12–19.

[10] Thompson and Yeo, *Unknown Mayhew*, p. 467.

[11] G. Unwin, *Industrial Organisation in the Sixteenth and Seventeenth Centuries* (1904, 2nd ed. 1957), pp. 5–6.

[12] G. Unwin, *The Gilds and Companies of London* (1908), p. 249.

sweating were to be found in the eighteenth century. The capital contained a large mass of labour, formally unskilled but more than willing to learn fairly basic skills at short notice. These skills could always be employed by those willing to subcontract. Campbell's button makers and milliners were so employed. What is surprising is the extent to which subcontracting and dilution did not take place during the eighteenth century.

But first it is necessary to discuss what is meant by the term 'skill', and especially the term 'semi-skilled', for it was the semi-skilled workers who were most pressed by domestic outworkers during the first half of the nineteenth century. The concept of skill is by no means straightforward.[13] A definition based on a combination of manual dexterity or skill allied with knowledge, which is only available through some kind of learning process, usually an apprenticeship, is suitable for the more skilled workers, the nineteenth-century 'trades-men' or labour aristocrats. The distinction between these men on the one hand, and labourers on the other hand, was fundamental: it was only during the 1890s that the term 'semi-skilled' was used, as an acknowledgement that there were and always had been grades of skill below that of the artisan.[14] Unfortunately, the semi-skilled trades are those least susceptible to historical analysis. Weavers, it was said in 1838, 'could be struck into existence in a month'. So they could, but they were not 'proper' weavers 'and Mr. Athow [a manufacturer] calls them shuttlethrowers and not weavers: still, such parts as they cannot do themselves they get others to do for them, and they manage to do all the rest of their work'.[15] Setting up a loom required considerable skill. If by tailoring is meant understanding the entire process of the trade, from measuring the client and cutting out the cloth to providing the finished suit this was indeed skilled; stitching the pieces together was much less skilled. Even in the Port of London, where brute strength was frequently said to be all that was required, there was an almost infinite variety of skills. Stevedores knew how to load ships so that they would not capsize and were obviously a class apart, but different groups of men specialised in different materials – wood, coal, sugar and so forth – with a wide variety of skills between them.[16]

Hence the problem of understanding exactly what is meant by that

[13] C. More, *Skill and the English Working Class, 1890–1914* (1980), pp. 15–26.
[14] E. J. Hobsbawm, 'Artisan or labour aristocrat?', *Econ. Hist. Rev.*, 2nd ser., 37 (1984), pp. 355, 358.
[15] Bythell, *Sweated Trades*, p. 160.
[16] J. Lovell, *Stevedores and Dockers* (1969), pp. 37–48.

common phrase of the time, the 'overstocking' of a trade. It was supposed to mean that too many people wanted to work in it relative to the demand for the final product, and that wages were accordingly depressed below a level considered appropriate. Exactly which part of the trade was overstocked was rarely made clear. There were many trades which, although dominated at the top by a highly skilled elite, were always liable to be flooded by a wave of less skilled labour. As said earlier in this chapter, what is particularly noticeable about eighteenth- and nineteenth-century London is this mass of labour, not formally skilled, but willing and able to learn certain skills at relatively short notice. Such labour may be called semi-skilled, but the extent of skill involved should by no means be underestimated. How many readers of this book could work a Jacquard loom, even if the pattern had been set up by somebody else, or sew materials together at the speed that was required of London tailors, or unload a ship between two tides without much damage to either the goods or people? The question is whether the *preponderance* of the work required an extensive knowledge of the trade. Many nineteenth-century artisans spoke and behaved as though a tidal wave of the unskilled was about to break over their flimsy ramparts. That their ramparts were about to be broken was often quite correct, but they underestimated the skills that were required to break them.

The rest of this chapter examines four of the trades whose members complained to Mayhew with much warmth and feeling, and who insisted on looking back to an earlier and not long departed golden age: the tailors, shoemakers, silkweavers and furniture makers, following them across a century and a half of work experience.

The defences against sweated labour

'In a Taylor's Shop, there are always two Sorts of Workmen' wrote Campbell in 1747,

first the Foreman, who takes Measure when the Master is out of the Way, cuts and finishes all the Work, and carries it Home to the Customer: This is the best Workman in the Shop, and his Place the most profitable; for ... he has generally a Guinea a Week, and the Drink-Money given by the Gentlemen on whom he waits to fit on their Cloaths. The next Class is the mere working Taylor; not one in ten of them know how to cut out a Pair of Breeches: they are employed only to sew the Seam, to cast the Button Holes, and to prepare the Work for the Finisher. Their Wages, by Act of Parliament, is twenty Pence in one Season of the Year, and Half a Crown the other; however a good Hand has Half a Crown and Three Shillings: they are as numerous as Locusts, are out of Business about three or four Months in the Year, and generally as poor as Rats.[17]

Shoemaking was similar, requiring only a minority of skilled workmen who could cut the leather into the correct shape, and then give it to other workmen to stick together. In 1792 the shoemakers' union complained that, unlike almost any other trade, 'the servant without a character, or the soldier worn out in the service, who can command a guinea or two, will at any time be taught the business'.[18] Collyer's Directory of 1761 suggested that it took between four and six weeks to learn how to make a shoe,[19] and it was so easy that around 1815, if the memory of a nostalgic shoemaker writing fifty years later is to be trusted, there was a sudden craze among society women to try their hand at making shoes – 'shoemaking became the rage from the palace to the garret, as knitting and crocheting was recently the whim in all ranks of female society'. Even Queen Caroline was said to have attempted it.[20]

Despite the vulnerability of these trades, and the occasional aberrations of high society, the journeymen maintained their fight against dilution with a fair degree of success. The different structures of these trades led to correspondingly different types of labour and union organisation which, broadly speaking, cover the range of organisation in which different groups of working men in London could be found. In the strongest position were the furniture makers and the tailors, with a strong organisation on the shop floor, itself made possible by their skills but also by the cost of their product. Weakest were the dispersed silkweavers, with no shop floor to organise and therefore reduced to riot, or rather to collective and sometimes violent demonstrations, until they received their Acts of Parliament taxing imports and, subsequently, regulating wages. Between these groups were the shoemakers, weaker on the shop floor than the tailors or furniture makers, continually threatened with outwork and with a correspondingly weaker organisation and trade union, continually and unsuccessfully seeking to raise themselves to the levels of the better organised trades. All these methods provided some protection to the

---

[17] Campbell, *London Tradesman*, pp. 192–3.
[18] 'Articles of the Friendly and United Society of Cordwainers, instituted at Westminster on 4 June 1792', in A. Aspinall, *The Early English Trade Unions* (1949), p. 83.
[19] Collyer, *The Parents' and Guardians' Directory*, p. 249.
[20] O'Neill, 'Fifty years' experience', 2, p. 122. There was little change during the next half century: R. A. Church, 'Labour supply and innovation 1800–1860: the boot and shoe industry', *Business History*, 12 (1970), p. 29.

workmen during the eighteenth century but much less during the nineteenth century: the change in their circumstances should, therefore, be examined more closely.

Tailors

The journeymen tailors of the capital stood at the apex of the clothing trades. Below them stood a mass of impoverished workers and precarious employers. Their masters were not like the hapless glovemakers who complained, early in the eighteenth century, that 'they are generally so poor that they are supplied with leather upon credit, not being able to pay for that or their workfolk's wages till they have sold the gloves'.[21] The men were not in the position of the shirtmakers employed by Messrs Silver & Co. from 1794, 'since which and up to the present time [1843] the same relative prices have been paid for making shirts for home use, namely from 2/4 to 3/2 for making a frilled or a full-fronted linen shirt',[22] which may not have been unreasonable during the period of falling prices at the end of the Napoleonic Wars, but was another matter during the first twenty years of the firm's existence, and which, it is no surprise to learn, was carried out by 'a vast number of women and children both in the metropolis and in the country'.[23] Nor is it surprising to learn that as Messrs Silver's business expanded they began to use the cheaper labour to be found outside London, though they did not need to move very far: 'we established a person at Deptford, who got 20 to 40 dozen [shirts] per week at from 1/6d. to 1/10d. for a frilled shirt, and 10d. if plain, and these prices continued to be paid by us for a series of years'.[24]

The male journeymen tailors were proud to be above all that. They kept the threat of dilution at bay, or at least so their successors of the middle years of the nineteenth century believed. There are three aspects of this trade that are of particular interest for an understanding of how this threat was contained: retail bespoke, the house of call, and the channelling of female labour into particular branches that did not compete directly with the men.

'In the vicinity of the metropolis', wrote Eden in 1797,

working-people seldom buy new cloaths: they content themselves with a cast-off coat, which may usually be purchased for about 5s. and second-hand waistcoats and breeches. Their wives seldom make up any article of dress, except making and mending cloaths for the children.[25]

[21] Quoted in S. and B. Webb, *The History of Trade Unionism* (1920), p. 43.
[22] P.P. 1843, 14, p. 833.
[23] P.P. 1843, 13, pp. 446–7.
[24] P.P. 1843, 14, p. 833: Children's Employment Commission.
[25] F. M. Eden, *The State of the Poor* (3 vols., 1797), I, p. 554.

The second-hand market was enormous. It was much remarked on during the nineteenth century and must have been as important a century earlier. Dickens can be found meditating in Monmouth Street, 'the only true and real emporium for second-hand wearing apparel',

venerable from its antiquity, and respectable from its usefulness. Holywell Street we despise; the red-headed and red-whiskered Jews who forcibly haul you into their squalid houses, and thrust you into a suit of clothes, whether you will or not we detest.

The inhabitants of Monmouth Street are a distinct class; a peaceable and retiring race, who immure themselves for the most part in deep cellars or small back-parlours, and who seldom come forth into the world, except in the dusk and coolness of the evening ... Their habitations are distinguished by that disregard of outward appearance, and neglect of personal comfort, so common among people who are constantly immersed in profound specu-lation, and deeply engaged in sedentary pursuits.

'A Monmouth Street laced coat' was a by-word a century ago ... but it is the times that have changed, not Monmouth Street.

He was in fact wrong: Monmouth Street was one of the few streets that Francis Place admitted to have declined since the eighteenth century to become 'one of the meanest and poorest streets of its width and length in London'.[26]

A century before Dickens' time the top end of the second-hand clothes market stretched sufficiently far to include brisk men of the world like Boswell, who on New Year's Day 1763 bought a suit of old clothes for 11s., a suit in good enough condition for him to pursue his various conquests, in particular one Louisa. As a master tailor Francis Place found that he was doing his share in this market: for his part it consisted of bespoke suits rejected by customers, 'sold to a jew for not much more than one-third of its price, because a man or his wife or his mistress disliked it when it was made up'. Quite a long way down the scale were 'rag fair breeches' which were 'made from skins which were damaged either by sea water or by worms, and it required considerable judgment to purchase – prepare – and make the leather into breeches'.[27]

Where there was a mass market or, more accurately, a standardised mass market, there was dilution and the large-scale employment of women and children. Often this market catered for the colonies:

[26] C. Dickens, *Sketches by Boz*, chapter six: Meditations in Monmouth Street; *Auto-biography of Francis Place*, p. 63n.

[27] *Boswell's London Journal, 1762–3*, ed. F. A. Pottle (Harmondsworth, 1966), pp. 140–1; *Autobiography of Francis Place*, pp. 74, 217. See also B. Lemire, 'Consumerism in pre-industrial and early industrial England: the trade in secondhand clothes', *Journal of British Studies*, 27 (1988).

apparently ready-made footwear went to America on quite a large scale, there are some references to sailors' clothing, and so forth. But the home market for new clothes was much more limited. It was not entirely retail bespoke – Dr Earle has found a Londoner who died early in the eighteenth century possessed of a thousand suits – but it was very largely so.[28] New suits, unlike shirts, were intended to fit well, and this limited their mass manufacture. In the absence of a mass market for suits, the tailors worked for individual customers. This, in turn, meant that a tailor could set up for himself without very much capital, his main expenses being the rent of his shop and the cost of its upkeep, while his most important requirement was con- tinuous short-term credit from those from whom he purchased his materials. The shopkeeping master tailor, who sold single bespoke garments at retail, employed working tailors and organised the divi- sion of labour himself, is supposed to have been a rather new phenomenon in the seventeenth century, before which master tailors were simply craftsmen who made up the customer's cloth directly.[29] The outcome of this new system was a proliferation of small masters which, if it made unionisation among the men difficult, made it equally difficult for the masters to combine effectively, and so perhaps made them more readily prepared to agree on fixed wage rates for the trade, the more so since there was no middleman to take a cut out of the master tailor's profits.

But these were slender safeguards, and towards the middle of the eighteenth century the favoured position of the journeymen tailors looked like coming to an end. 'Many Master Taylors', the journeymen petitioned the House of Commons in 1752,

in order to have their work done cheap, get a great number of young, raw and unexperienced lads out of the country, who, for better instructions, are glad to work at low prices; and by such means, great numbers of the best and most experienced journeymen taylors are forced to go into all parts of the kingdom, to the great prejudice of themselves, their wives and children; whereby the business is not so well done as formerly in London and Westminster; and the trade every year declines through the avarice of some Master-Taylors, who, the more effectually to facilitate their encroachments on the journeymen's labour most fallaciously insinuate that they only want to be relieved from being obliged to pay 2s. 6d. a day to every journeyman, if ever so bad a workman; a necessity they never laboured under.[30]

---

[28] Peter Earle, personal communication. The American traffic is referred to by D. Davis, *A History of Shopping* (1966), p. 220. No reference is given.
[29] P. K. Newman, 'The early English clothing trade', *Oxford Economic Papers* (1952).
[30] Quoted in Galton, *Select Documents*, p. 51.

This was a reference to an Act of Parliament of 1720[31] which attempted to fix the daily wages of London tailors but did so at a level which, according to Campbell in 1747, was regularly exceeded. The implication of the petition is that some employers were turning to piecework.

We do not know the consequences. In 1756 the tailors went on strike, and remained out for at least a month.[32] In 1767 there is the first recorded literary mention of 'flints' and 'dungs', the flints working by the day and the dungs by the piece, all battling somewhat heroically in mock epic verse.[33] This division might have been the occasion for a breakdown of trade union organisation amongst the tailors, but it was not, and whether they worked by the day or by the piece the tailors saw their wages increasing until 1813. 'Great animosity formerly existed' between the flints and the dungs, wrote Place in 1818,

the Dungs generally working for less wages, but of late years there has not been much difference in the wages, the material difference being the working by the piece or day, instead of by the day only; and at some of the latest strikes both parties have usually made common cause.

The flints, he continued, always took the lead in trade disputes.[34]

Without doubt, the major strength of the tailors' union was the house of call. Tailors without work went to particular public houses and waited until there should be a demand for them. A labour exchange suited both masters and men in an industry in which the demand for labour fluctuated so heavily, and if it was complained that the men drank away their earnings, they also had a unique opportunity to form a trade union of their own. Houses of call were a common feature in many London trades,[35] the public house serving as the rendezvous for a drinking club, friendly society and trade union. They were the nuclei of the tailors' union, and until the 1830s the system functioned well, with the flints and the dungs managing to co-ordinate their efforts, and the employers not having sufficient incentive to lead a really well-prepared and concerted attack against the union, a difficult business at the best of times, the union being, in the masters' own words, 'a combination subsisting for nearly a century and ripened by experience . . . and not to be over-turned by a sudden, irregular and ill-concerted attack'.[36]

[31] 7 Geo. I stat 1 c. 13; Galton, *Select Documents*, p. 18.
[32] G.L.R.O. MJ/SP/1756/Oct./27.
[33] In Samuel Foote's play, *The Tailors: a Tragedy for Warm Weather*. Soporific enough in the British Museum Reading Room in winter.
[34] *Gorgon*, 3 October 1818.
[35] B. Harrison, *Drink and the Victorians* (1971), pp. 53–4; see above, pp. 120–1.
[36] Galton, *Select Documents*, p. 92.

The ill-concerted attack of 1810 from which this complaint dates left little in its wake beyond a report from the Committee of Master Tailors. This charged that the men did not allow a master to change his men from the day to the piece, or vice versa, without first giving a month's notice of his intentions, 'which is tantamount to his not being supplied for that month, or at least his being subject to a very bad supply, and to every other vexation, which the men well know how to inflict'. Secondly, the journeymen insisted on the master applying at his local house of call.

If a master, in the busy time of the year, cannot be supplied with additional men, he dare not, however he may offend his customers by their work not being done to the time he has pledged himself, give out a single garment to be made without incurring the threat (which in many cases has been put into execution) of not being supplied for one calendar month for the first offence, two months for the second, and . . . for the third, if hardy enough to offend a third time, he must retire from business altogether.[37]

Eight years later Francis Place explained that every house of call had a book into which men's names were entered in order of seniority, and when there was a call for men, those more senior went first. In addition, a house of call had a benefit club for sickness and old age, and

a mere trifle for supporting the combination. They have also occasionally a much larger subscription for the purpose of maintaining their own members, who cannot be employed when trade is dull, and to these they usually allow about eight or nine shillings a week.[38]

Those who received such relief were not permitted to apply to their parish for any further relief.[39]

The corollary to the house-of-call system was a union rule that prevented a married man with children from giving his wife or his children any work to do at home, and insisted that the man himself must work at his employer's workshop.[40] The family unit had no charm: it merely depressed wages. However, the journeymen tailors limited their aspirations in this field, principally in three ways. In the first place, while they did their best to keep women out of men's tailoring they, in their turn, appear to have kept out of ladies' dress-making. Secondly, the union men kept away not only from shirt-making and such like, but also from government contracts, where the work was regularly done at home. Military, and to some extent colonial, demand served for the lower middle-class and working-class

[37] *Ibid.*, pp. 89–90.   [38] *Gorgon*, 3 October 1818.
[39] British Library, Additional MS 27,800 (Place Papers), fo. 131.
[40] Galton, *Select Documents*, p. 90.

demand of the late nineteenth century. Army contracts were on a very large scale, and occupied many tailors – over 8,000 according to the largest army clothier in 1833,[41] when the demand was very much smaller than during the war years. In 1813 and 1814 alone, nearly 400,000 uniforms and over 443,000 greatcoats were supplied, many of them made in London. In 1808 the greatcoat contract was opened to competitive bidding (instead of the traditional contract given hitherto), with the result that the price fell, the tailors were paid less and consequently did the work in a hurry, and did it badly. The greatcoats soon fell to pieces and, after a few years, the army returned to the more respectable clothiers who had refused to lower their estimates to bankruptcy prices.[42] This situation was by no means new in the Napoleonic Wars, although the scale of the demand was unprecedented. In 1761 some of the principal naval contracts were reputed to be worth several thousand pounds, and were largely carried out by women, the role of the journeymen being confined to cutting out the cloth and giving it to the women to sew together.[43]

Thirdly, the houses of call kept their 'Log'. The prerequisite for being on the Log was that one would work particularly quickly, more quickly than the less skilled tailors were able to do.[44] The latter were thus automatically relegated to the ranks of the badly paid mass production trade that, throughout the eighteenth century, existed side by side with adequately paid small-scale retailing. However, quite early during the course of the nineteenth century the two branches came to be competing with each other more than before. During wartime the competition was alleviated, after Waterloo it became more visible, by the 1830s it was overwhelming. The flints had not done badly during the war years, their wages rising to 36s. a week in 1813, the same as their traditional peers, the bricklayers and carpenters. The twelve-hour day also remained. Their problems came with the depression and the fall in prices after the war years. Place was already out of date when in 1818 he said that there was not much animosity between flints and dungs: the demand for labour during the war years prevented serious enmities, but after the war enmity broke out with renewed strength. The dungs were undercutting the flints and, more importantly, there was an expansion in the number of small masters or 'sweaters', often working at home and employing their own families, or other women and children, for as little as 3s. to 8s. a week.[45] Others

---

[41] *S. C. on Army and Navy Appointments*, P.P. 1833, 7, Q. 610.   [42] *Ibid.*, Q. 573.
[43] Collyer, *The Parents' and Guardians' Directory*, pp. 255–6.
[44] Prothero, *Artisans and Politics*, p. 44.
[45] Thompson and Yeo, *Unknown Mayhew*, pp. 220, 240.

employed journeymen at reduced rates for a fourteen- or even sixteen-hour day.[46] As Mayhew would insist, low pay produced overwork, which in turn intensified the competition.[47] By the mid 1820s the flints were feeling the pressure, their pay often being reduced from the 'official' rate of 6d. an hour to 5d. by various means. A strike in 1827 against female labour was beaten – and for the tailors to lose a strike was unprecedented. They lost another strike in 1830.[48] The tailors were further under attack by the expansion of shops offering ready-made clothing. According to a letter in the *Pioneer*, the great expansion of such shops dated from the 1820s:

These individuals generally require all their premises to make what they term a show, but have in very few instances room for a workshop. The consequence is, that they persuade men to take their work to their own homes, telling them that their wives, etc. might assist them . . . I know a great many instances of seven or eight men, sweaters or dampers as they are termed, the wife of one of them, and half a dozen children being huddled together in one small apartment.[49]

The skilled male tailors were outraged:

have not women been unfairly driven from their proper sphere in the social scale, unfeelingly torn from the maternal duties of a parent, and unjustly encouraged to compete with men in ruining the money value of labour?[50]

The tailors, therefore, had many reasons to be bitter by the 1830s. Theirs was one of the largest unions in the Grand National Consolidated Trades' Union (GNCTU), with some 9,000 members, and one of the most impatient to go on strike, thereby establishing a claim on the funds of the GNCTU. They duly did so, and their strike was not only an attempt to raise wages, but also to restore the tailors' union to the position it had held earlier. The houses of call were no longer exercising the same control over the trade that had existed when Place wrote his account in 1818. 'The first step necessary', said the committee of journeymen tailors in 1833, would be 'the formation of a Union, to consolidate, under one interest, the whole body of the trade.'[51] When giving notice to strike, the committee instructed that no 'brother . . . shall work for an employer anywhere but on his [the employer's] premises . . . or on any other terms than by the day or hour'.[52] There would only be one union for the entire trade, no more flints and

---

[46] *Ibid.*, p. 257.   [47] Thompson and Yeo, *Unknown Mayhew*, p. 467.

[48] T. M. Parsinnen and I. J. Prothero, 'The London tailors' strike of 1834 and the collapse of the Grand National Consolidated Trades' Union: a police spy's report', *International Review of Social History*, 22 (1977), pp. 67–80.

[49] *Pioneer*, 14 March 1834; B. Taylor, *Eve and the New Jerusalem* (1983), p. 103.

[50] *Ibid.*, p. 191.

[51] Galton, *Select Documents*, p. 180.   [52] *Ibid.*, p. 184.

Table 7.1. *Declared values of woollen fabrics exported as a percentage of the 1814–16 valuation*[53]

	Woollens	Worsteds	Mixed wool/cotton
1816	100	100	100
1824–6	75.4	65.2	38.7
1834–6	66	69.3	38.7
1844–6	77.7	58.3	30.5
1854–6	61.5	46.9	18.3

dungs. All work, without exception, was to be done on the employer's premises. To share out the available work, hours would be reduced; daily pay would be increased, but not, in fact, by sufficient to compensate the most skilled tailors for their loss of earnings. Women, of course, would have to go. However, to counter criticism that those men who worked more slowly would be paid the full rate, the union accepted that those who worked too slowly would be paid less, provided that a union committee gave its approval for each case.

At the end of April their strike began. The union claimed to have 9,000 members. However, the 1831 census had returned 14,500 tailors in the capital,[54] many women were brought into the striking workshops, and their products were publicly displayed around town.[55] With strike funds exhausted and the executive of the GNCTU refusing more money, while the masters were requiring a denunciation of the union as the price for returning to work, the tailors were forced to surrender and their union left the GNCTU. All the ills were exacerbated. In 1824 there was supposed to be only one dung to every four flints; in 1849 there were three flints to every twenty dungs.[56]

The process that is clear here is the development of mass production, not by machinery but by the division of labour and by greater specialisation. Adam Smith would have recognised it, and it had presumably long been the case with standardised articles such as shirts and underwear. What is significant is – as said earlier – that precisely the same process was taking place in other major European cities at precisely the same time. Two factors were involved. The first

53 R. Davis, *The Industrial Revolution and Foreign Trade* (Leicester, 1979), p. 23.
54 Prothero, *Artisans and Politics*, p. 342; *Crisis*, 17 May 1834. W. H. Oliver, 'The Consolidated Trades Union of 1834, *Econ. Hist. Rev.*, 2nd ser., 17 (1964–5), p. 85, gives 4,600 tailors.
55 Taylor, *Eve*, p. 115; *Crisis*, 17 May 1834.
56 Taylor, *Eve*, p. 104; Galton, *Select Documents*, introduction; Oliver, 'Consolidated Union', p. 95.

was the increase in demand following the cheaper grain of the post-war years. The second – and much more significant in the long run – was the fall in the price of the material from which the suits were made. A good indication of the extent of this fall is to be found in the data presented by Ralph Davis on the declared and official values of exports. The official values did not change. The declared values did change, thereby providing an indication of changes in prices. Table 7.1 shows the trend, giving an indication of price changes.

It was the falling price of cotton yarn and woollen yarn that made possible the great expansion of demand for clothing on the continent as well as in England.[57] With the mass market came the changes in work practice, the division of labour, the mass production. London responded to the industrial revolution by expanding its traditional methods of manufacture.

Shoemakers
The strength of the tailors' position had been that, in the absence of a standardised mass market, they insisted for as long as possible on all the work being done on the employers' premises. Cabinet makers were in the same position. Silkweavers were at the other extreme, working predominantly under the domestic system. Shoemakers were intermediate. Some of their work was done on the employers' premises but there was more mass demand than for men's suits, while there was also a large demand for exports and for the army.[58] Much of the work was done at the shoemaker's own home, by his wife and his children, although the really skilled work, which involved cutting out the leather to fit the feet of the customer, was inevitably carried out on the premises. Stitching the pieces together was less skilled and was usually done at home; the finishing was done in the shop.[59] There were no houses of call and their union, as would be

[57] Imlah, *Economic Elements*, pp. 208–13, has cruder figures, showing the same trend:

	Cotton manufactures	Woollen manufactures	
1814–15	100	100	100
1816–20	75	77	92
1821–25	49	55	79
1826–30	36	42	65
1831–35	33	33	62
1836–40	32	29	67
1841–45	27	23	56
1846–50	23	20	51

[58] Church, 'Labour supply and innovation', pp. 26–7.
[59] Collyer, *The Parents' and Guardians' Directory*, pp. 248–9.

expected under such circumstances, appears to have had occasional bursts of activity throughout the eighteenth century, meeting with indifferent degrees of success. By the mid eighteenth century the shoemakers were threatened by mass production and appear to have lost some of their work to the provinces. Corbyn Morris wrote in 1751 that:

A practice hath lately prevailed of working in the country, manufactures for sale in London, which formerly employed great numbers of journeymen in this city. This is visible in the article of shoes, in which there are fewer by many hundreds retained at work than there were twenty years ago ... and this method will probably be followed in many other branches of consumption – especially as the carriage from the country to London, by the improvement of the roads becomes easier.[60]

And on Saturday nights in 1764 London labourers were to be observed taking their week's pay to 'Yorkshire and other shoe-houses in almost every public street in London'.[61]

The erosion continued. By the beginning of the nineteenth century the mass production of standardised footwear was fairly extensive at Northampton and Stafford, as well as existing on a more limited scale at Kettering, Wellingborough and Daventry.[62] The rout of the London shoemakers did not come until well into the nineteenth century, but the pressure was felt long before and had served to keep their wages down to almost the lowest in Campbell's list of 1747, at a mere 9s. or 10s. a week, little more than a common labourer would earn at the standard rate of 2s. a day.[63] However, the pressure was not as decisive as it would become later. During the 1720s and 1730s the London trade could still indulge in the luxury of a dispute between the small shoemakers and their larger rivals who controlled the Cordwainers' Guild and who hoped, by enforcing the guild's rules against the cutting of leather, to drive the small men out of business.[64] There is no information how this affected the journeymen, beyond a rule made by the guild in 1722 purporting to lay down a seven-year apprenticeship for all entrants to the trade,[65] a rule presumably intended to make life difficult for the small men who would have difficulty paying the wage that the minority of qualified men would demand.

---

[60] Quoted in *London Life*, p. 368.   [61] Anonymous, *Low Life*, p. 6.

[62] J. H. Clapham, *An Economic History of Modern Britain* (3 vols., 1930–8), II, p. 320.

[63] See above, p. 170. On the assumption that the labourer was not employed for six days in the week.

[64] *London Life*, pp. 196–8; C. H. W. Mander, *A Descriptive and Historical Account of the Guild of Cordwainers of the City of London* (1931), p. 89.

[65] London School of Economics, Webb Trade Union Collection, A. 7, fo. 167.

But such rules were never enforceable in so large and diffuse a trade and by 1738 the Cordwainers' Guild had admitted defeat on all counts. The dispute had not prevented the journeymen from having a union of their own and, if the complaint that an employer of forty years' standing made in 1738 is to be trusted, it was not an inactive union. He was, he said, compelled to pay 2s. 3d. for work formerly done for 14d., and the journeymen 'will stand still sooner than reduce their wages'.[66] Conceivably the union may have been attempting to enforce the regulation of apprenticeship in some of the larger shops. Certainly it was attempting this in 1766 when some, though not all, of the London journeymen shoemakers went on strike. Saunders Welch, the London magistrate, mediated successfully,[67] and when the men returned to work they returned 'hearty thanks to those Masters who so zealously promoted the lawful right of the Trade in general, and in suppressing every person from carrying on the trade who had no Right hitherto'.[68]

Whatever their success – and it was difficult to enforce such a rule when so much work was done at home – their union was complaining once more in 1792 that anyone who wanted to do so could enter the trade.[69] Once more they resolved to end this state of affairs. Initially their attempts were remarkably successful, apparently by involving most of the boot-closers, these being the skilled men who worked at the employers' premises. The union's strength evidently lay in the largest shops, and it had enforced a closed shop there by 1804 when it sought to forbid the employment of more than one apprentice for each journeyman – some of the journeymen were threatening to secede from the union in opposition to this rule. However, by 1811 they seem to have given up the attempt for a while and are not even to be found seeking to restrict employment or union membership to men who had served an apprenticeship. In the same year John Brown, a Cambridge shoemaker whose apprenticeship ended prematurely when he assaulted his master, was permitted to join a shop on condition of joining the union. In his autobiography, John Brown spoke a good deal of the union but very little of apprenticeship.[70] In 1824, when it was much weaker than in 1804, the union was again making some efforts to limit its own members to one apprentice each but was

[66] Quoted in *London Life*, p. 198.
[67] J. T. Smith, *Nollekens and his Times* (1828), I, p. 108; see below, pp. 222–3.
[68] *St James' Chronicle*, 5 June 1766.
[69] Aspinall, *The Early English Trade Unions*, p. 83.
[70] N. Mansfield, 'John Brown: a shoemaker in Place's London', *History Workshop*, 8 (1970), pp. 129–36.

avowedly making no attempt to limit the number of apprentices that a master might take.[71]

The London masters claimed in 1839 that it was in 1809 that they had begun cutting out boots and shoes and sending them to North-ampton to be made up at little more than half the London price;[72] the journeymen themselves saw the turning point in their trade, the point when Northampton shoes began to arrive on a large scale, as coming in 1812, after a disastrous strike in that year.[73] Both sides over-estimated the significance of these years – the change would have come about in any case – but both sides were at one in claiming that it was during the second decade of the nineteenth century that provin-cial pressure became sufficiently overwhelming to bring about drastic changes in the methods of shoe production in London. In 1812 the shoemakers of the West End were being paid more than the men in the City, and when the latter went on strike to end this differential the West End shoemakers broke away and formed a union of their own.[74] Defeated, they all went back to work, women and children entered the trade on a scale much larger than hitherto and of course were not given men's wages, but there were still further cuts in wage rates for most of the shoemakers in 1817.[75] Even this did not prevent the Northampton shoe manufacturers from acquiring a warehouse in 1818 and installing an agent to receive their shoes and press their sale on the London market. We do not know the details, nor do we know whether the flints and dungs amongst the tailors had the same geographical dividing line, although with the West End being the centre of the luxury trade this would not be surprising.[76] However, the significance of Northampton was not only in the competition that it provided – the virtual wiping out of the London trade did not occur until after 1860[77] – but also that, in adapting itself to this competition the London trade extended the employment of women and children far beyond its original bounds. The pressure for such extension had

[71] *S.C. on Artisans and Machinery*, P.P. 1824, 5, p. 136.
[72] *Reports of the Assistant Commissioners on the Handloom Weavers*, P.P. 1840, 23, p. 121.
[73] Thompson and Yeo, *Unknown Mayhew*, pp. 282, 294–6.
[74] *Ibid.*, pp. 282, 294–5. We do not know about wartime contracts for boots.
[75] Church, 'Labour supply and innovation', p. 292, reference to Webb Collection in n. 65 above; *Trades Newspaper*, 21 August 1825. Twelve West End shops did not reduce their wages, in order to secure the best workmen: *London Life*, p. 199.
[76] The case for this is strengthened by the existence in 1792 of the 'Master Shoemakers of the City and Liberty of Westminster', who induced the Cordwainers' Guild to pass a resolution in that year purporting to forbid any guild master from employing 'any Journeymen concerned in this Combination till good order be restored': Mander, *Cordwainers*, p. 92.
[77] P. G. Hall, 'The East London footwear industry: an industrial quarter in decline', *East London Papers*, 5, no. 1 (1962), pp. 3–21.

always existed; the 'dishonourable' part of the trade had long submitted to it, but its extension to the 'honourable' part of the trade on such a large scale appears to have been new. The skilled men could not combine strongly enough to prevent themselves being outflanked. Entry into the trade was too easy, there were no houses of call to regulate the supply of labour. This depressed the shoemakers' earnings, but they were still able to protect themselves to some extent – the extent to which a mass standardised market did not exist. Much of the work was still done to individual specifications, which meant working on the employers' premises, and which gave the men a certain bargaining position that they would lose when they merely delivered goods to the warehouse. But the London context itself was relentlessly becoming less dominant. More and more of the shoes sold in the capital were being manufactured outside the town in regions which did not mechanise any more than the capital, but where labour costs were lower, and which themselves colonised areas with even lower wage rates. Central supervision was only required at the cutting-out stage.[78] In the autumn of 1825 the London shoemakers are to be found striking, claiming that tailors were paid 36s. a week for a twelve-hour day, while they only received 16s.–18s. for a fourteen- to fifteen-hour day.[79] In 1826 some London shoemakers, anticipating Owenite co-operation, were preparing to open shops in different parts of London 'not for purposes of gain, but to procure a fair remuneration for our labour'[80] – the action not of a triumphant artisinate, but of a desperate group whose wages were, it was claimed in 1834, more than double those of the Northampton shoemakers[81] and who were fighting to uphold a situation that only the minority of the more skilled men could hope to enjoy. The growing employment of women was, in these circumstances, certain to take place; there were enough women in the trade for them to attempt to form a union in 1834, at the height of the trade union formation of that year, although the attempt met with indifferent success.[82] In that year, only 3,000 shoemakers were affiliated to the GNCTU – less than a fifth of those who called themselves shoemakers in the 1831 census, less than a seventh of those who did so in 1841.[83] Disgusted at having to await

[78] Church, 'Labour supply and innovation', p. 28. These were mainly in Northamptonshire and Staffordshire.
[79] *Trades Newspaper*, 9 October 1825, 25 December 1825. The edition of 21 August 1825 mentions 21s.–24s. a week for a sixteen-hour day, but this does not include waiting for work at the shop of the employers, 'who, not paying us by the time but by the job, never take into account the many hours they cause us to lose this way'.
[80] *Trades Newspaper*, 6 August 1826.   [81] *Poor Man's Guardian*, 8 February 1834.
[82] *Crisis*, 6 March 1834.
[83] Prothero, *Artisans and Politics*, p. 342; Oliver, 'Consolidated Union', p. 85.

the end of the tailors' strike before they could begin their own, they voted by 782 to 506 to leave the GNCTU.

It is noteworthy that the decisive break came when it did. A union as weak as the shoemakers' was in no position to resist a determined attack, but such an attack did not take place until 1812. The defeat of the union was in part a consequence of the difficult economic situation of that year, but it was the development of the market that ensured that the defeat of the union would be so disastrous. That the men's wages failed to rise was not, in itself, so important; it was the entry of women and children to the trade on a scale much larger than hitherto that mattered much more.

Furniture makers

The trade of furniture making was better paid and more prestigious than tailoring or shoemaking, or at least it was in the eighteenth century, but its practitioners, too, claimed to have undergone a similar degradation, at about the same time as the other two trades. The furniture trade comprised numbers of artisans in separate trades – carvers, gilders, upholsterers, carpenters and others – and in true form they all did their best to keep their demarcation lines well fortified.[84] Like the members of those trades described earlier, few in the furniture trades were subject to much new machinery until the mid nineteenth century.[85] Sawyers were the exception: in 1768 a mechanical saw-mill in Limehouse was attacked and partially destroyed by 500 sawyers who when told that the mill had not injured them replied that 'it partly might be so, but it would hereafter if it had not; and they came with a resolution to pull it down, and it should come down'.[86] Nevertheless, the circular saw was introduced on a fairly wide scale during the last quarter of the eighteenth century, and by the second decade of the nineteenth century it was driven increasingly by steam power.[87] By the mid nineteenth century the sawyers had been effectively superseded by machinery. But this was unusual: the threat to artisans was not from machinery but from the rise of the 'cheap and nasty trade' in the East End during the course of the nineteenth century. During the eighteenth century, furniture making was a respectable occupation, carried out mostly in a few parts of the City of London and Westminster. The shops – elite establishments charging high premiums for apprentices and known to refer to

---

[84] P. Kirkham, 'Furniture making in London, c.1700–1870: craft, design, business and labour', London University, Ph.D. thesis, 1982, p. 67.
[85] *Ibid.*, p. 205.   [86] Rudé, *Wilkes*, p. 94.
[87] Kirkham, 'Furniture making', p. 206.

apprentice upholsterers as 'articled young gentlemen'[88] – made their own furniture and sold it directly to the individual customer. The shops themselves were a creation of this period.[89] At the beginning of the century there existed specialist cabinet-making shops, specialist upholsterers and so forth, while craft and business ran more or less on parallel lines. From around 1740 there was an amalgamation and the 'general' furniture shop came into existence. These shops were usually run by men with a background in a variety of furniture-making crafts. They became more widespread, and by the end of the century this was the established mode for organising production.[90]

Such shops were high-class establishments, and some were quite large. By the third quarter of the eighteenth century the leading West End general firms were employing between forty and fifty people each; by the early nineteenth century this had risen to between eighty and a hundred. By the mid nineteenth century the largest shops were employing between 100 and 350 persons.[91] However, in the process, the larger comprehensive manufacturing companies came to be run by men who had not practised the craft and by 1830 it was not even considered necessary that they should have been trained in it.[92] Nevertheless, apprenticeship premiums remained high and the training was good.

Side by side with these firms was the disreputable trade. During the eighteenth century it was not very large, it was largely concentrated in the East End, it tended to buy the goods from wherever it could obtain them, and concentrated on marketing, not manufacture. The masters charged lower fees for taking apprentices, and with reason.[93] The pressure to increase productivity and to reduce costs forced these firms into making only a limited range of goods and into subdividing the craft; apprentices were trained to a reasonable competence in only one aspect of what had hitherto been a wide ranging craft. The slop trade – ready-made furniture manufactured at home and brought to the showroom – was claimed in the mid nineteenth century to have taken off during the 1820s, the years when real wage rates for London working men in regular employment rose most considerably, while conditions in the furniture trade deteriorated considerably after about 1835, taking a distinct turn for the worse by 1848.[94] By 1850 the sub-divisions in the 'slop' cabinet-making trade were, according to Mayhew, 'as numerous as the articles of the cabinet-maker's calling',

[88] *Ibid.*, pp. 330–2.   [89] *Ibid.*, pp. 107–8.   [90] *Ibid.*, p. 118.

[91] *Ibid.*, pp. 136, 147; Kirkham and Hayward, *William and John Linnell*, I, pp. 45, 139–40.

[92] Kirkham, 'Furniture making', p. 165.

[93] *Ibid.*, pp. 92, 333; Collyer, *The Parents' and Guardians' Directory*, p. 87.

[94] Kirkham, 'Furniture making', p. 15.

and he therefore considered it unnecessary to list them all. The 'honourable' shops took relatively few apprentices and trained them well; in the dishonourable sector cheap apprentice labour became the norm by the 1820s.[95] This, of course, produced more pressure to cheapen other forms of labour, and the final degradation came by the mid century, when the small 'dishonourable' master could not even afford to keep apprentices and used his own children, who were cheaper.[96] It had not always been like that. The journeymen cabinet makers and their employers had agreed on a price book that was published in 1768 and updated successively in 1793, 1803, 1805, 1811 and 1824. The 1811 book had evidently been two years in the making, and masters and men were reimbursed for their time in preparing it. Chairmakers obtained books in 1736, 1761, 1802 and 1808, and added to the 1808 book in 1811 and 1823.[97]

The fate of these price books was the same as the fate of the 'official' wage rates of the tailors or bricklayers. Some men earned the rate set out in them; an increasing proportion did not. The crucial factor was the change in the nature of the market. By the 1820s the market for new furniture was much wider than it had been a century earlier; much of this market was less wealthy and less discriminating than hitherto, so its demands were met by the poor and increasingly sweated labour of the East End. The process of sweating spread relatively rapidly, and in due course the quality shops of the West End were being put under pressure, frequently sending out their work to garret masters. Adam Smith's law that the division of labour was limited by the size of the market was vindicated. The market expanded, employment expanded; the new market, more price conscious than before, created a tidal wave of employees that threatened to sweep away the defences that the skilled workers had erected during preceding centuries. Capital per employee was not increased, but the volume of labour and the subdivision of labour were increased.

Silkweavers

At first sight, silkweavers – the last group of workers to be considered, and a large one[98] – would appear to belong to Breuilly's third category of craft workers, those whose trades were destroyed by industrialisation. That this was the case with cotton and woollen weavers is undeniable, but it was not the case with silkweavers. Silk was fragile, and the industry was therefore not extensively mechanised until late

95 *Ibid.*, p. 97.   96 *Ibid.*, p. 98.   97 *Ibid.*, pp. 287–93.
98 Earle, *Making*, pp. 19–21.

in the nineteenth century. The problem was French competition and, to an increasing extent, provincial competition. The French were combated with a prohibition on imports imposed in 1766 and not changed to a tariff until 1826, a change that much of the industry was unable to survive. When the tariff itself was finally abolished in 1860 the silk industry in London and in most of England virtually collapsed. However, until then, provincial rather than foreign competition was a more pressing problem for the London silk trade.

As a group, silkweavers lacked even the limited status accorded to the more skilled tailors and shoemakers. But it is significant that their fall from some small state of grace occurred at about the same time as that of the other trades examined in this chapter. The silkweavers are significant because their history combines so many of the characteristics of other trades examined earlier. They demonstrate not only the vulnerability of a trade, but also the failure of so many industries in the capital to invest and mechanise in depth. By delivering their goods to the warehouse, the Spitalfields weavers represent very nearly the full outwork system, and compare closely with the domestic system in other parts of England during the eighteenth century. Furthermore, the silkweavers met most of the late nineteenth-century criteria of sweated labour. Looms were cheap, costing less than £2 in 1840, and if a weaver could not afford to buy a loom he or she could always rent one for about 1s. 4d. a month.[99] Much the greatest part of the work was accordingly done at the weavers' own homes; they could not, therefore, exclude women or children. The least skilled part of the work was silktwisting, commonly carried out in London workhouses from the 1730s[100] and not the sort of thing for which London, with its high cost of living, was suitable. The labour of the capital's women and children was best used either in the service sector or in the finishing sector of manufacturing, as in neither of these cases was there provincial competition. Silktwisting accordingly left London. Weaving, however, remained, and with it all the classic conditions that were to be attributed to sweated labour during the succeeding century. 'Some of the masters only keep a loom or two at work and such a master may set up with £50 or £100. But there are others who are great dealers and employ from £500 to £5,000 in the trade. These last require from £20 to £100 with an apprentice who will be chiefly employed in the counting house.'[101] Thus Collyer in 1761. The small masters were very small indeed, and very much in the power of those who could advance them credit; as was said specifically in 1826, and

[99] *Reports of the Assistant Commissioners on the Handloom Weavers*, P.P. 1840, 23, p. 235.
[100] *London Life*, p. 185.   [101] Collyer, *The Parents' and Guardians' Directory*, p. 251.

had been said in a similar vein during the preceding century: 'When a glut arises in the market, such employers and employed are immediately involved in one common mass of misery.'[102]

Apprentices were taken on as cheap labour: in 1769 the *Public Advertiser* claimed it as 'a certain fact that there are several weavers in Spitalfields who have from ten to twenty apprentices each'.[103] But since apprentices were supposed to be taken on for at least five years, if not seven, whether the trade was good or bad, this would not have been very common. In fact, the weavers did not do so badly during the first half of the eighteenth century, at any rate compared with what came later. 'The wages of weavers in general are but poor, the best hands among the journeymen seldom able to get above 15s. a week' was Collyer's opinion in 1761, a prosperous year. The pay of a bricklayer or carpenter was 15s., which was not bad. However, the less skilled weavers received some 12s. a week, which was the pay of a labourer, and were paid it at the end of their work – which might take weeks – living on credit for the duration.[104] Nevertheless, the weavers appear to have found conditions more or less tolerable during the first two-thirds of the eighteenth century. Keeping them tolerable involved the occasional riot – since the weavers could not form a strong trade union, violent demonstrations were the most effective method of drawing attention to their grievances and attracting the intervention of the magistrates, as the next chapter shows. In 1719 the Spitalfields weavers were fortunate enough to have their grievances coinciding with the grievances of most of the country's textile industry, and all campaigned together against the import of East Indian calicoes. They were more vociferous than most – any woman thoughtless enough to walk through Spitalfields wearing a calico gown was liable to have it ripped off her back. With protests pouring in from many other parts of the country as well as a publicity campaign organised by Daniel Defoe, Parliament duly passed an Act purporting to forbid the wearing of calicoes.[105] In 1736 their aims were more limited: they rioted with the building workers to prevent Irishmen being employed at lower than customary wages. The masters agreed to stop the practice.[106]

---

[102] Bondois-Morris, 'Spitalfields', p. 367.   [103] *London Life*, pp. 182–3.

[104] For weavers' wages in the 1760s, see Rothstein, 'The silk industry', chapter two; Bondois-Morris, 'Spitalfields', p. 294; Collyer, *The Parents' and Guardians' Directory*, p. 251; *London Life*, p. 181.

[105] A. P. Wadsworth and J. de L. Mann, *The Cotton Trade and Industrial Lancashire* (Manchester, 1931), pp. 133–4. There is an account of the rioting of the 1720s and the 1760s in Rothstein, 'The silk industry', chapter five and Rothstein, 'The calico campaign'; Plummer, *Weavers' Company*, pp. 292–314.

[106] Rudé, 'Mother Gin', pp. 201–21. See below, p. 222.

Conditions became less than tolerable with the end of the Seven Years War in 1763, which marked the turning point from occasional to endemic large-scale rioting. First, employers and weavers together asked for a prohibition on all imports of French manufactured silks and duly obtained it in 1766. Then the weavers asked for higher piece rates. The underlying problem was provincial competition, which could only be met by growing specialisation; the immediate problem was lack of work and low profit margins, import prohibition notwithstanding. In 1767 a book of piece rates, informally agreed between masters and men, was cast aside by some of the masters, and the rioting duly broke out again. It reached the point of the formation of a club (perhaps a trade union, perhaps not) known as 'The Cutters', that sought to levy a tax on anyone who owned or possessed a loom, and which sent letters addressed in terms such as: 'Mr. Hill, you are desired to send the full donation of all your looms to the Dolphin in Cock Lane. This from the conquering and bold Defiance to be levied at four shillings per loom.' The magistrates duly broke it up.[107] At last in 1773 the weavers obtained an Act allowing magistrates to fix piece rates. The Act did more – it also limited the number of apprentices per journeyman to two – but it did not exclude women, as both sides had agreed to do during a very temporary truce in 1769, when they brought out a book of piece rates that permitted women to work only at items specifically mentioned and poorly paid, unless it was wartime, when 'every manufacturer shall be at liberty to employ women or girls in the making of any sort of works as they shall think most fit and convenient without any restraint whatsoever'.[108]

Women duly entered the trade on a particularly large scale during the 1790s, when trade expansion coincided with a recruitment campaign and a general shortage of labour.[109] But the weavers were fortunate for in 1801 the Spitalfields Acts were extended to cover women.[110] However, silk weaving was expanding in the North and the Midlands; more and more of the trade left Spitalfields and the principal problem faced by the journeymen was not female competition so much as slow expansion and provincial competition. By 1818, wages for the more skilled journeymen had fallen from those of carpenters and bricklayers to those of labourers.[111] They survived in

[107] Plummer, *Weavers' Company*, pp. 315–26.

[108] *Ibid.*, p. 325; *London Life*, p. 183. They could, for instance, work on handkerchiefs, where provincial competition was becoming intense. There had been an earlier list in 1762, before the bad times: Plummer, *Weavers' Company*, pp. 322–3.

[109] See above, pp. 100–1.   [110] 51 Geo. III c. 7.

[111] For 1818 wage rates, see the evidence presented to the *S.C. to whom the Several Petitions of the Ribbon Weavers of Coventry and Leek ... were Referred*, P.P. 1818,

the capital, albeit at the cost of growing impoverishment, unable to make themselves more skilled, but depending on the Acts, and depending even more on the prohibition of French silk imports. But the Spitalfields Acts went in 1824, the import prohibition in 1826. The 1826 depression struck very hard – it was already being anticipated in 1825 when retailers were selling off their remaining stocks of English goods, although the prohibition was not due to be lifted until 5 July 1826.[112] In January 1826 the overseer of the poor of Bethnal Green had over 1,200 persons on outdoor relief, and within a few days a delegation from the parish visited Huskisson, to be assured that their problems were merely temporary and that a duty of 30 per cent was preferable to prohibition and smuggling.[113] Over the next five years the weavers' piece rates fell by half.[114] There are hints that the arrival of unsmuggled French silk imports overturned a tacit national price structure which reflected the division of labour between areas. It was not only Spitalfields that kept agreed prices until the 1820s. The Essex silkweaving towns such as Braintree, Bocking, Halstead, Colchester, and Coggeshall normally set their weavers' piece rates at two-thirds the level of Spitalfields;[115] in Coventry there were books of prices that were usually observed until 1823, but not thereafter.[116] During the 1820s the informal regulation that had sometimes preceded the 1773 Act was not repeated, and in the provinces the informal agreements disappeared.

In London, the distress was dire. The weavers became a byword for dire poverty, as described by Mayhew in 1849 and by Dickens in 1854: 'There is not one resident whom the world would call respectable. There are not more than half a dozen families able to keep a servant; and there is not one man, I believe, able to tenant a whole house . . . They are comparatively wealthy who afford to rent two rooms.'[117] Finally the Cobden–Chevalier Treaty of 1860 finished off almost the whole business.[118] The silk industry, like so many others in London,

---

Evidence of Messrs Elks, Hale, Gibson, Moore, Ballance suggests that average wages were 15s.–17s. a week, costs 3s.–4s.6d., so a net income of 11s.6d.–12s.6d.

[112] *Trades Newspaper*, 15 January 1826.   [113] *Ibid.*, 29 January 1826, p. 454.

[114] For wages in 1831, see *S.C. on the Present State of the Silk Trade*, P.P. 1831–2, 19, especially evidence of Ballance and Wallis. Also D. J. Rowe, 'Chartism and the Spitalfields silk weavers', *Econ. Hist. Rev.*, 2nd ser., 20 (1967), pp. 489–90.

[115] *R.C. on the Handloom Weavers. Report of Assistant Commissioners*, P.P. 1840, 23, p. 125.

[116] J. Prest, *The Industrial Revolution in Coventry* (Oxford, 1960); P. Searby, '"Lists of prices" in the Coventry silk industry, 1800–1860', *Bulletin of the Society for the Study of Labour History*, 27 (1973).

[117] Thompson and Yeo, *Unknown Mayhew*, pp. 122–36; C. Dickens, *Household Words*, 9, no. 212, 15 April 1854, 'The Quiet Poor'.

[118] Warner, *Silk Industry*, pp. 78–90.

typified the tendency among the industries of the capital to invest in width, not depth.

London overheads and mass production

As soon as a product came to be made for a mass market, its manufacture was liable to become sweated. That is to say, Adam Smith's law of the division of labour being limited by the extent of the market would apply, but it would apply as much to entrepreneurs as it would to artisans. In all the four trades observed, the expanded market was supplied not by large integrated businesses but by a multitude of small masters, often giving out work to be done at home, competing with each other on price and cutting down on quality as much as possible. This tended to mean the labour of women and children, and in the London context it is usually undocumented, since such work left no trade union in its wake. Trade unions existed, almost by definition, in trades that were not carried out in the home, in trades where the earnings were in the middling or higher range and in trades where the members of the trade would at least be able to hope that they might support a wife and children – in other words, they existed when the labour force was male. The shipwrights, the millwrights and the coachmakers often met these requirements, as did a goodly number of the tailors and furniture makers. The shoemakers aspired in this direction, at least during the eighteenth century. The silk-weavers did not.

Once a product had been cheapened sufficiently to enable its mass production, there was little that could be done to stop the rot. The Spitalfields Acts and the import prohibition delayed matters in Spitalfields, but could not prevent silk from being manufactured elsewhere in the country. The tailors, the shoemakers and the furniture makers were undermined, though prompt action, strong organisation and luck could conceivably delay their fate by as much as a generation.

Why was it that the response to market opportunity took the form of such a proliferation of small employers? Why did not integrated firms come into existence with more capital to meet the economies of integrated production? The answer, as outlined in chapter one, is in the very nature of the metropolitan economy, with its high rents, great fluctuations in demand to discourage long runs of production, and the proximity to an enormous but volatile fashion market, ensuring concentration on finished products and leaving primary or intermediate production to be carried out elsewhere. The finishing trades could adapt themselves successfully to these conditions, conditions which militated against heavy capitalisation but which militated strongly for an 'urban proto-industrialisation', using wherever possible the household as the unit of production – particularly underemployed labour within the household – and furthermore decomposing the productive process into a series of operations none of which added much value to the production, none of which paid their practitioners much, but which it remained unprofitable to integrate. Additional income came from the occasional earnings of all the other members of the household. Where these conditions applied for a particular London trade – for instance silkweaving, watch and clock making or coach building – that trade expanded. Where they did not apply – as with silktwisting, ribbon making, framework knitting or some shoemaking – the trade tended to leave.

But while this was the tendency, chapter two has shown that many things stood in the way of this tendency working itself out rapidly. There were processes at work within London that affected the willingness of different groups there to do certain kinds of work and the ability of other groups to stop them. These will be examined in the next chapter.

The defences of the inferior artisans

The equilibrium that was referred to in the previous chapter could also be interpreted as meaning the maintenance of some autonomous areas for labour. There are of course always such areas, and, as frequently said, their survival depends on many factors – and these include suitable legal and political institutions. The eighteenth-century London artisan found himself with a range of institutions which had been created in an earlier age. He – it was only men to whom this applied – tried to use them to maintain his areas of autonomy and his standard of living. Improvements were desirable, but maintenance was essential. The artisans, and many of the smaller masters to whom they were so akin, were engaged in a ceaseless quest for stability. This meant the stability between contending forces, the temporary stability that could be wrested from the balance of economic forces and opportunities. From time to time the balance changed, and the position of the artisans changed with it. Always they were aware of the threat of the less skilled – which meant the threat of penury as well as of loss of status. As the nineteenth century would make clear, basic economic trends could not be opposed in the long run. But such trends could hardly be foreseen during the eighteenth century. The journeymen knew that from instability they would probably emerge the losers, but they also knew that the balance of stability needed to be constantly redefined. They used the institutions they inherited. None of these were ideal for maintaining stability – in a society as dynamic as that of eighteenth-century England this would hardly be expected – but some were of service. This chapter considers three such institutions: guilds, apprenticeship regulations and the magistracy. The guilds were inherited from an earlier regime and exercised an erratic and declining influence. Apprenticeship also had some legal justification and a strong moral

H

tradition which gave it strength, but it derived more strength from the fact that the journeymen wanted it and that it usually suited the masters to keep it. Magistrates were responsible for order, and had scant resources to impose it. They could interfere erratically, like the gods, but if the feeling among the men was sufficiently strong then an occasional descent into the arena was insufficient and the magistrates knew it. This might make them amenable to controls on competition.

Finally, this chapter considers a fourth influence, not an institution, over which neither employers nor workers had much sway, and that was recruitment in time of war. As already shown in chapter three, wars – the Revolutionary and Napoleonic Wars in particular – with their enormous demand for men, had a strong effect on the labour market. The ending of a war and the demobilisation of so many men had an even greater effect because it was more abrupt.

The old law: guilds

There is a large and confusing literature on the supposed decline of the London guilds during the seventeenth and eighteenth centuries. Guilds exercised many functions – in their golden age they were supposed to have had something to do with the regulation of apprenticeship, the admission of journeymen, the regulation of their trade and the government of their town. The golden age is as little likely ever to have existed as the static urban society, but it is undeniable that the loss of the various functions held by the guilds was piecemeal, depending on the function and the guild, thus making it difficult to discern common patterns. In the case of London it was made more complex by the tradition that one did not need to enrol in the guild of one's trade in order to become a freeman. Many of the Livery Companies, as the City's guilds were called, were basically honorific bodies throughout this period, but not all were so. During the late seventeenth and early eighteenth centuries quite a few were making serious attempts to find a role for themselves and this usually meant looking back to an earlier and somewhat traditional regulatory role.[1] If the Company had a legal jurisdiction for a number of miles outside the City it was an encouragement.[2] By the end of the

---

[1] Walker, 'Extent of guild control'; J. R. Kellett, 'The breakdown of gild and corporation control over the handicraft and retail trade in London', *Econ. Hist. Rev.*, 2nd ser., 10 (1957–8); W. F. Kahl, *The Development of the London Livery Companies: An Historical Essay and Select Bibliography* (Boston, 1960); W. F. Kahl, 'Apprenticeship and the freedom of the London livery companies, 1690–1750', *Guildhall Miscellany*, 7 (1956), pp. 17–20.

[2] Walker, 'Extent of guild control', p. 186.

eighteenth century most of the Companies had found new roles, which had little to do with these traditional functions and much to do with estate management, previously only one aspect of their activities. Some Companies, such as the Apothecaries' or the Goldsmiths', continued to exercise a degree of quality control well into the eighteenth century and were important to their members.[3] The bakers – whose trade was evidently rather traditional during the eighteenth century – kept their identity: unlike many other Companies, the Bakers' Company consisted largely of bakers and until the third quarter of the eighteenth century most of them were admitted by patrimony rather than redemption. The Ironmongers' Company, similarly, kept its identity.[4] In more dynamic trades, the role of the Company was rather different. The Weavers' Company held no attractions to the journeymen silkweavers of Spitalfields – although occasional unsuccessful attempts were made to remedy this – but it might be useful to the masters as a pressure group when dealing with the government.[5] For the smaller masters of many trades, membership of a Company was a financial burden which gave few benefits and often involved expenses, sometimes quite onerous. Age and economic progress had heightened rather than dulled the guilds' almost infinite variety, but it is evident that in the early eighteenth century there was a surprisingly large number of trades for which the existence of a Company could not be ignored, if only because the masters were obliged by antiquated laws to belong to it, and the journeymen insisted on making repeated and usually unsuccessful attempts to use the Company regulations on their own behalf. To others, of course, the Companies were stepping stones to City office.

It should not be forgotten that traditionally the main justification of the guild system was that it provided a system of urban government. As this role declined, the guild system would be expected to decline. If guilds were ever supposed to hold back the development of individual enterprise – and this is open to doubt – this was not how they regarded their role during the eighteenth century. If market forces led in a certain direction, the guild would adapt itself to those forces. Far from being inflexible institutions that held back the development of market forces, guilds were remarkably flexible in adapting themselves to such forces.[6] They survived, but at the cost of losing most of their functions except their paramount political function of playing a part in City government.

3 Earle, *Making*, p. 254–6; Walker, 'Extent of guild control', p. 188.
4 Walker, 'Extent of guild control', p. 214.
5 Plummer, *Weavers' Company*, p. 292–310.   6 Walker, 'Extent of guild control', pp. 390–1.

The eighteenth-century London Companies were very rarely in a position systematically to prevent gross exploitation of labour, even if they had wished to do so. They had little control over the fixing of wages or prices, they had very little control over who should enter a trade, and they were certainly not in a position to restrain either the growth of the large-scale entrepreneur on the one hand, or of outputting and sub-contracting on the other hand. During the seventeenth century there are some examples of a lingering desire to exercise some controls over their trades; during the eighteenth century the desire faded as rapidly as the ability. Eighteenth-century London guilds remained important political institutions; they had some social value to their members in providing social and professional contacts and good dinners, but their economic functions were another matter entirely. They were usually dominated by hard-headed employers, who had no intention of permitting guild regulations to stand in the way of making money, but who might be willing to use those regulations to safeguard their position *vis-à-vis* smaller employers.[7] In addition, the power of any individual guild was extremely limited and had become more limited during the seventeenth century, when there is said to have been a distinct tendency towards a merging of small employers and journeymen, under the heading of 'working members', 'artisans' or 'the handytrade', themselves increasingly under the influence of the larger capitalists who supplied the raw materials.[8] Companies could do little about this, even if they wished to do so. Some sought to defend themselves by insisting on financial qualifications for members, but their efforts frequently came to nought. If one Company chose to be scrupulous it was usually possible to join another Company with fewer scruples or greater penury. Alternatively, people could often work outside the City without joining a guild at all.

The principal aim of the eighteenth-century London Companies was survival. This being the eighteenth century, the question of why

[7] And this was not new, nor was it confined to London: 'the hard-headed businessmen who composed the corporation are not likely to have perpetuated a system that was a brake on the city's prosperity, and the revival of York's fortunes between 1550 and 1650, when the guild structure remained intact, suggests that it was no great hindrance': D. M. Palliser, 'The trade guilds of Tudor York', in P. Clark and P. Slack (eds.), *Crisis and Order in English Towns, 1500–1700* (1972), p. 112.

[8] This argument follows closely N. Carlin, 'Levelling the liveries: some aspects of the outlook of craftsmen in the London livery companies of the mid-seventeenth century', *Middlesex Polytechnic History Journal*, 1(4), pp. 3–25. Carlin speaks of 'the "emancipation" of the journeymen combining with the poverty of small masters to create a more unified artisan class': *ibid.*, p. 12. For the increasing capital required, see Earle, *Making*, pp. 106, 108.

they should survive was not considered. Survival meant maintaining their numbers, something that the City's largest guilds – the Twelve Great Livery Companies – found themselves failing to do during the first half of the eighteenth century, although the smaller and more specialised Companies seem to have managed it.[9] By the nineteenth century the Companies were making enough money from property not to need to worry too much about the lack of members, but during the first half of the eighteenth century this was not the case.[10] It was, after all, a period of depression in London building, so their rents are unlikely to have been very high.

The Carpenters' Company illustrates the dilemma of the guilds very clearly. It was not untypical. The failure of London carpenters to enrol in their Company was nothing new. It has been estimated that during the second half of the sixteenth century at least 60 per cent of London's carpenters had not done so.[11] By the seventeenth century the law that was supposed to compel them to join was of doubtful application, and the Company made little effort to enforce it: despite ordinances which in 1607 extended the Company's rights for two miles around the City and four miles in 1640 a smaller proportion of carpenters belonged to the Company than a century earlier.[12] There was, after all, little economic incentive for a carpenter to join his Company. If he was conscientious he would have to undertake tiresome searches, usually at his own expense, while for only a few of the largest master carpenters was the patronage awarded to the Company of much value – and even of this little had remained by the seventeenth century.[13] The reluctance to join the Company was not uncommon in other trades. Ephraim Flammer told the Weavers' Company in 1748 that although he had been 'duly brought up to the Weaving Trade which he had exercised many years...he did not consider it would be of any use to be admitted to the Freedom of the Company and therefore would not be at any expense to be admitted'. Neither did James Voisin, who 'had not money to pay the charges, nor ever should have, and peremptorily refused to be admitted'.[14] He could in

9 This is discussed by the various sources mentioned in n. 1 above.
10 Kellett, 'Breakdown'.
11 B. W. E. Alford and T. C. Barker, *A History of the Carpenters' Company* (1968), p. 32; L. D. Schwarz, 'London apprentices in the seventeenth century: some problems', *Local Population Studies*, 38 (1987), pp. 18–22.
12 Alford and Barker, *Carpenters*, pp. 69, 73.
13 *Ibid.*, pp. 42–4. The post of King's Carpenter fell into abeyance in 1269; the Company lost any automatic association with the post of Surveyor to the King's Works in 1565. Other examples date from the early sixteenth century. For more general comments on the guilds' decline, see Earle, *Making*, pp. 250–60.
14 Plummer, *Weavers' Company*, p. 355.

fact probably have afforded to get in by patrimony;[15] the problem was that the wealthier employers were under continuous pressure to devote much of their time and money to the Company, and by the late seventeenth century were paying £20 to be excused all offices. Worse still, such a man would be formally forbidden to have more than two apprentices, and usually forbidden to employ women. If threatened with legal action – which the Weavers' Company was doing to some recalcitrant employers as late as 1787 – he joined, but reluctantly.[16]

During the early part of the eighteenth century the Corporation could still be prevailed upon to act in the old manner. It issued an Act in 1712 declaring that it would punish unfreemen who attempted 'to use any manual occupation or handicraft or to sell or put to sale any Wares of Merchandizes by Retail in any Shop'; in 1717 when the journeymen blacksmiths prosecuted an employer for employing a 'foreigner' the Lord Mayor's Court referred the case back to the Blacksmiths' Company whose members were obliged to 'declare their opinion that the employing of foreigners should not be countenanced', although this was as far as they could be induced to go, announcing very firmly that it was not 'in their power to fix the wages and hours of journeymen's work' and accordingly left those issues 'to the parties in difference to determine betwixt themselves'.[17] Declarations against the employment of foreigners remained rather in the nature of pious intent followed by occasional and not very frequent bursts of activity. The Butchers' Company, for instance, made some forays against street sellers of meat and prosecuted them in 1726, 1728 and 1732, but by the 1760s seems to have restricted itself mainly to the prosecution of sellers of bad meat on public health grounds.[18] A serious check on 'foreigners' involved regular checking of premises. The Coopers' Company did this regularly. It was very time consuming and had its snags – 'Mr. Fennings in the Strand threatened to shoot one of the wardens through the head.' It was also expensive and it was rare for the wardens, themselves employers taking time off from their own business, to be reimbursed. The Weavers' Company, whose searchers were reimbursed, continued for longer, but the last general search was in 1736, and membership of the Weavers' Company promptly fell by nearly a quarter during the next four years; the Company carried out a specific search in Spitalfields in 1740 and another in 1744 to induce masters to join the Company, but did not

---

[15] *Ibid.*, pp. 19–20. Half a century earlier, redemption by patrimony would have cost him less than £1.

[16] *Ibid.*, pp. 289–90.   [17] Dobson, *Masters and Journeymen*, p. 49.

[18] A. Pearce, *The History of the Butchers' Company* (1929), pp. 112–16.

follow it up. It must have been very unpopular: the searchers were paid 4d. by each member who had the privilege of being searched, and out of this the searchers had breakfast and supper, the Company itself making up any deficiency in the bill. The Watchmakers' Company, whose members paid 4d. a quarter for being searched, gave up its searches 'soon after' 1735. In 1750 the City decided to abandon the whole attempt and a system of licensing non-freemen was introduced, with a considerable effect on membership, at least for a while, and a very welcome effect on the Companies' finances, although this by no means prevented complaints of 'the number of shopkeepers at the time following the said trade within the City and not free of the said Company exceeding that of the present members thereof' as the Watchmakers' did in 1766.[19]

The reasons for joining a City Company were not really economic: they were to avoid the nuisance value of not doing so, and – at least as important – they were social and political. 'Now a Youth having taken up his Freedom', said Campbell in 1747,

if he is a popular Man, he may in two or three Years have the Honour to be appointed Renter Warden or Steward, which entitles him to the Privilege of treating the Fraternity unto an elegant and expensive Entertainment on Lord Mayor's Day.[20]

City politics were the liveliest in the land, and the Common Hall, where the less wealthy met, was an enjoyable place in which to exercise one's right of free speech. What Common Hall said did not usually make much difference – it usually had to defer to the more select Common Council or the Court of Aldermen – but it was one of the more democratic institutions of the eighteenth century.

It was this last factor that is a major reason for a Company such as the Carpenters' surviving the Great Fire. From an economic point of view it is surprising that it should have done so, because in the aftermath of the Fire even the pretence of its functions was peremptorily removed. In order to attract labour, carpenters who were not freemen of London were given the same rights as freemen – for seven years in the first instance, but this could be extended. The Company appealed to have the right to check the indentures of all carpenters working in the City to ensure that all had served a seven-year apprenticeship, but this was refused.[21] Nevertheless the Company survived – partly because it managed to keep some revenue from its property,

---

[19] Plummer, *Weavers' Company*, pp. 47–8, 53–5, 355; Atkins and Overall, *Clockmakers of the City of London*, pp. 235–42, 385–93; Kellett, 'Breakdown'.
[20] Campbell, *London Tradesman*, p. 305.
[21] Alford and Barker, *Carpenters*, pp. 84–5.

partly because those apprentices who had completed their indentures in London still sometimes sought to register the fact with the Company, and partly because of its political role which, though minor, was still significant. It also took some trouble to maintain its nuisance value to those employers who had not joined, in which it was also typical of other Companies, especially those that were short of money.

If merely forcing tradesmen to join a Company was difficult enough, regulating them would have been much more difficult. It was not attempted, and those whose opinions mattered had little interest in doing so. The historians of the Carpenters' Company, for instance, conclude that during the second half of the seventeenth century the Company 'gradually came to represent, with decreasing effectiveness, small independent master carpenters who formed a transitional class between three unavoidable alternatives: the most able could aspire to become building contractors or "architects"; a larger, but still minor proportion could concentrate on specialist branches of the craft, of which joinery was the most prominent; while the majority were forced to suffer reduction to the status of journeymen employees'.[22] It was the same with the Masons' Company: a petition of 1750 claimed that eighty of the 120 free journeymen who had come out of their time, but without sufficient capital to set up for themselves, had become the direct employees of twenty-one master-masons. The latter were concerned, not with the competition of 'foreign' masons, but with combinations amongst their own journeymen who, taking advantage of the fact that the masters were supposedly forbidden to employ unfreemen, had 'entered into unlawful Combinations, busying themselves more to prevent others from Working than to procure or Deserve Employment for themselves', so that the freedom which had once been 'a great and invaluable Franchise – by Securing Imployment to the honest Citizen' was now coming 'to destroy Subordination and to Raise an intractable Spirit in the lower class of Freemen'.[23] The weavers, who received a new Charter as late as 1707 re-affirming their traditional rights and giving them jurisdiction up to ten miles around the capital, concentrated on enrolling employers, a sensible policy and the only possible one in the circumstances.[24]

The old law and the new reality: apprenticeship

The guilds' failure to control apprenticeship is an excellent example of their weakness. Apprenticeship was a vital area for the guilds to

---

[22] *Ibid.*, p. 89.   [23] Kellett, 'Breakdown', p. 388.
[24] Plummer, *Weavers' Company*, pp. 278–91.

control, if quality control or the limitation of numbers was to mean anything at all. Guild members were supposedly restricted in the number of apprentices whom they could employ, usually to no more than two.[25] This had various purposes: it limited the potential use of apprentices as sweated labour thereby preventing other masters from being undercut, it made it more likely that the apprentices would be taught properly and less likely that the market would be flooded with more labour than it could comfortably absorb, so it protected the master craftsman. However, many years ago, Unwin suggested that many London crafts experienced a substantial increase in out-working during the sixteenth and seventeenth centuries,[26] an increase related to the growing numbers of young men who failed to complete their apprenticeships but were nevertheless able to set up for themselves in households of their own.[27] Subsequent research has indeed confirmed a very high drop-out rate for apprentices – as high as 60 per cent during the sixteenth century and likely to be as high during the first half of the seventeenth century.[28]

The problems faced by the London Companies are well illustrated in the history of the Carpenters' Company. Flouting the spirit, if not the letter of the regime, it compiled new rules in 1607 whereby the master and wardens of the Company were permitted three apprentices each, members of the livery two, and ordinary freemen one.[29] This did not prevent a clause permitting the master and wardens to waive all these rules and permit any freeman to have an additional apprentice for a fine of 2s.6d. However, freemen who had not practised the craft for at least three years were not permitted to have more than one apprentice, while those who had practised for more than three but less than seven years were limited to two apprentices each.[30]

These loopholes were not sufficient. Since apprenticeship to any one London Company gave a man the Freedom of the City, a carpenter could be formally apprenticed to any freeman of London, duly registered with that freeman's Company – Mercers', Bakers', Woodmongers', etc. – and then employed by a carpenter. This took place on a large scale in the mid 1650s, when there was a building boom, and the Carpenters' apprenticeship regulations rapidly became unworkable.

[25] Unwin, *Gilds*, pp. 264–6.   [26] Unwin, *Industrial Organisation*, pp. 5–6.
[27] Unwin, *Gilds*, pp. 225–6.
[28] Schwarz, 'London apprentices', pp. 18–22.
[29] Alford and Barker, *Carpenters*, p. 70.
[30] *Ibid.*, p. 70.

Whereas divers persons of this Company have at present great imploym^t in building (worke being now very plentifull & still increasing) & yett by the strict rules of the ordinances of this Company are limitted in their apprentices whereby they are in want of workemen & so are not able many times to performe their worke undertaken in due time To the great prejudice of themselves & damage of their worke masters wch hath caused divers suit^{r}s to repaire unto the Court for apprentices extraordinary who upon deniall of their requests have gone privately to other Companys & procured them to be there bound & afterwards assigned over to them & such apprentices doe afterwards come to be made free of other Companyes & have & doe daily multiply and increase To the great injury and destruction of this Company (if not timely remedied) whereupon this Court for prevencon of that evill for the future as much as in the Comp lyes & upon reading of the ordinances wch enables the M^r & wardens for reasonable cause to allow an apprentice extraordinary doth think fitt & so order That liberty be given by the M^r & wardens to any person desiring the same that hath worke sufficient to imploy an apprentice extraordinary in to have & take one apprentice over & above the number limited by the ordinances And likewise that the same liberty by given to any person requesting the same (though not compleatly three yeares a freemen) to have & take an apprentice Soe as such persons be thought capable thereof by the M^r & Wardens.[31]

The guilds decayed, their controls over apprenticeship withered away, but the institution of apprenticeship remained. Its strength was not in the law of 5 Elizabeth to which artisans were appealing during the early years of the nineteenth century. This law purported to make an apprenticeship virtually compulsory and would, if strictly observed, have kept 'unqualified' labour out of these trades. That was why the artisans appealed to it, and that was why their employers disliked it. 'When this Act was made', said Lord Kenyon, giving judgement during the 1780s,

those who framed it might have found it beneficial, but the ink with which it was written was scarce dry, ere the inconvenience of it was perceived; and the Judges falling in with the sentiment of policy entertained by others, have lent their assistance to repeal this law as much as it was in their power.[32]

So successful were they that by the early eighteenth century little of it was left outside the City of London. In the City it had a sporadic and usually rather slight influence, occasionally interrupted by some striking but short-lived successes.[33] Any effectiveness it may have had in the City of London finally disappeared in 1750 – the year when the Corporation introduced a system for licensing non-freemen – when a

---

[31] *Ibid.*, pp. 74–5.

[32] T. Peake, *Cases determined at Nisi Prius, in the Court of King's Bench, from the sittings after Easter term 30 G.III to the sittings after Michaelmas Term 35 G.III* (2nd ed., 1810), p. 148.

[33] See above, p. 214, for the blacksmiths in 1717. Such cases are not infrequent in the guild histories; the difficulty is to know how frequent they were.

'club' of journeymen painters prosecuted a master for employing an unapprenticed painter. The master was found guilty, but it was a Pyrrhic victory, for Common Council promptly passed an Act permitting unapprenticed non-freemen to be employed if freemen were unavailable, subject only to a licence from the Mayor.[34] This regularised the existing situation. Surrounded by the out-parishes, whose population was increasing rapidly and where the jurisdiction of the guilds was often minimal, or non-existent, while the population of the City was stagnant, the City masters could not permit the enforcement of regulations that might damage their own trade, even if their inclinations were in that direction, which was seldom. If the insistence on apprenticeship and the limitation of numbers was to have any effect at all, it had to extend over the metropolis as a whole, and even then it would remain effective only as long as the provinces were not serious competitors. Hence the interest of the London trades in extending the scope of 5 Elizabeth, and their involvement with the Parliamentary campaign of 1813–14, which culminated in the repeal of the legislation they wished to strengthen.[35]

The repeal of 1814 did not change the basic pattern: throughout the eighteenth century it had been for the journeymen to enforce apprenticeship if they were strong enough to do so, and this remained the case. During the eighteenth century, they had, more often than not, been unsuccessful in this endeavour. 'No Trade Union', the Webbs have remarked,

has been really able to enforce a limitation of apprentices if new employers are always starting up in fresh centres; if the craft itself is frequently being changed by the introduction of new processes or machinery; if alternative classes of workers can be brought in to execute some portions of the operation.[36]

Which, of course, was happening all the time.

The tailors did not seek to enforce apprenticeship. The hatters, strong enough to enforce a closed shop by 1775, were rewarded with a special Act of Parliament in 1777 to prevent their limitation of apprenticeship numbers. In 1797, two journeymen printers were indicted for

---

34 W. Besant, *London in the Eighteenth Century* (1902), pp. 223–4. A copy of the Act is in C.L.R.O., P.A.R. 7, pp. 141–6. Kellett sees this as a successful attempt by the guilds to increase their membership: 'Breakdown', pp. 389–91. This may have been one of its purposes, but the Act did end any remaining limitation on apprenticeship. See also Dobson, *Masters and Journeymen*, p. 49.
35 T. K. Derry, 'The repeal of the apprenticeship clauses of the Statute of Apprentices', *Econ. Hist. Rev.*, 1st ser., 3 (1931–2), pp. 67–87; Prothero, *Artisans and Politics*, pp. 51–61.
36 S. and B. Webb, *Industrial Democracy* (1902), p. 479.

conspiring to restrict the number of apprentices to three for seven presses,[37] while in 1803 the curriers resolved that nobody who had served his apprenticeship with a master 'having more than one apprentice besides him' should be permitted to work in London.[38] But these were exceptional. Some workshops did their best to ensure that men entering a trade should have served an apprenticeship – they might be flexible about this in prosperous and secure times though not otherwise – but few had much success in limiting the numbers of apprentices.

There are some suggestions that there was a large-scale breakdown of the apprenticeship system during the second third of the eighteenth century, a reflection of changed conditions for the trades. Walker finds that many of the manufacturing guilds (e.g. cordwainers or smiths) suffered a serious decline in membership during the 1730s and 1740s. However, examining the length of apprenticeships served according to settlement certificates Snell has found that until 1746–50 the seven-year period of apprenticeship remained normal, but there was a clear and continuing decline from the mid century. Walker attributes the breakdown of many guilds to the pressures of the slump of the 1730s and 1740s. Snell, whose data shows decline during a slightly later period, attributes it to the subsequent boom and the efforts by masters to use cheap labour to expand production. This leads him to question whether there was a serious depression in the smaller towns examined by Walker during the 1730s and 1740s.[39]

If either Snell or Walker were right it would be of great interest for the study of the London trades. Furthermore, as they are not studying the same data, it is not unreasonable to put their conclusions together and suggest that the second third of the eighteenth century saw both a decline in admissions to freedoms and in length of apprenticeship served. However, both these studies suffer from two problems. The first is that of sample size. Snell specifically refers to the small size of his sample for London, while Walker analyses only a number of the smaller Companies.[40] Secondly, there is the problem of long-term cycles. Snell considers it quite plausible that apprentices ended their indentures prematurely because they found the prospects for setting up on their own increasingly bleak, while the wages for those who did not set up on their own were increasingly poor, so there was little incentive for them to serve out their full time. They may indeed have

[37] Webb, *History of Trade Unionism*, pp. 27–30; E. Howe and H. E. Waite, *The London Society of Compositors. A Centenary History* (1948), pp. 66–83.
[38] Dobson, *Masters and Journeymen*, pp. 58–9.
[39] Walker, 'Extent of guild control', pp. 298–300; Snell, *Annals*, pp. 238–43.
[40] Snell, *Annals*, p. 234.

found their prospects extremely bleak, but such an argument ignores the extraordinarily high-drop-out rate of the seventeenth century. This could be ignored if most of those who dropped out were women, but there appears to be no evidence to sugget that this was the case.[41] In short, there is insufficient evidence to revise the conclusion of the previous chapter that the decline of the semi-skilled trades took place during the nineteenth and not the eighteenth century.

Magistrates

The guilds decayed, the apprenticeship laws withered away although apprenticeship survived, but the magistrates remained. Magistrates were not necessarily antipathetic to trade regulation: the Spitalfields Act of 1773, passed largely at their behest, did include a clause limiting the number of apprentices to two per master.[42] After all, magistrates had an interest in stability. But they could not stand out against economic realities: an Act that regulated the silk industry in the entire metropolis was one thing, but there were few such Acts; enforcing higher costs on masters who happened to be living in the City of London, and not in the out-parishes, was another. Nevertheless, the tradition that magistrates should intervene in wage negotiations, and if necessary seek to regulate the price of labour, was by no means dead in the eighteenth century. During the first quarter of the eighteenth century Parliament would, on occasion, pass Acts specifically permitting wages to be fixed, but Parliament usually required the prior consent of the local employers to such an Act, and it might take a riot to obtain such consent. The Colchester weavers rioted in 1715, with four troops of guards being required to restore order, but an Act was passed in 1716 meeting some of their grievances.[43] The London tailors, being better organised, merely struck in 1720 and duly obtained their Act the following year.[44]

During the course of the eighteenth century such Acts became less frequent. Legal loopholes remained: in 1751 the London tailors petitioned the magistrates to increase their wages, as permitted under the 1721 Act, and they won a small concession.[45] However, the legal powers of the magistrates came to matter less than their moral influence, and this was easier to exercise when there was no competition from outside the region. London magistrates and others in authority

[41] Snell, *Annals*, pp. 243–52; Schwarz, 'London apprentices'.   [42] 13 Geo.III c.68 c.7.
[43] J. Sharpe, *Crime in Early Modern England, 1500–1750* (1984), p. 138.
[44] Galton, *Select Documents*, pp. 1–23.
[45] Galton, *Select Documents*, pp. 46–8.

might well take their duties extremely seriously, especially when the working men were a force to be reckoned with. Collective bargaining by riot could be highly effective when both sides knew the rules of the game. In 1736 Lieutenant Collet of the militia, on patrol with eighteen men, confronted some 700 or 800 rioters:

> He desired to know the cause of their complaint; to which one who seem'd to be the Captn. of the Mobb made answer in the name of the rest that Mr. Goswell, the builder of Shoreditch Church, had paid off his English labourers and imployed Irish because they worked cheaper and several of the Master [silk] Weavers imployed none but Irish by which means the English Manufacturers were starving, and that they chose rather to be hang'd than starved.
>
> To which Mr. Collet replyed that if they wanted redress in this or any other matter their proper Method was to get a Petition drawn to Parliament & no doubt all English Manufacturers would find Encouragement there upon proper Application and that he would find them a Gentleman to settle their case properly and assist them in obtaining Relief. That, as for Mr. Goswell, he had already discharged his Irish Labourers and Employed English in their Stead and he doubted not but the Weavers would be prevailed upon to do the same. That Mr. Chetham (who, as they said Employed near 200 Irish and against whom the Mobb was particularly incensed) had promised him that he would discharge his Irish workmen as soon as they had finished the several pieces of work they had in Hand. After this short Parley the Mobb gave 2 or 3 huzzas and the Ring-leaders thanked Mr. Collet for his advice – and immediately dispers'd and have never gathered in these parts since.[46]

Saunders Welch's daughter

often spake of his going, in 1766, into Cranbourne-alley unattended, to quell the daily meeting of the journeymen-shoemakers, who had struck for an increase in wages. Immediately her father made his appearance he was recognised, and his name shouted up and down the Alley, – not with fear, but with a degree of exultation. 'Well,' said the ring-leader 'let us give him a beer-barrel and mount him;' and when he was up they one and all gave him three cheers and cried 'Welch! Welch, for ever!' In the mildest manner possible, Mr. Welch assured them that he was glad to find they had conducted themselves quietly; and at the same time, in the most forcible terms, persuaded them to disperse, as their meetings were illegal. He also observed to the master-shoemakers, who were listening to him from their first floor windows, that as they had raised the prices of shoes on account of the increased value of provisions, they should consider that the families of their workmen had proportionate wants. The result was, that the spokesmen of their trade were carried into the shops, and an additional allowance was agreed upon. The men then alternately carried Mr. Welch on their shoulders to Litchfield-street, gave him three cheers more, and set him down.[47]

[46] G. Rudé, *Paris and London in the Eighteenth Century* (1970), p. 207.
[47] Smith, *Nollekens*, pp. 83–4.

Subsequently the newspapers carried a notice:

The Journeymen Shoemakers at a General Meeting with their Masters, on Tuesday the 27th. of May last, at the White Hart Tavern in Holborn, think it their Duty to return their publick Thanks to that worthy Magistrate by whose repeated Advice they think so salutary a work has been brought about. They likewise return their hearty thanks to those Masters who so zealously promoted the interest of Journeymen as well as Masters, in the just support of the lawful Right of the Trade in general, and in suppressing every Person from carrying on the trade who had no Right thereto.[48]

The Spitalfields weavers found things more difficult. They had profited from the warfare of the mid eighteenth century, which drove their French competitors off the seas, but in 1763 the French returned, to compound the rather dismal trade prospects. It took the Spitalfields weavers ten years of rioting and loom cutting to obtain their Act. The London magistracy, much concerned though it was with law and order and inclined to search for the 'ringleaders' of popular protests, was not doctrinaire, in the nineteenth-century *laissez-faire* sense. In the case of Spitalfields, however, they needed persuasion, probably because masters and men failed to agree. The magistrates were happy to lend their assistance to the hanging of a number of Spitalfields weavers, but nevertheless the Spitalfields Act had the support of both the Lord Mayor and Sir John Fielding: in May 1772 the latter informed the government that the magistrates chiefly concerned with Spitalfields had met at Bow Street on the previous day and that 'the Committee of the journeymen weavers and several of the masters attended there, when the Bill. . .was read and approved by the magistrates, masters and men'. Fielding, accompanied by three justices of the Spitalfields district, personally delivered the Bill to Lord North, informing the Prime Minister that in his opinion 'the masters will have more reason to rejoice than the men [if the Bill was passed], as it frees them from their outrages' and would probably 'turn the journeymen weavers' road from the Palace to the Quarter Sessions'. The Act was duly passed, and peace broke out.[49]

When the Act was repealed fifty years later, the views of the magistrates were barely considered. London was much better policed than had been the case half a century previously, and in any case the Spitalfields weavers had been peaceful for so long that they were hardly considered a danger. More importantly, however, economic conditions had changed: Spitalfields was facing competition from elsewhere in the country. Parliament was no longer willing to prohibit

48 *St James' Chronicle*, 3–5 June 1766.
49 Plummer, *Weavers' Company*, pp. 327–8; Dobson, *Masters and Journeymen*, pp. 58–9.

the import of silk, preferring a tariff of 30 per cent.[50] There was little that the magistrates could do. They were prepared to follow the point of view of the majority of the employers, and if this led towards a limitation of competition, they would give it their seal of approval. They were prepared to put moral pressure on the minority of employers who would not follow this lead. But when the masters would not or, given the restraints of national and international competition, could not give a lead, the magistrates were powerless.

Demography and war

The institutions and customs described so far in this chapter were designed to stabilise the London trades, while all about was changing. But there was another set of factors, that can loosely be referred to as demographic, which also exercised a considerable influence on the structure of the labour force and in particular on the division of labour between the sexes and between adults and children, a division that lay at the heart of the fine gradations so carefully insisted upon by the male trades. There were three major 'demographic' influences. The first was the changing sexual balance within the labour force. This is a highly speculative field of enquiry, but it is unlikely to have exercised a major effect. Secondly, there was the increasing size of families, which did have a major influence, although the nature of the sources makes it difficult to find supporting evidence. Finally, there was the very considerable impact of recruitment for the armed forces, the effects of which were sudden, massive and relatively well documented.

The age and sex structure of the population before the nineteenth century is a topic about which little is known, but it is possible to draw some speculative conclusions from statistics on the number of apprentices who were enrolled in London during the seventeenth century.[51] Making certain assumptions that verge on the heroic, women aged fifteen and over appear to have formed rather less than half the population of this age group in the capital in 1700, compared with 54 per cent in 1821. The evidence supporting this speculation is rather thin.[52] With the second force for change – the effects of increased

---

[50] See above, p. 205.

[51] The assumptions for the seventeenth-century figures are put forward in Schwarz, 'London apprentices'. The figure for 1700 emerges as women aged fifteen and over forming 47–8 per cent of the population in 1700; women of all ages formed 48–9 per cent in 1700.

[52] R. A. P. Finlay, *Population and Metropolis. The Demography of London, 1580–1650* (Cambridge, 1981), pp. 140–1, asserts that seventeenth-century London contained

family size on the supply of labour – one is on stronger ground. Unless the real income of the father was increasing, an increased burden of dependency inevitably increased the pressure on mothers and children to procure some additional income, although the increased burden would itself make it more difficult for mothers to go out to work. In London money wages were not rising faster than prices – let alone fast enough to compensate for larger family sizes – until after the Napoleonic Wars. This was far more significant than possible changes in the sex ratio of the adult population.

But the pressure that women and children exercised was cut short by war. The general impact of war on the labour market has been discussed in chapters three and four, but the specific impact of the Napoleonic Wars on the labour of women and children in London is fairly well documented, and it was very considerable. The two decades after 1790 saw many years of relatively full employment, if not of labour shortage in some spheres, and this made the employment of women and even children necessary, while weakening any opposition on the part of the journeymen to such employment. In the Spitalfields silk industry, for instance, not only was there an influx of women, but there was also a shortage of children, so machinery had to be used instead.[53] In fact, the employment of juveniles provides a good illustration of the impact of war, not only of the Revolutionary and Napoleonic Wars, but also of previous wars. For parish overseers, with children to apprentice, wars were blessings sent from heaven. That there were not very many jobs available for pauper children did not trouble the overseers for much of the eighteenth century, as hardly any of the children in their care survived to the age when they would be apprenticed. Then in the 1750s Hanway came to take an interest in the children's fate, and in 1767 Parliament intervened to preserve them with an Act requiring those under the age of six to be sent out of London to be nursed, and which laid down minimum payment for the nurses.[54] Now that the children were surviving, they were becoming a problem.

The Marine Society arranged for some of the children over the age of thirteen and taller than 4 feet 3 inches to join the navy; those not so

---

a preponderance of males. However, it may be dangerous to rely excessively on the Bills: between 1821 and 1830 female burials in the parish registers – with all their faults usually assumed to be more reliable than the Bills – came to 49 per cent of all burials, but in 1821 women formed 53 per cent of the capital's population.

[53] *London Life*, p. 184. This was the 'wooden draw-boy', apparently a preliminary version of the Jacquard loom.

[54] *Ibid.*, pp. 58–9; J. S. Taylor, *Jonas Hanway, Founder of the Marine Society. Charity and Policy in Eighteenth-Century Britain* (1985), pp. 112–17.

tall served on merchant ships.[55] The industrial revolution helped even more, as it provided a steady outlet of apprentices to the cotton factories. Between 1802 and 1811 5,815 children were apprenticed by parishes within the Bills of Mortality, of whom 2,026 were bound to 'persons in the country', three quarters of them being in the cotton industry.[56] Then in 1816 Parliament again demonstrated its inconvenient tendency to safeguard London apprentices, and pronounced it to be illegal to apprentice them more than forty miles from the metropolis.[57] The overseers found that both their principal outlets – the war and the cotton industry – were cut off almost simultaneously. 'During the war', said the principal overseer of Whitechapel in 1834, the apprenticeship of parish children was attended with

> much less difficulty and considerably less expense. We have about 25 young persons fit to go out, but by all the exertions of the overseers they cannot find means to get them off...We have constant complaints from private individuals, stating that as the parishes give high premiums, they as private individuals have not the means of getting their children off, which brings them again to find means of getting them into a workhouse for that purpose.[58]

Children who were not in workhouses likewise found more employment during the Napoleonic Wars. Robert Chalmers, police magistrate of Southwark, told the House of Commons Committee on Emigration in 1826 that 'London has got too full of children'. He produced figures showing the number of prisoners in Cold Baths Fields prison for the previous twenty years, distinguishing those over and under the age of twenty-one, and continued that

> it would appear that during the war, there being more employment for children, the rate of juvenile delinquency was much less; but after then, and from the number of children who had no means of getting employment, the number of crimes were greatly increased.
>   How were the children employed in war time? – They were taken on board ships, men of war, more sailors were employed, and young people were in great request; they are now in very little request indeed; there certainly is a very great stagnation for the employment of children in London, the parish workhouses are filled with those children. Another reason I would assign for the increase of juvenile offences is, the crowded state of the London workhouses, from whence those children are glad to escape; which crowded state arises principally from the last Apprentice Act of the 56 of G. III c. 109.[59]

---

[55] Taylor, *Jonas Hanway*, pp. 70–2; I. Pinchbeck and M. Hewitt, *Children in English Society* (2 vols., 1969), I, pp. 113–14.
[56] *London Life*, pp. 423–5.   [57] 56 Geo. III c. 109.
[58] *R.C. on the Poor Laws*, P.P. 1834, 29, p. 393.
[59] *S.C. on Emigration*, P.P. 1826, 4, pp. 83–4.

This was the Act that prevented the parishes from sending their children to the cotton factories.

The wars also permitted the dilution of the labour force at a time when the men might not object so strongly. Wartime contracts were often carried out by a female labour force, especially during the early nineteenth century, both because of the size of the order and because of the number of men enrolled. The tailors' union – always alert to the threat – beat back an attempt by employers in 1810 and 1814 to introduce women into their workshops.[60] This whole subject, of considerable importance, remains under researched: future research will presumably not only uncover more evidence, but will hopefully provide some indications of what happened to the composition of the labour force and to the employment of women when peace broke out.

The search for stability

The industrial revolution involved the production of semi-finished goods at a price much cheaper than hitherto, for a much larger market. The London trades were among the largest users of what came out from the factories; they were immediately affected. With new goods becoming available at a price that had until now been attained only in the second-hand market, there was an inevitable expansion of demand, and consequently a demand for more labour. But it was not necessarily for the most skilled labour, nor was it necessarily for London labour. A wealthy clientele continued to order its goods at the shop, and doubtless this clientele expanded in number. The shop-based workforce to meet this bespoke demand presumably also expanded. But the greatest expansion in demand came from those who only visited a shop in order to buy the goods on display, possibly having them modified a little. This demand was met to a growing extent by the underemployed labour so abundant in London: this labour was home based and often part time. If this process had taken place in the countryside during the eighteenth century, historians would have called it 'proto-industrial', but it took place in London during the nineteenth century. The skilled craftsmen in these trades – for instance those who cut out the material, or who could execute the more intricate designs – were not superseded, but the less skilled men faced increasing pressure from the labour of women and children and from the provinces. The women and children became better off: their rates of pay may not have increased, but there was more work for them. The men in these trades did not

[60] Parsinnen and Prothero, 'The London tailors' strike', p. 70.

usually become better off. They sought to maintain their status and their income, but had little power to do so. Guilds were quite unsuitable for that purpose; unions sought to enforce apprenticeship regulations, but had little success during the eighteenth century and in 1814 even the law that had ineffectively sought to enforce apprenticeship was repealed. Magistrates – even Parliament, though to a declining extent over the course of the eighteenth century – did their best to fix wage rates, but the magistrates' power was basically limited to bringing together masters and men and using their moral authority as honest brokers. They had some success when there was little provincial competition; they were therefore more effective during the eighteenth century than during the nineteenth.

Meanwhile, by the second half of the eighteenth century family sizes were beginning to increase, and, since the earnings of men did not increase, the pressure of child labour increased accordingly. There is also some slight suggestion – it is too weak to call it evidence – that the number of women in the labour force also increased.

But the wave of the underemployed did not break over the semi-skilled London trades until after the battle of Waterloo. The mass recruitment of the Revolutionary and Napoleonic Wars created a general tightness on the labour market that postponed these effects, while goods continued to cheapen themselves. A mass market came into existence, formed by those who previously had not been able to afford such things, but the things themselves were being made by an artisinate that felt itself to be becoming worse off than before. This was the paradox of the industrial revolution in London. Sweated labour was not new but during the nineteenth century it seems to have spread considerably, presumably by mopping up much hitherto underemployed labour. At the same time, those who were not making the goods, but merely buying them, experienced a rising standard of living by the 1820s – mainly because the price of bread was lower than during the wartime years, but to a certain extent because the price of the goods themselves was lower. A tailor might work for more days during the year than his father or grandfather would have done during the eighteenth century, and he might find himself earning less for each day that he did work. On the other hand, his wife would also be working, though not earning much.

But important though the semi-skilled tradesmen were, they were not a majority of the working-class population. For most – both the more skilled artisans above them and the labourers below – real wages were probably improving during the first half of the nineteenth century, even if the fitfulness of this improvement must have rendered it difficult to enjoy. This was the reverse of the situation of the second half of the eighteenth century when a mass market was only coming into existence, when the trades often had some defences, while real wage rates were falling from the mid century. The equilibrium so treasured by the eighteenth-century inferior artificers worked to their advantage; during the nineteenth century this equilibrium vanished.

Conclusion: downstream from industrialisation

In a much-quoted statement, J. L. Hammond described the industrial revolution as 'a storm that passed over London and broke elsewhere'.[1] The storm broke at the top of the river, upstream in the production process, where raw materials were changed into semifinished goods – bales of cloth, bars of iron – or finished capital goods such as steam engines. It all took place a long way from London, the goods came down to London, and London adapted itself to them. It did so, not by building factories and competing directly – the cost of factory production in London would have rendered this prohibitive. With its higher costs – its more expensive land and labour, its more expensive coal and the alternative outlets for local finance – manufacturing in London could not compete if its production processes were identical to those of the provinces and the material that it processed cost as much as in the provinces. Where London could compete was by taking advantage of its proximity to the market, its low transport costs and its ample supply of labour. It specialised at the 'downstream' end of production, but it could only do so by continually adapting, both to constantly fluctuating markets within the capital and also to falling costs outside the capital. The tendency was to move up-market – fustian manufacture left London during the course of the seventeenth century, framework knitting during the early eighteenth century, the mass production of silk and handkerchiefs increasingly by the late eighteenth century, shoes likewise.

London manufacturing existed in an equilibrium. Not, on the whole, badly affected by imports, it could continue on its traditional path as long as the nature of the market did not change fundamentally. As long as this market was relatively small-scale and seg-

[1] 'The industrial revolution and discontent' (review of *London Life*), *New Statesman*, 21 March 1925.

mented, the pressures on the trades to change could be withstood. When the market expanded – which it did when industrialisation reduced the price of the goods and sent great volumes of cheap cloth to the capital – then the pressures for mass production grew. The industrial revolution produced an increase in the number of hand-loom weavers, but it also produced a very large – and longer-lasting – increase in the number of needlewomen and tailors. The handloom weavers declined into pauperism; so did many of the tailors, whose precarious gentility was the product of an earlier age. It was better for the labour force when the processed materials cost more: London was famous for its finished goods with a high value-added content, added by a skilled labour force – goods such as coaches, mathematical instruments or watches. This was what its manufacture was best suited for, and it was to this end that so many of the trade routes of the kingdom directed themselves. Such a situation was good for craftsmen, but less good for the mass of less skilled male labour, and even worse for women.

In this respect, eighteenth- and nineteenth-century London was what many other European cities of the time became during the course of the nineteenth century: a centre that imported the cheap goods of the North and Midlands of England, and turned them to its own use. Capital was not deepened, it was widened. Except for specialised fields, or for isolated periods at the peak of a boom or at the height of a recruitment drive, the overall supply of labour was not limited. What limited manufacturing growth was the rate of growth of demand. Productivity did not increase very much, nor usually did wage rates. Similarly, wages did not fall much when prices fell, but they were laggardly in rising when prices rose, and the major factor that affected real wages was the price of bread. When this was rising, as it was for half a century, real wages showed a tendency to fall; when the price of bread fell, real wages rose. Cheaper clothing made some difference, but cheaper food made a much greater difference.

However, manufacturing was never of supreme importance in the capital. There was a great deal of it, because London was so large a town: in 1851 the number of men and women involved in manufacturing in London was almost equal to the entire population of Liverpool, the second largest city in Britain at the time, and greater than the population of Manchester or Glasgow.[2] Nevertheless, this number constituted a lower proportion of the labour force than was the case in

[2] The total male and female population engaged in manufacturing in London in 1851, according to appendix one, was 373,557. For town populations, see Mitchell, *British Historical Statistics*, pp. 26–7.

many towns, while services employed a noticeably higher proportion. Services had always dictated the principal contours of manufacturing in London. They had raised the price of land, and had competed for labour, as well as providing a market for the relatively expensive finished goods the provision of which was the response of the trades to these increased costs. Within the capital's middling classes, and these formed about a fifth of the population at the end of the eighteenth century, it was the service sector that was the wealthiest – bankers, merchants, lawyers, doctors and the more select among the retailers, such as drapers and mercers. There was nothing new about this: it had been as much the case in the 1690s as it was in the 1790s, and it would remain thus, although the professions had expanded particularly rapidly during the late seventeenth and early eighteenth centuries.

Within this fifth of the population wealth was spread very unevenly. During the 1770s some two-thirds of those who declared a trade were insuring property worth less than £600, while the top quarter of the trade owned over half the wealth insured, often much more. This is a situation that is likely to have endured for a long time. The remainder – about 7 per cent of the capital's population – would have had enough reserves in their businesses to cushion themselves against most unanticipated shocks, as would the 3 per cent or so of the population in the highest 'upper' income group. These were largely in the service sector – the higher ranks of the professions, or large-scale traders such as merchants, drapers or mercers. There were a few manufacturers, largely in the capital-intensive drink trade, but as capital-intensive production was unusual in London, so were wealthy manufacturers. Most entrepreneurs, in manufacturing and in the services, worked on a small scale, with their capital well towards the lowest limit of what commentators considered acceptable, and very often below that limit. But whatever their level of capitalisation, during the eighteenth century the individual trades usually kept about the same position in the hierarchy of trades as they had enjoyed or endured during the seventeenth century, and this hierarchy quite probably extended well into the nineteenth century as well.

Everything is relative, and of course £600 – even if largely obtained on credit – was far beyond the aspirations of those earning a guinea a week, the sum considered by Dr Johnson in 1775 to be reasonable for a working man, and which was, in fact, about 3s. a week more than a bricklayer, carpenter or reasonably skilled tailor earned at the time if he had a full week's work.[3] 'The Uncertainties of Life and Trade'[4] were

---

[3] J. Boswell, *Life of Johnson* (1960 ed.), I, p. 533.
[4] The title of *London Life*, chapter six.

powerfully felt by the mass of people in eighteenth- and nineteenth-century London, where every year the question arose of how many would be laid off when the peak of seasonal demand had passed, and where for many their 'official' trade was only carried out during a part of each year. During the rest of the year they swelled London's adaptable, reasonably educated, semi-skilled labour force extending the casual labour market and the poverty-stricken 'overstocked' parts of the service sector, available whenever wanted. For women, of course, it was worse than it was for men: women were more restricted in the jobs that they were permitted to do and, by immemorial tradition, were paid a pittance for doing them. Usually one managed, unless the winter was particularly bad or there was a slump, or both.

Certain nineteenth-century observers, frequently of a pedantic nature, with Francis Place foremost among their number, were very concerned to show that there had been considerable 'improvements' in London from an earlier and more barbaric age. It was Francis Place on whom Dorothy George placed particular reliance. There were indeed many improvements on which to dwell. The streets were better illuminated and often cleaner, while houses were less likely to collapse into those streets. Many of the more notorious neighbourhoods had been demolished and their inhabitants dispersed. There was more cheap cotton clothing, so people were better dressed. There was better sanitation, at least in parts of the town. As a corrective against a rather naïve disenchantment with the industrial age the views of Victorian optimists had their value. But an excessive reliance on Place has its dangers. It is remarkable how concerned his autobiography is with moral, rather than simply material improvement. He took pains to stress the dissoluteness and free spending so prevalent in the days of his youth, it grieved him that the more people earned the more dissolutely they spent it,[5] it grieved him that the children of respectable tradesmen should have played in the streets with more dissolute children, it grieved him that adults drank so much, and he was also brought to grief by Fleet marriages and state lotteries.[6] Like a good Victorian, he applauded the improvement of slums[7] (meaning their demolition), even though the evicted inhabitants simply went off to overcrowd slums elsewhere. He was not blind to physical improvements and sometimes he wrote about them[8] and

---

[5] Quoted in *ibid.*, p. 264.

[6] For instance printers were drinking less in 1824: *ibid.*, p. 383 n. 18.

[7] *The Autobiography of Francis Place*, pp. 227–30.

[8] *Ibid.*, pp. 107–8, also quoted in *London Life*, p. 113. For the decline of rickets, see *ibid.*, p. 71.

he was certainly not blind to poverty. But most of the improvements quoted from him by Dorothy George are, strictly speaking, moral. After all, moral improvement was a prerequisite for everything else: as he wrote in 1834, in the past if people had earned more they would simply have become more dissolute.[9]

That the 1774 Building Act, which insisted on the use of stone and which *was* enforced, improved the quality (as well as raising the cost) of houses is undeniable, but the removal of urban sewage was hardly as universal as Dorothy George sometimes thought. The wealthier areas looked after their own and did so fairly efficiently;[10] the poorer areas remained to be condemned during the course of the nineteenth century in terms as graphic as anything that was used to condemn the eighteenth century. Dorré's and Booth's London also had its 'narrow courts . . . [where] the dirt and filth used to accumulate in heaps and was but seldom removed . . . circulation of air was out of the question, the putrid effluvia was always stagnant', a state of affairs that Place was confident in 1826 would scarcely be believed 'in a few years from this time'.[11]

The improvements in sanitation that Place and Dorothy George stressed were partial.[12] Much was indeed improved, cleaned, lighted and paved, especially the wealthier areas and the main roads. The poor had to wait longer. In the 1840s, certain streets in Whitechapel had no sewers; as for washing clothes, 'they merely pass dirty linen through very dirty water'.[13] Much of the City was just as bad, as John Simon, its Medical Officer pointed out in 1849: 'Animals will scarcely thrive in an atmosphere of their own decomposing excrement, yet, such, strictly and literally speaking, is the air which a large proportion of the inhabitants of the City are compelled to breath.' The death rate was thirty per thousand, and in some districts as high as forty per thousand, the seventeenth-century level.[14]

Travel within Victorian London was no easier than it had ever been – thieves escaping from pursuit regularly jumped out of carriages to make their way on foot. The air was no purer: the number of foggy

[9] As n. 5.
[10] Sheppard, *Infernal Wen*, pp. 222–50, 278–92; S. and B. Webb, *History of Local Government: Statutory Authorities for Special Purposes* (1923), *passim*.
[11] *Autobiography of Francis Place*, p. 108, also quoted in *London Life*, p. 113.
[12] For two classic sources on nineteenth-century sanitation, or rather the lack of it, see E. Chadwick's two celebrated reports: *Report on the Sanitary Condition of the Labouring Population*, P.P. 1842, 26 and *Report on the Results of a Special Inquiry into the Practice of Interment in Towns*, P.P. 1843, 12.
[13] Sheppard, *Infernal Wen*, pp. 255–7.
[14] *Ibid.*, pp. 270–1. See chapter seven of the book for a good overview of London's sanitation.

days was rather greater than half a century earlier, while the amount of smoke in the atmosphere had been rising steadily with the rising imports of coal.[15] The Thames did not improve: traditionally, human waste had gone into outdoor privies which were discharged into cesspools; from the 1770s water closets spread, duly connected to the nearest culvert or river from which most people took their drinking water.[16] It all ended up in the Thames, more and more of it as the population grew. At the beginning of the 1820s it was still possible to catch the occasional salmon in London; by 1827 even eels – particularly hardy fish – were said to be dying from lack of oxygen.[17] This all culminated in the 1850s, when it became mandatory to connect cesspools to sewers, which duly discharged their contents into the Thames.[18] The climax was duly reached during the particularly hot summer of 1858, the year of the Great Stink, when the corridors of the Houses of Parliament were draped with sheets soaked in chloride and lime and on one occasion the various members of a House of Commons committee were observed to be 'rushing out of one of the rooms in the greatest haste and confusion . . . foremost among them being the Chancellor of the Exchequer (Disraeli), who with a mass of papers in one hand and with his pocket handkerchief clutched in the other, and applied closely to his nose, with body half bent, hastened in dismay from the pestilential odour, followed closely by Sir James Graham, who seemed to be attacked by a sudden fit of expectoration'.[19] 'Improvement' was not unadulterated.

Nevertheless, the really great improvement was with the death rate. For most of the eighteenth century mortality had remained at the non-plague levels of the seventeenth century or some forty per thousand, much higher than the national average. During the second quarter of the century it may even have attained fifty per thousand.[20] By 1841 the CDR in London was down to twenty-three per thousand, virtually the same as the national average. Dating the fall is speculative, but it appears that the most significant decline began around the last quarter of the eighteenth century, continuing into the nineteenth century. This was not the period of greatest improvement in

[15] P. Brimblecombe, *'The Big Smoke.' A History of Air Pollution in London since Medieval Times* (1987), pp. 114, 172.

[16] L. B. Wood, *The Restoration of the Tidal Thames* (Bristol, 1982), pp. 21–2.

[17] *Ibid.*, p. 18; Bill Luckin, *Pollution and Control. A Social History of the Thames in the Nineteenth Century* (Bristol, 1986), p. 12.

[18] Wood, *Restoration*, pp. 21–2.

[19] B. Weinreb and C. Hibbert (eds.), *The London Encyclopedia* (1983), pp. 237, 330 for the Great Stink; for the rout of the committee: *The Times*, 3 July 1858, quoted in Sheppard, *Infernal Wen*, p. 282.

[20] Landers and Mouzas, 'Burial seasonality', p. 69.

the capital's living standards – quite the contrary. Nevertheless, the traditional killers of smallpox and 'fevers' were no longer so prevalent. Deaths from consumption were high, but the proportion of the population dying from consumption was lower than during the eighteenth century, and its importance as a cause of death is not because it was more virulent or more widespread than previously, but because the decline of other diseases kept people alive for long enough for consumption to get to them in their middle age or later. Even cholera did not change the picture very basically. The largest fall, however, was in infant mortality, which appears to account for about half the decline in the CDR during this century and a half; the decline in consumption, smallpox and fevers account for most of the rest. London, which had begun the eighteenth century as the great devourer of lives from the country, a town that absorbed an inordinate part of the country's natural population increase and proceeded to kill it, was by the mid nineteenth century as healthy as the rest of the country, and no longer a death trap. No longer were half the children born to Londoners dying before reaching the age of fifteen; looked at from another angle, if consumption, smallpox, fever and typhus had been at their seventeenth-century levels in 1841, then an additional 20,000 Londoners, or 1 per cent of the population, would have died during that year.

The pulse of population growth also had a great effect – sometimes an overwhelming effect – on the development of the metropolitan economy. During the seventeenth century a high death rate was compensated by mass immigration to London from many parts of the kingdom; during the first half of the eighteenth century the death rate remained as high as before, but the immigration came from a more restricted area, and by the late 1720s there are signs that the overall population of the capital was not growing much, if at all. Combined with the effects of war, this was enough to depress the metropolitan economy more than the rest of the country – agricultural depressions there may have been, and falls in the national growth rate, but for London the fall in the growth rate was more severe. The years from 1725 were years of stagnation, turning into depression in the late 1740s. To a certain extent the problems can be attributed to the impact of wars and the particular orientation of the capital's trade, but this explains neither the length nor the depth of the stagnation and, of course, there was no war until 1739. A great deal of blame must go to low population growth. If there was a period when the provinces 'broke loose' from London, it was during the second third of the eighteenth century. They certainly seem to have broken loose as regards growth rate. *If* (and it is a big if) the national growth rate data can be trusted, then the stagnation of this period was principally confined to the London region.

Immigration into the capital picked up again by the 1760s, the death rate was falling by the last quarter of the century, and the economy of the capital was growing, probably at about the national averge – not spectacularly like Lancashire, but not stagnating either. Without a fall in the death rate this might not have been possible. By the late 1820s London growth rates slowed down again. This had nothing to do with population growth, and the slow-down appears to have been more of a sectoral affair. It picked up again during the 1840s.

The impact of industrialisation on London was complex. The eighteenth century saw an enormous underclass, an apparently inexhaustible reserve army of labour, always threatening to flood over the precarious ramparts of the semi-skilled trades, and not quite succeeding in so doing. For those with a certain amount of protection, economic growth was experienced fairly even-handedly during the eighteenth century. Obviously some trades rose more than others, but on the whole the hierarchies, while regularly disturbed, were not overthrown. The term 'equilibrium' – in the sense that no one force was powerful enough to disturb the whole order – has some meaning. London contained a mass of labour, male and female, formally unskilled but willing and able to learn fairly basic skills at short notice. The adaptability of this labour posed a problem for the trades. Unable to prevent outsiders from practising 'their' trade, tradesmen traditionally sought to control entry to the trade, and then to control the conditions of work. Earlier methods of control – guilds and apprenticeship regulations – had become ineffective by the eighteenth century. Magistrates remained of some efficacy and were prepared to intervene, if only to preserve peace and order, but could only do so if the trade in which they intervened remained reasonably protected from competition from outside London. This sometimes ceased to be the case, as the silkweavers and shoemakers discovered. But even when there was no competition from the provinces, the industrial revolution had its effect. Not only did it increase the national demand for services such as the law – of which London took the lion's share – and give money to large numbers of the gentry and bourgeoisie who visited London in order to spend it, but it also cheapened the production process upstream, out of London. The materials that were sent to London were thus potentially within the range of a much larger market than hitherto. It became profitable for employers to reduce the cost of tailors and others; the 'official' wage rate usually remained intact, but departures from it were increasingly frequent. During the eighteenth century, when the materials cost more, there was less pressure to depart from the 'official' wage.

In an economy where productivity and the conditions of production did not change markedly and were not expected to do so, wage rates were, not surprisingly, sticky. Of course wage rates – even after making allowance for unemployment – are only one feature of incomes: there is a gulf between rates per hour and pay per week; there is an even larger gulf between wage rates and living standards. The nature of the wage and the organisation of production are of considerable importance. Not everybody depended upon a money wage and only a money wage for their total remuneration, and some depended upon it hardly at all. Nevertheless, the data on money wages is what we have, and with all its drawbacks the movement of money wage rates gives an indication of the movement in real wages which, provided they are not regarded as very accurate over the short run, are unlikely to be seriously misleading. Between 1717 and 1792 money wage rates barely changed. This may only be indicative, but such stability does appear to be very strongly indicative of sticky earnings. During the eighteenth century the major influence on the real wage rate – and that means, on the whole, the major influence on the cost of living – was the price of bread. There was not very much starvation in eighteenth-century London – at least not for fit adult men – and bread absorbed a much lower proportion of family earnings than was the case in, for instance, Paris.[21] But movements in the price of bread were much more important than movements in the price of manufactured goods, and bread prices were consistently rising from the mid eighteenth century. North of a line from the Severn to the Wash real wage rates did not fall or, if they did fall, this was corrected during the 1770s, if not earlier. South of that line real wage rates fell. There was no labour shortage except, occasionally, during wartime years.[22]

After 1815 things were different. The cost of bread remained the major influence, and the period of good harvests for so many years after 1815 was one of the important factors in reducing the cost of living after 1815, but so was the return to gold and the postwar deflation as well as the fall in the price of manufactured goods, which had a persistent influence, not only on the cost of living but on the traditional hierarchies themselves. As in the 1980s there was a great increase in wealth for many, perhaps an increase in poverty for many others, certainly an increase in relative deprivation. It was *not* simply a

[21] Rudé, *Paris and London*, pp. 53–4.   [22] Schwarz, 'Trends in real wage rates.'

matter of the rich becoming richer and the poor poorer. The rich did become richer, but so did many of the poor, if healthy and lucky enough to have a regular job – and they were more likely to be healthy during the nineteenth century than before, while the trade cycle was no worse. It was the lower orders of the trades, the less skilled trades, that tended to feel the changes, that experienced the overturning of the traditional hierarchies. Some continued unaffected, others found their earnings depressed and their labours increased, while those hitherto outside the slightly charmed circle – mostly women – found a chance to make a little money that had previously been inaccessible. The situation of the less skilled artisans had always been conditioned by the nature and composition of demand; during the first half of the nineteenth century demand changed and it changed because of the factories. 'Sweating' was not new, but there had been no purpose in exploiting labour to reduce by a few pence a product that only a few could afford and which was not highly price-elastic. A purpose duly came. During the half century after 1815 the divisions within the London trades increased, even as the poorest found themselves with more money and better health. But the greatest effect of the increased wealth that industrialisation and Britain's role in the world brought to London was to strengthen the dominance of the service sector, where London led the world.

Seventeenth- and eighteenth-century sources on occupations and incomes

Seventeenth-century data

Two historians have recently sought to analyse occupations in London during the late seventeenth century: Beier, who has carried out an extensive survey of the occupations entered in burial registers between 1641 and 1700, and Alexander, who has analysed the occupations entered in the City for the poll tax of 1692.[1] Neither of them was primarily concerned with providing a systematic basis for comparison with later periods, and the greater the effort that one undertakes to make such a comparison the more one is impelled to question its validity. In the first place, occupations changed their nature – retailing in particular was in the process of becoming a much more specialised occupation – and the distinction between production and retailing, which is not always valid even in 1851, is not at all valid two centuries previously. Secondly, a large town, such as London, combining so many functions, not dominated by any single activity or source of income, will produce a highly variegated pattern of employment, whether examined for the seventeenth or the nineteenth centuries. When even the largest occupations occupy only a relatively small proportion of the labour force (with the obvious exception of domestic service for women), a comparison of figures different by one or two percentage points across a gap of a century and a half has a very doubtful significance. A presentation of data from the seventeenth and the nineteenth centuries can point to the varied nature of employment in London (at any rate for men), indicate the most general trends, such as the importance of manufacture at each of these points in time, and point towards more detailed changes that further

[1] 'Beier, Engine of manufacture', pp. 141–67; Alexander, 'Economic and social structure', especially pp. 78–9.

study may or may not confirm. It may well be the case that the significance of London's occupational structure is not the extent to
which this did or did not change over the long run, but the extent and
manner in which the capital was different from other parts of the
country. Efforts to achieve a more precise analysis across such a long
period of time may well prove chimerical.

Beier has examined burial registers for a wide variety of City
parishes between 1641 and 1700, and has aggregated them in a format
that makes suitable allowance for the different size of parishes.[2] That
his findings cover a long period does not matter, as there appears to
have been little major change in the structure of the workforce during
these years.[3] What matters much more is a problem that is
inescapable when occupations were not scattered randomly across
the capital, but were often carried out in very restricted geographical
locations. A different sample might produce significantly different
results. The occupational structure of seventeenth-century Southwark, for instance, was very different from that of the City Within. A
complete coverage is a counsel of perfection, which it would be
unreasonable to expect, but the drawbacks of samples should be
borne in mind.[4]

When this data is compared with data for the nineteenth century,
two major problems promptly arise. First of all, the seventeenth-
century data does not distinguish between the sexes. This did not
matter for Beier's original purpose, which was to demonstrate the
wide extent of manufacturing in the capital, but it does matter when
comparisons are made with later periods. Baptismal and burial
records are particularly likely to omit maidservants, who were usually
young, unmarried and not in the habit of dying in large quantities.
Male servants are usually excluded, for the same reason that female
servants were excluded: between 1641 and 1700 servants are believed
to have formed nearly a quarter of the population (but some of them
were apprentices), and in 1851 they formed 22.5 per cent of the total
employed population. Secondly, there is the problem of comparing
categories across time: nineteenth-century occupations do not always
fit easily into seventeenth-century categories. Beier's category of
'merchants' had to be omitted, because it included grocers, mercers,
merchant tailors, brokers and factors, a difficult group to fit consist-

[2] Beier, 'Engine of manufacture', *passim*. See also M. J. Power, 'The East London
working community in the seventeenth century', in P. J. Corfield and D. Keene (eds.),
Work in Towns, 850–1850 (Leicester, 1990), p. 105.
[3] Beier, 'Engine of manufacture', pp. 147–51.
[4] For Southwark, see J. Boulton, *Neighbourhood and Society: a London Suburb in the
Seventeenth Century* (Cambridge, 1987), p. 66.

Table A1.1. *London occupations, 1641–1700, compared with census returns, 1851*

	1641	1851 census	
		Male	*Female*
Building	8.3	13.0	9.7
Clothing	26.2	18.6	32.3
Decoration/furnishing	4.0	5.8	5.1
Distribution/transport	9.8	19.6	14.7
Labouring	7.5	9.9	7.3
Leather	11.5	1.2	1.1
Metals	19.7	7.8	5.9
Civil officers and professions	2.2	9.7	10.2
Victualling	19.7	14.3	13.6
Total	100	100	100
Number in table above	10,300	507,185	246,173
Number not fitting in above categories	1,959	204,260	157,389
Total number	12,259	711,445	403,562

Note: Totals may not add up precisely because of rounding.

ently into the mid nineteenth century.[5] Nevertheless, when all adjustments are made, 84 per cent of Beier's sample, 71 per cent of the employed male and 61 per cent of the employed female population of 1851 remain available for comparison, and are so compared in table A1.1.

Very considerable care indeed must be exercised in interpreting table A1.1 (which is why it has been relegated to an appendix). It is a mistake to attach too much weight to an exercise that must by its very nature be highly uncertain even if – which is by no means certain – a comparison of occupations across a gap of a century and a half is considered valid. But it has its uses, provided that the results are not regarded as more than indicative. Males and females have been separated in 1851, and it is best to compare males across the two centuries as well as to allow a fairly wide margin of error. Accepting all these precautions, table A1.1 nevertheless shows rather limited changes. Over the two centuries there were increases in the categories for building, for transport and distribution – which presumably reflect a larger as well as a wealthier town and port – an unsurprising fall in

5 I would like to thank Dr Beier for his assistance in finding suitable categories for the 1851 data.

Table A1.2. *London occupations, 1690s, compared with census returns,*
1851

	City 1690s		London 1851	
	Persons	*Householders*	*Men*	*Women*
Dealing	45.1	45.7	13.6	8.0
Manufacturing	32.5	33.5	34.1	32.8
Services (excluding				
domestic service)	12.1	10.0	12.0	5.6
Building	6.6	7.2	10.0	0.03
Transport	3.5	3.4	11.7	0.2
Total	99.8	99.8	81.4	46.6
Number	12,063	10,361	711,445	403,562

leather, a considerable rise in the importance of the professions, and a suspicious fall in the importance of victuallers and clothing. The victuallers' supposed decline is suspicious because it is not supported by other sources, while the seventeenth-century figure for clothing is particularly likely to be inflated by those women who were included. The other changes are less open to question.

Secondly, there are statistics from the poll tax and the population enumeration of London during the 1690s. The 1692 poll tax record often gives the name of the head of the family and his (or occasionally her) occupation, and indicates the existence of a wife and children. It is an excellent source when used with due care. The surviving records are mainly confined to the City, relate mostly to men, and, by definition, to one year only. Until recently, they had only been used for a few parishes within the City; however, Alexander has recently used them to survey the entire City of London.[6] His breakdown of occupations is based on the Cambridge Group's classification, which is discussed later in this appendix, and has been used in chapter one of

---

[6] Alexander, 'Economic and social structure', especially pp. 78–9. See also Glass, 'Socio-economic status and occupations'; D. V. Glass, 'London inhabitants within the walls, 1695', *London Record Society Publications*, 2 (1966); D. V. Glass, 'Notes on the demography of London at the end of the seventeenth century', *Daedalus*, Spring 1968; R. Wall, 'Mean household size in England from the printed sources', in P. Laslett and R. Wall (eds.), *Household and Family in Past Time* (1972), provides household sizes only; Wall, 'Regional and temporal variations', pp. 89–113, also gives the number of servants and lodgers and is based on a more representative sample of City parishes. Servants and lodgers are also given for four parishes within the Walls in Macfarlane, 'Studies in poverty', pp. 65ff.

this book. He has been successful in finding the occupations for just under half the population surveyed, and somewhat more than half the households. The categories are different from Beier, so cannot be compared, but can be compared with 1851. The main outlines are in table A1.2. The two biases – the bias of the City, wealthier than everywhere else except the wealthier parts of Westminster – and the bias of selecting the wealthier half of the population – is apparent in the dominance of dealers. But as far as building and transport are concerned, they bear out the conclusions already reached about their growing importance during the intervening century and a half. Beier's insistence on the importance of manufacturing in London is further borne out – even in a square mile where the dealing sector was so important. The proportion remains remarkably stable.

A more detailed analysis of Alexander's subcategories contains relatively few surprises, although once again there is the fall in victualling trades, from some 10 per cent in 1692 to 1.7 per cent in 1851. The changes in the proportion that most of his categories form is not great, with no obvious trend in any direction, except in the 'arts/entertainments' area of the service sector and a corresponding decline in the proportion of dealers in textile and apparel by 1851. It might be expected that the greater diversity of trades in the London of 1851 would have tended to lead to a decline in the importance of any individual sector, as far as male employment was concerned, but the data is unable to provide a sufficiently detailed measurement of this. For women, of course, the continued dominance of domestic service was an enormous exception to this trend.

Insurance policies

The computerised index of the fire insurance policies issued by the Sun Fire Office and the Royal Exchange Assurance between 1775 and 1787 has been described elsewhere.[7] To summarise, we have access to a list of some 300,000 policies giving the insured person's name, address, occupation and the value of his or her policy. Out of this number, 43,568 policies refer to London. These need to be handled with some care. In the first place they are new policies, not routine renewal policies. In the 1790s the Sun believed that the average policy

---

[7] L. D. Schwarz and L. J. Jones, 'Wealth, occupations and insurance in the late eighteenth century: the policy registers of the Sun Fire Office', *Econ. Hist. Rev.*, 2nd ser., 36 (1983), pp. 365–73.

lasted for seven years.[8] Some obviously did not last for this long, and there are quite a number of policies that are virtual duplications of each other, identical in every respect – name, address, occupation – except value of policy. These could be additional policies, or they could be revaluations of older policies. Without an examination of the policy registers there is no means of knowing, and even that would not necessarily be conclusive. Fortunately this does not make much difference when considering the incidence of occupations, or their geography. In chapter two, when the policy values for the members of different trades were considered, the problem was ignored, each entry being regarded as an entity in its own right, thereby biasing the data in the direction of greater equality. However, for appendix two, where the occupations of those that took out insurance policies are given, there was little option but to take the first policy and to disregard the others. This happened for 3,532 persons. A more serious bias, however, is when a person with the same name held properties in various parts of London. The insurance registers will not help at all in this respect and even detailed work on directories will not help much. John Robinson, a tailor, insured himself for £500 in Chapel Street; there is also a policy for £100 under the name of John Robinson, a tailor, in Drury Lane. A Thomas Smith, tailor, of Gracechurch Street was worth £600; Thomas Smith, tailor of Old Street, was worth £500. Were they the same persons? We have no means of knowing. This problem would be serious if fine tuning was involved, but, as is shown below, the data is in fact so approximate, that the fault is not crucial. For considerations of geographical location it obviously does not matter at all.

Thirdly, they are the problems of multiple occupations, of which there are a large number. A 'haberdasher and milliner' is easy to classify, but what of a 'cook and bricklayer', a 'butcher and cloaths salesman', a 'tailor and dealer in coals' or, spectacularly, Martin Vancutchett: 'watchmaker, surgeon, dentist, patentee for string band'? Fortunately, only a few people divided themselves so much. When classifying occupations and examining their distribution it was decided to take the first occupation entered, and to stick to it rigorously. In any case, when the occupations are grouped into larger categories the problem of multiple occupations lessens considerably.

At the end of this process there remain 40,126 non-duplicating

[8] Correspondence of Sun's secretary with William Pitt; P.R.O., PRO/30/8/187, fos. 238ff. (Contrary to rumour, this document was well known to Schwarz and Jones in 1983, but a detailed comparison was omitted on grounds of space. I would like to thank Dr Charles Jones for information on the source of this rumour.)

policies, each of which is treated as referring to a discrete individual. This is a large number, by eighteenth-century standards, and is larger than most directories. With an average family size of four it would come to 160,000 persons, or about 20 per cent of London's population, virtually a complete coverage of those with middling or higher incomes. Obviously we cannot go below this level since the policies refer only to those who owned or rented an entire house, and omit lodgers, servants and such like. Unfortunately, as a summary of bourgeois occupations it is flawed by the fact that 14.7 per cent of those who insured themselves gave their occupation as 'Gent', and 3.6 per cent as 'Esq.' – more respectable in appearance than a mere 'Gent' – a further 3 per cent were self-proclaimed spinsters and 5.6 per cent returned themselves as widows. Presumably as a result of this, professional men formed only 3.8 per cent of those who gave an occupation. The remaining records will therefore be skewed disproportionately towards shopkeepers, and it is not surprising that nearly half of those who did return a specific occupation were involved in some form of distribution. This means that, like the poll tax data of 1692, the insurance data has to be regarded as only indicative of the capital's bourgeoisie, not as a conclusive census. A detailed view of the occupations given in the policies for 1775–87, based on Armstrong's classification, is given in appendix two; it may be of use to some, but it must be handled with considerable care. At any rate, the problem of whether the valuation is correct does not arise.

Of one thing, however, we can be sure, which is that the policies that are being analysed, although new and not routine renewal policies, are nevertheless an accurate reflection of all the policies. In 1796, when corresponding with the Treasury, the Sun provided a breakdown of all its policies. It is close enough to the new policies' list as to be almost identical; the regional breakdown is also very similar.[9]

Patrick Colquhoun

It is high time that Colquhoun was relieved of his reputation as a serious statistician. It is surprising that this reputation survived his claim in 1796 that there were 50,000 prostitutes in London – as Chadwick pointed out in 1839 this would have meant about one prostitute for every three adult males, assuming all were lascivious (married or not), and that every third or fourth woman would be a prostitute! In fact, the police estimated in 1839 that London prostitutes

[9] *Ibid.*

numbered barely a tenth of Colquhoun's figures – 5,500 – and the population of London had grown some two-and-a-half fold since Colquhoun's statement.[10] In his colourful book on the depradations committed on shipping in the Thames he combined some very precise information, such as enumerating the 8 members of Trinity House, 35 ropemakers (presumably employers) and 120 master coopers, alongside bold statements asserting there were 33,000 'seamen and boys, riggers, etc.' and some 57,000 'clerks, apprentices, journeymen and labourers'.[11] By such means he reched a total of 120,000 men employed on the riverside,[12] which would have been about 40 per cent of all adult male Londoners. Colquhoun's figures are not realistic; what matters is that, as a well-informed person, he could believe that such a high proportion of Londoners worked on the riverside at some time or other during the year. He had no way of testing these figures, and in any case employment at the Port was so seasonal that, without an indication of the time of year, they are meaningless. Elsewhere in the same volume the ships' crews are only 27,444, lightermen fall from 3,390 to 1,500, watermen from 6,500 to 900, while revenue officers increase from 600 to 1,400.[13]

Census

The 1851 census is of considerable value in producing a reasonably accurate indication of the occupations of Londoners. It is far better than anything that preceded it, and it marks a good stopping point for this study, despite its drawbacks, which are well known to historians. In the first place, it did not distinguish retailers adequately from producers. This may be a reflection of the fact that many producers sold their own goods, and it is important to bear this in mind when considering tailors, shoemakers, jewellers and such like. A more significant drawback is its failure to enquire systematically into the field of employment, and the further one descends down the social scale the more important this becomes. We have a fairly precise idea of what barristers did, but labourers could have been anywhere and employed at anything. The Port of London, which employed many

10 P. Colquhoun, *A Treatise on the Police of the Metropolis* (1796), p. 340; L. Radzinowicz, *A History of English Criminal Law and its Administration from 1750* (1948–), III, p. 243; Bosanquet, *The Rights of the Poor*, p. 24; *R.C. on Constabulary Force: First Report of the Commissioners*, P.P. 1839, 19, p. 15. To be fair to Colquhoun, Chadwick exaggerated a little: there were probably around 300,000 adult males in London at this time, so the proportion would have been one in six. Francis Place's views on moral reformation since his youth may be seen in this light.
11 Colquhoun, *A Treatise on the Commerce and Police*, pp. xxx–xxxii.   12 *Ibid.*, p. xxx.
13 *Ibid.*, p. 198.

labourers, remains a closed book when approached from the census – we can discover the numbers involved in building and repairing ships, the number of coopers, warehousemen and so forth, but not the number of labourers.

A related problem lies with those – and they were many – who followed their census occupation for only a part of the year. We have to assume that 'shoemaker' means what it says, and then speculate elsewhere on the proportion of shoemakers that worked only part-time at their trade, swelling the ranks of 'labourers' during the rest of the year, perhaps helping with the harvest for a month, unloading the West India fleet during another month, and earning some money on a building site during a third month. All this detracts from the value of the census, but there is no doubt that it remains incomparably the best source on occupations for the century and a half under consideration. However, it needs to be classified.

There are, of course, many ways of classifying the census, but the Cambridge Group's classification as developed by Armstrong[14] has the supreme advantage that others can make use of the work. The problem with using the excellent schema developed for London in 1851 by Bédarida and Sheppard[15] and in 1861 by Stedman Jones[16] is that it is not clear in any of these studies exactly how the various categories are compiled. This is of little significance when London is being examined on its own, but it does matter when London is compared with the rest of the country. The Armstrong categories have some curious aggregations, especially the putting of those in banking, insurance and finance together with general labourers under the heading of 'industrial services', and in the present summary they have been separated. They have been criticised by Lee for 'overstraining the credibility of precise disaggregated figures', but Lee's own categories are too wide for present purposes.[17] A detailed breakdown of the 1851 census is given in appendix three.

[14] W. A. Armstrong, 'The use of information about occupation', in E. A. Wrigley (ed.), *Nineteenth-Century Society* (Cambridge, 1972), pp. 255–310.
[15] F. Bédarida, 'Londres au milieu du 19e siècle: une analyse de structure sociale', *Annales, Economies, Sociétés, Civilisations*, 23 (1968), pp. 268–95; Sheppard, *Infernal Wen*, pp. 387–9.
[16] Stedman Jones, *Outcast London*, pp. 350–8. See also Crossick, *Artisan Elite*, pp. 40–5.
[17] C. H. Lee, *British Regional Employment Structures, 1841–1971* (Cambridge, 1979), p. 5. He also includes Middlesex within London.

Occupations insured with Sun Fire Office and Royal Exchange Assurance, 1775–87

Classifications are those of the Cambridge Group: see appendix three for details.

Building
1.	Management	106	
	Architects	22	
	Surveyors	84	
2.	Operatives	2,442	
	Bricklayers	366	
	Builders	106	
	Carpenters	1,255	(excluding ships' carpenters)
	Glaziers	111	
	Masons	134	
	Painters and glaziers	242	
	Paperhangers	13	
	Plasterers	101	
	Plumbers	114	
3.	Roadmaking	15	
	Paviours	15	
Total		2,563	

Manufacturing
1.	Engineers	8	
2.	Gunmaking	83	
3.	Shipbuilding	219	
	Shipwrights	193	
	Mastmakers	15	
	Ships' chandlers	11	
4.	Iron and steel	215	
5.	Non-ferrous metals	169	(brass 67, tin 78, pewter 24)
6	Gold, silver jewellery	402	(jewellers 101, goldsmiths 125, silversmiths 176)
10.	Furs and leather	252	(fur 37, leather 215)
11.	Tallow chandlers	265	
12.	Hair, brushes, etc.	33	

13.	Wood workers	404	(coopers 261, sawyers 35, turners 108)
14.	Furniture	807	(chairmakers 20, bedjoiners 6, undertakers 40, cabinet makers 421, upholsterers 197, carvers 123)
15.	Carriage and harness	411	(carriage 230, harness 121, wheelwrights 60)
19.	Weavers	339	(silk 126, 'weavers' 210, stocking weavers 1, framework knitters 2)
20–1.	Flax, hemp, lace	143	(rope 52, sailcloth 91)
22.	Dyeing	69	
23.	Dress	2,525	
	Glovers	50	
	Hatters	173	
	Hosiers	20	
	Mantua makers	174	
	Milliners	265	
	Peruke makers	254	
	Robe makers	13	
	Seamstresses	10	
	Shoemakers	520	
	Staymakers	112	(moved from Armstrong's machinery category)
	Stocking trimmers	11	
	Tailors	943	
25.	Sugar refiners	131	
26.	Baking	720	
27.	Drink preparation	284	(brewers 224, distillers 60)
29.	Watches, instruments, toys	447	(clock makers 63, watch makers 293, musical instrument makers 44, mathematical instrument makers 47)
30.	Printing, bookbinding	237	
Total		8,163	

Transport

1a.	Warehouses and docks	223	
	Packers	27	
	Warehousemen	154	
	Wharfingers	42	
1b.	Messengers, porters		
	Porters	67	
2.	Ocean navigation	647	
	Mariners	420	
	Master mariners	195	
	Pilots	32	

3.	Inland navigation	279
	Lightermen	141
	Watermen	138
5.	Roads	388
	Carmen	48
	Carters and carriers	5
	Coachmasters	171
	Coachmen	54
	Chairman	4
	Stable keepers	106
Total		1,604

Dealing

1a.	Coal merchants, dealers	188	
1b.	Coal heavers	2	
2.	Raw materials	356	
	Corn factors/dealers	259	
	Timber merchants	97	
4.	Dress	1,341	
	Drapers	676	
	Haberdashers (often inc. hosiers)	529	
	Mercers	95	
	Slop sellers	41	
5.	Food	2,016	
	Butchers	578	
	Cheesemongers	358	
	Coffee dealers (often also victuallers)	117	
	Fishmongers	57	
	Fruiterers	73	
	Grocers	624	(Inc. greengrocers)
	Milksellers	55	
	Oilmen	45	
	Poulterers	71	
	Tea dealers	38	
6.	Tobacco	177	
7.	Wine, spirits, hotel	543	
	Wine and brandy merchants	285	
	Vintners	146	
	Inn and hotel keepers	112	
8.	Lodging and coffee houses		
	Coffee houses (inseparable from coffee dealers, above)		
9.	Furniture		
	Pawnbrokers	215	
10.	Stationery, publications	308	(stationers 147, bookbinders 161)

11.	Household utensils, ornaments	213	
	Hardwaremen, ironmongers	177	
	Chinamen	36	
12.	General dealing	4,942	
	Shopkeepers	46	
	Chandlers	870	
	Victuallers	3,911	
	Salters	5	
	Perfumers	110	
13.	Unspecified	2,349	
	Merchants	706	
	Brokers, agents	456	
	Auctioneers	56	
	Salesmen/women	278	
	'Dealers'	804	
	Factors	49	
Total		12,650	

Public service and professions

1.	Customs	39	
7.	Law	169	
8.	Medicine	478	
	Apothecaries/chemists	240	
	Surgeons/doctors	178	(often inc. apothecaries)
	Doctors	60	
9.	Engravers	116	
10.	Musicians	78	
13.	Education	132	(schoolmasters 85, schoolmistresses 47)
Total		1,012	

Other

	Hairdressers	271	
Total		26,263	

Unspecified

	Esq.	1,450
	Gent	5,893
	Spinsters	1,215
	Widows	2,228
Overall total		37,049

Total non-duplicating policies	40,126	
Multiple policy holders	3,532	
Excluded	3,077	= 7.7% of total

Total number of policies:	44,844

Table A2.1. *Sectoral distribution of occupations insured with Sun Fire Office and Royal Exchange Assurance, 1775–87*

	Number	%
Building	2,563	9.8
Manufacturing	8,163	31.1
Transport	1,604	6.1
Dealing	12,650	48.2
Public service and professions	1,012	3.9
Personal service	271	1.0
Total	26,263	100.0

Note: Totals may not add up precisely because of rounding.

1851 census: Armstrong classification

The classifications in this appendix are those put forward by W. A. Armstrong, 'The use of information about occupation', in E. A. Wrigley (ed.), *Nineteenth-Century Society* (Cambridge, 1972), pp. 255–310. In certain cases the appendix provides details of some of the more important sub-classifications, but exhaustive detail to the extent made possible by Armstrong would only be confusing. So, for instance, while the appendix does say that there were in London in 1851 11,679 male workers in iron and steel, of whom 7,807 were blacksmiths, it does not provide details of the remaining 3,872. On the same principle, when a number of sub-categories are given, as, for instance, among building operatives, other smaller sub-categories are omitted, so the sub-categories included may well not add up to the total in that classification.

	Number		% of national total	
	Male	Female	Male	Female
Agriculture	22,963	1,527	1.43	0.91
Mining	4,181	91	1.28	1.06
Building				
1. Management	4,564		21.73	
2. Operatives	64,331	129	16.21	64.5
Bricklayers	13,919		20.74	
Carpenters	23,453		15.02	
Masons	4,578		5.82	
Plasterers	4,378		27.89	
Plumbers, painters and glaziers	15,369		26.36	
Builders, house decorators		129		18.4
3. Roadmaking	1,664		3.97	
Total	70,559	129	15.35	14.3

	Number		% of national total	
	Male	Female	Male	Female
Manufacturing				
1. Machinery	8,321		13.46	
2. Tools	2,557		7.48	
3. Shipbuilding	5,069	4	18.91	
Shipwrights	3,273		13.99	
4. Iron and steel	11,679	153	5.69	0.91
Blacksmiths	7,807	23	8.29	3.83
5. Non-ferrous metals	11,274	292	19.88	4.49
6. Gold, silver, jewellery	5,706	144	80.37	16.0
7. Earthenware	1,372	160	3.94	1.37
8. Coal and gas	1,702		21.54	
9. Chemicals (see no. 22)	2,630	376	30.94	47.0
10. Furs and leather	6,263	1,600	25.88	84.21
11. Glue, tallow	4,311	332	65.32	
12. Hair, brushes, etc.	3,055	1,712	22.3	39.81
13. Wood workers	14,202	27	19.14	1.0
14. Furniture	18,658	2,431	40.12	45.87
15. Carriage and harness	9,605	175	16.14	19.44
Carriagemakers	4,948	81	32.1	40.5
16. Paper	2,648	1,267	24.52	18.36
17. Floorcloth				
18–21. Textiles	21,625	16,894	4.96	3.59
22. Dyeing	1,735		6.65	
23. Dress (incl. footwear)	59,181	103,835	15.17	22.33
Boot and shoemakers	30,855	7,158	14.62	24.4
'Shoemaker's' wife		12,616		
Hatters	2,494	2,434	9.44	36.33
Bonnet and capmakers		3,046		6.55
Milliners		43,928		17.42
Seamstresses		21,210		35.71
Staymakers		2,466		
Tailors	22,479	8,292	18.47	47.8
24. Sundries connected with dress	841	1,221	11.52	20.02
25. Food preparation	1,200	3	3.44	0.60
26. Baking	13,762	1,150	25.77	10.85
Bakers	11,580	543	25.39	8.9
Confectioners	2,182	607	27.97	13.49
27. Drink preparation	7,604		27.65	
Brewers	2,617		15.3	
28. Smoking	901	193	17.67	14.85
29. Watches, instruments, toys	9,354	517	39.8	39.77
Watch and clock makers	4,847		28.35	
Musical instrument makers	2,929		83.69	
Scientific instrument makers	1,578	93	54.4	18.6

		Number		% of national total	
		Male	Female	Male	Female
30.	Printing, bookbinding	14,002		46.06	
	Printers	10,365		46.69	
	Bookbinders	2,850		50.0	
31.	Unspecified	1,662		13.19	
	Total	240,919	132,486	13.94	12.91
Transport					
1a.	Warehouses and docks	4,108	84	12.34	2.9
1b.	Messengers, porters	33,214	262	37.19	7.28
2.	Ocean navigation	18,193	29	23.47	14.4
3.	Inland navigation	5,721	176	15.55	7.04
4.	Railways	3,816	4	15.2	4.0
5.	Roads	17,452	133	24.27	6.33
	Total	82,504	688	24.71	6.04
Dealing					
1a.	Coal merchants, dealers	2,412	186	22.54	
1b.	Coal heavers	4,020	3	32.68	0.43
2.	Raw materials	2,411	223	15.26	55.75
3–4.	Clothing materials, dress	11,427	3,541	13.51	37.27
	Drapers, mercers	1,816	958	4.84	15.7
	Hosiers, haberdashers	1,314	470	41.06	18.8
5.	Food	36,295	8,112	21.81	26.86
	Butchers	9.586	216	15.82	13.5
	'Butcher's wife'		3,100		
	Cheese and butter	2,715		75.42	
	Fishmongers	2,571		36.21	
	Grocers	7,853	698	13.47	5.21
	Greengrocers	3,885	980	44.66	20.85
	Oil and colourmen	1,632		85.89	
	Milksellers	3,938	1,262	36.80	34.11
	Poulterers	631		31.55	
6.	Tobacco	756	478	47.25	
7–8.	Wine, spirits, hotel, lodging	12,169	9,635	15.91	30.3
9.	Furniture (pawnbrokers)	1,451		23.03	
10.	Stationery, publications	4,824	3,626	39.54	
	Publishers, booksellers	2,435	3,136	40.58	
	Stationers	2,389	490	61.26	49.0
11.	Household utensils, ornaments	4,500	414	27.78	18.82
12.	General dealers	8,031	4,887	20.13	16.57

	Number		% of national total	
	Male	Female	Male	Female
13. Others and unspecified	12,186	1,178	35.22	
Auctioneers	897		25.63	
Commercial travellers	2,907		34.61	
Total	100,482	32,283	22.93	29.78
Industrial service				
1. Banking, insurance	18,186	8	40.68	8.0
Commercial clerks	16,420		43.79	
2. General labour	50,173	410	15.46	5.69
Total	68,359	418	18.51	5.73
Public service and professions				
1. Central government	11,535	74	30.04	6.17
East India Co.	1,214		35.71	
2–3. Local government	1,752	152	15.5	15.2
4–5. Armed forces	19,047		22.23	
6. Police and prisons	6,367		38.82	
7. Law	12,794	8	39.73	
8. Medicine	8,698	8,168	25.58	9.53
9–12. Art, amusement,				
literature, science	16,993	1,303	68.52	52.12
13. Education	4,742	12,499	16.94	18.68
14. Religion	2,810	529	9.34	58.78
Total	84,738	22,733	28.16	23.01
Domestic service				
Indoor, permanent	20,348	165,195	20.70	21.06
Outdoor, occasional	16,392	48,012	31.89	25.65
Total	36,740	213,207	24.54	21.95
Total occupied population	711,445	403,562	12.45	16.80
Independent	11,660	30,308	19.11	20.15
Undefined	16,230	18,157	24.63	
Vagrants, paupers, etc.	4,197	7,975	4.18	
Family dependants				
Adults (wives, widows, etc.)		345,542		12.07
Children (incl. 'scholars')	367,184	449,992		12.64
Total	399,271	851,974	13.02	12.63

1851 census: summary tables

A. Occupied female population ('000)

	England and Wales	London	England and Wales excluding London
Agriculture	169.3	1.5	167.8
Mining	8.6	0.1	8.5
Building	0.9	0.1	0.8
Manufacture	1,026.2	132.5	893.7
Transport	11.4	0.7	10.7
Dealing	108.4	32.3	76.1
(Banking, insurance)	(0.1)	(0.008)	(0.1)
(General labour)	(7.2)	(0.4)	(6.8)
Industrial services total	7.3	0.4	6.9
(Central and local government)	(2.2)	(0.2)	(2.0)
(Other services or professions)	(96.6)	(22.5)	(74.1)
Public service and professions total	98.8	22.7	76.1
Domestic service	971.5	213.2	758.3
Total	2,402.4	403.6	1,998.8

Note: Totals may not add up precisely because of rounding.

B. Occupied male population ('000)

	England and Wales	London	England and Wales excluding London
Agriculture	1,607.2	23.0	1,584.2
Mining	326.6	4.2	322.4
Building	459.8	70.6	389.2
Manufacture	1,728.6	240.9	1,487.7
Transport	333.9	82.5	251.4
Dealing	438.3	100.5	337.8
(Banking, insurance)	(44.7)	(18.2)	(26.5)
(General labour)	(324.6)	(50.2)	(274.4)
Industrial services total	369.3	68.4	300.9
(Central and local government)	(49.7)	(13.3)	(36.4)
(Armed forces, police)	(102.1)	(25.4)	(76.7)
(Other services or professions)	(149.1)	(46.0)	(103.1)
Public service and professions total	300.9	84.7	216.2
Domestic service	149.7	36.7	113.0
Total	5,714.3	711.4	5,002.9

Note: Totals may not add up precisely because of rounding.

C. Occupied male and female population ('000)

	England and Wales	London	England and Wales excluding London
Agriculture	1,776.5	24.5	1,752.0
Mining	335.2	4.3	330.9
Building	460.7	70.7	390.0
Manufacture	2,754.8	373.4	2,381.4
Transport	345.3	83.2	262.1
Dealing	546.7	132.8	413.9
(Banking, insurance)	(44.8)	(18.2)	(26.6)
(General labour)	(331.8)	(50.6)	(281.2)
Industrial services total	376.6	68.8	307.8
(Central and local government)	(51.9)	(13.5)	(38.4)
(Armed forces, police)	(102.1)	(25.4)	(76.7)
(Other services or professions)	(245.7)	(68.5)	(177.2)
Public service and professions total	399.7	107.5	292.2
Domestic service	1,121.2	249.9	871.3
Total	8,116.7	1,115.0	7,001.7

Note: Totals may not add up precisely because of rounding.

D. *Summary of data for figures 1.1, 1.2 and 1.3: occupations in London and rest of England and Wales (both sexes)*

(1) Percentage of working population of London engaged in various occupations.
(2) Percentage formed by Londoners of all people engaged in that economic activity, England and Wales.
(3) Percentage of working population of England and Wales, excluding London, so engaged.
(4) Percentage of working population of 'urban provincial England' so engaged.
(5) Number, for London.

	(1)	(2)	(3)	(4)	(5)
Agriculture	2.2	1.38	25.02	2.2	24,490
Mining	0.38	1.27	4.73	6.16	4,272
Building	6.34	15.34	5.57	7.27	70,688
Manufacture	33.49	13.55	34.01	44.36	373,405
Transport	7.46	24.09	3.74	4.88	83,192
Dealing	11.91	24.28	5.91	7.71	132,765
(Banking, insurance)	(1.63)	(40.61)	(0.38)	(0.5)	(18,194)
(General labour)	(4.54)	(15.25)	(4.02)	(5.24)	(50,583)
Industrial services total	6.17	18.26	4.39	5.74	68,777
(Central and local government)	(1.21)	(26.04)	(0.55)	(0.72)	(13,513)
(Armed forces, police, prisons)	(2.28)	(24.89)	(1.1)	(1.43)	(25,414)
(Other services or professions)	(6.15)	(27.9)	(2.53)	(3.3)	(68,544)
Public service and professions	9.64	26.89	4.17	5.45	107,471
Domestic service	22.42	22.29	12.44	16.23	249,947
Total	100.0	13.74	100.0	100.0	1,115,007
Number	1,115,000		7,001,693	5,371,480	

Note: Totals may not add up precisely because of rounding.

E. Summary of data for figures 1.4, 1.5 and 1.6: female occupations in London and rest of England and Wales

(1) Percentage of employed females in London engaged in various occupations.
(2) Percentage formed by London females of all females engaged in that economic activity, England and Wales.
(3) Percentage of employed females in England and Wales, excluding London, so engaged.
(4) Percentage of employed females in 'urban provincial England' so engaged.
(5) Number, for London.

	(1)	(2)	(3)	(4)	(5)
Agriculture	0.38	0.90	8.39	0.38	1,527
Mining	0.02	1.06	0.43	0.46	91
Building	0.03	14.33	0.04	0.04	129
Manufacture	32.83	12.91	44.71	48.61	132,486
Transport	0.17	6.04	0.54	0.58	688
Dealing	8.00	29.78	3.81	4.14	32,283
(Banking, insurance)	(0.002)	(8.0)	(0.004)	(0.01)	(8)
(General labour)	(0.1)	(5.69)	(0.34)	(0.37)	(410)
Industrial services total	0.10	5.73	0.34	0.38	418
(Central and local government)	(0.06)	(10.27)	(0.1)	(0.11)	(226)
(Other services or professions)	(5.58)	(23.3)	(3.71)	(4.03)	(22,507)
Public service and professions total	5.63	23.01	3.81	4.14	22,733
Domestic service	52.83	21.95	37.94	41.24	213,207
Total	100.0	16.80	100.01	99.97	403,562
Number	403.562		1,998,838	1,838,595	

Note: Totals may not add up precisely because of rounding.

F. *Summary of data for figures 1.7, 1.8 and 1.9: male occupations in London and rest of England and Wales*

(1) Percentage of employed males in London engaged in various occupations.
(2) Percentage formed by London males of all males engaged in that economic activity, England and Wales.
(3) Percentage of employed males in England and Wales, excluding London, so engaged.
(4) Percentage of employed males in 'urban provincial England' so engaged.
(5) Number, for London.

	(1)	(2)	(3)	(4)	(5)
Agriculture	3.23	1.43	31.67	3.23	22,963
Mining	0.59	1.28	6.44	9.13	4,181
Building	9.92	15.35	7.78	11.02	70,559
Manufacture	33.86	13.94	29.74	42.11	240,919
Transport	11.60	24.71	5.03	7.12	82,504
Dealing	14.12	22.93	6.75	9.56	100,482
(Banking, insurance)	(2.56)	(40.68)	(0.53)	(0.75)	(18,186)
(General labour)	(7.05)	(15.46)	(5.49)	(7.79)	(50,173)
Industrial services total	9.61	18.51	6.02	8.52	68,359
(Central and local government)	(1.87)	(26.73)	(0.73)	(1.03)	(13,827)
(Armed forces, police, prisons)	(3.57)	(24.89)	(1.53)	(2.17)	(25,414)
(Other services or professions)	(6.47)	(30.88)	(2.06)	(2.92)	(46,037)
Public service and professions total	11.91	28.16	4.32	6.12	84,738
Domestic service	5.16	24.54	2.26	3.2	36,740
Total	100.0	12.45	100.0	100.01	711,445
Number	711,445		5,002,855	3,532,885	

Note: Totals may not add up precisely because of rounding.

Bibliography

Manuscripts

British Library
   Place Papers
City of London Record Office
   P.A.R. (*Printed Acts, Reports*)
Greater London Record Office
   MJ/SP: Middlesex sessions papers, 1770–1820
   P/91/1335: *Register of the Workhouse, St Leonard Shoreditch*
   MA/MN 196, 197, 198: Returns and certificates of recruitment
   P/93/CTC/1/55: *Minute Book of the Spitalfields Soup Society*
Guildhall Library
   Occupations insured with the Sun Fire Office and Royal Exchange Assurance, 1775–87
Port of London Authority Library
   London Dock Company, *Minute Books, 1800–15*
   West India Dock Company, *Minute Book*
Public Record Office
   PRO/30/8/280–1: Chatham Papers: assessed tax returns
   PRO/30/8/187: Chatham Papers: correspondence of Sun Fire Office's secretary with William Pitt
   T47.8: Employers of manservants in England and Wales in 1780
   E182/639, 641, 644, 645, 648, 653: Returns of income tax for Tower Division
London School of Economics
   Webb Trade Union Collection
Mile End Library, Local Collection
   Register of the Workhouse, Poplar and Blackwall
Shoreditch Library collection
   P/L/P/4: *Abstract of Accounts of the Poor 1825–6*

Official and parliamentary papers

Journal of the House of Commons
House of Lords Sessional Papers
Second Report from the Committee Appointed to Enquire How Far the

Orders of the Last Session Respecting the Poor ... had been Complied With (1777), *Eighteenth-Century Reports*, 9.

Fifth Report of the S.C. on the High Price of Provisions, *Eighteenth-Century Reports*, 9.

Returns of Income Tax: 1803–10: P.P. 1812–13, 12.
1812: P.P. 1814–15, 10.
1814: P.P. 1856, 4.

S.C. *to Whom the Several Petitions of Shipbuilders and Others Interested in the Building and Equipment of Ships ... Were Referred*, P.P. 1813–14, 8.

S.C. *on the Police of the Metropolis*, P.P. 1816, 5.

S.C. *to Whom the Several Petitions of the Ribbon Weavers of Coventry and Leek ... Were Referred*, P.P. 1818, 5.

Second Report of the House of Lords Committee on Foreign Trade, P.P. 1821, 6.

S.C. *on Artisans and Machinery*, P.P. 1824, 5.

S.C. *on the Combination Laws*, P.P. 1825, 4.

S.C. *on Emigration*, P.P. 1826, 4.

S.C. *on the Present State of the Silk Trade*, P.P. 1831–2, 19.

S.C. *on Army and Navy Appointments*, P.P. 1833, 7.

R.C. *on the Poor Laws. Appendix A: Reports of Assistant Commissioners* (E. Chadwick), P.P. 1834, 29.

R.C. *on the Poor Laws. Answers to Town Queries*, P.P. 1834, 35.

S.C. *on the Port of London*, P.P. 1836, 14.

R.C. *on Constabulary Force: First Report of the Commissioners*, P.P. 1839, 19.

R.C. *on the Handloom Weavers. Reports of Assistant Commissioners*, P.P. 1840, 23.

Report on the Sanitary Condition of the Labouring Population (E. Chadwick), P.P. 1842, 26.

Report on the Results of a Special Inquiry into the Practice of Interment in Towns (E. Chadwick), P.P. 1843, 12.

R.C. *on Children's Employment. Appendix to Second Report of the Commissioners*, P.P. 1843, 13, 14.

Returns Showing the Number of Vessels and Tonnage Entered Inwards and Cleared Outwards at Each of the Twelve Principal Ports of the United Kingdom, P.P. 1851, 52.

Average Price of Bread in London, 1738–1800, P.P. 1903, 68.

Average Price of Bread in London, 1801–15, 1820–1903, P.P. 1904, 79.

Census of Population: 1801, 1811, 1821, 1831, 1841, 1851.

Peake, T., *Cases Determined at Nisi Prius, in the Court of King's Bench, from the Sittings after Easter Term 30 Geo. III to the Sittings after Michaelmas Term 35 Geo. III* (2nd ed., 1810).

A Collection of the General or Yearly Bills of Mortality within the London District Parishes Published by the Company of Parish Clerks for the year ending December 14 1658 to December 11 1749.

Contemporary journals and newspapers

Annual Register
Charter
Commercial and Agricultural Magazine
Crisis
Gentlemen's Magazine

Gorgon
London Chronicle
Morning Post
Pioneer
Poor Man's Guardian
St James' Chronicle
Spectator
The Times
Trades Newspaper

Works originally published before 1880

Anonymous, *A General Description of all Trades* (1747).
Anonymous, *Low Life* (1764).
Bosanquet, S. R., *The Rights of the Poor and Christian Almsgiving Vindicated* (1841).
Boswell, J., *Life of Johnson* (1960 ed.).
Boswell's London Journal, 1762–3, ed. F. A. Pottle (Harmondsworth, 1966).
Campbell, R., *The London Tradesman* (1747).
Clode, C. M., *The Military Forces of the Crown* (2 vols., 1869).
Collyer, J., *The Parents' and Guardians' Directory* (1761).
Colquhoun, P., *Observations and Facts relative to Public Houses in the City of London and its Environs* (1794).
    A Treatise on the Police of the Metropolis (1796).
    General Report of the Committee of Subscribers for a Fund for the Relief of the Industrious Poor (1800).
    A Treatise on the Commerce and Police of the River Thames (1800).
    A Treatise on Indigence (1806).
Defoe, D., *A Tour Through the Whole Island of Great Britain*, ed. P. Rogers (Harmondsworth, 1971).
    Moll Flanders (Everyman ed., 1930).
Dickens, C., *Household Words* (1850–9).
    Sketches by Boz (1836).
Eden, Sir F. M., *The State of the Poor* (3 vols., 1797).
Farr, W., 'Bills of mortality: registration of births, deaths and diseases', *British Medical Almanack* (1836).
Felkin, W., *A History of the Machine-Wrought Hosiery and Lace Manufactures* (1867).
Fielding, J., *An Account of the Origin and Effect of a Police set on Foot by the Duke of Newcastle* (1758).
    A Description of the Cities of London and Westminster (1776).
Foote, S., *The Tailors: a Tragedy for Warm Weather* (1767).
Gay, J., 'Trivia, or the art of walking the streets of London', in G.C. Faber (ed.), *The Poetical Works of John Gay* (1926).
'The voyage of Don Manoel [sic] Gonzalez in Great Britain', in J. Pinkerton (ed.), *A General Collection of the Best and Most Interesting Voyages and Travels in all parts of the World* (1808–14).
Graunt, J., *Natural and Political Observations on the Bills of Mortality* (1759).
Gwynn, J., *London and Westminster Improved* (1766).
Howitt, W., *The Rural Life of England* (2 vols., 1838).

Kearsley, G., *Kearsley's Table of Trades* (1786).
Lovett, W., *Life and Struggles* (1876).
McCulloch, J. R., *A Dictionary of Commerce and Commercial Navigation* (1840).
Maitland, W., *The History and Survey of London* (1739, 1745, 1756 and 1760 eds.).
　The History and Survey of London, continued down to the Year 1772 by the Rev. J. Entick (1772).
Malthus, T. R., *An Essay on the Principles of Population* (5th ed., 1817).
Marshall, J., *Mortality of the Metropolis* (1832).
Mayhew, H., *London Labour and the London Poor* (4 vols., 1861).
Middleton, J., *View of the Agriculture of Middlesex* (1798).
Morris, C., *Observations on the Past Growth and Present State of the City of London* (1751).
O'Neill, J., 'Fifty years' experience of an Irish shoemaker in London', *St Crispin*, 1–2 (1869–70).
Parrot, R., *Reflections on Various Subjects Relating to Arts and Commerce* (1752).
Pitt, Sir W. M., *An Address to the Landed Interest on the Deficiencies of Habitation and Fuel for the Use of the Poor* (1797).
Smith, A., *Wealth of Nations*, ed. E. Cannan, (6th ed., 2 vols., 1961).
Smith, J. T., *Nollekens and his Times* (1828).
Society for Furthering the Education and Bettering the Condition of the Poor, 'An account of the soup society in Spitalfields', *Philanthropist*, 2 (1812).
Statistical Society of London, 'An investigation into the state of the poorer classes in St George's-in-the-East', *Journal of the Statistical Society of London*, 11 (1848).
Stevenson, W., *General View of the Agriculture of the County of Surrey* (1809).
Vaughan, W., *On Wet Dock, Quays and Warehouses for the Port of London* (1793).
Wales, W., *An Inquiry into the Present State of Population in England and Wales* (1781).

Works published after 1880

Aldcroft, D. H. and Fearon, P., *British Economic Fluctuations, 1790–1939* (1972).
Alexander, D., *Retailing in England during the Industrial Revolution* (1970).
Alexander, J., 'The economic structure of the City of London at the end of the seventeenth century', *Urban History Yearbook* (1989).
Alexander, Sally, 'Women's work in nineteenth-century London: a study of the years 1820–50', in A. Oakley and J. Mitchell (eds.), *The Rights and Wrongs of Women* (Harmondsworth, 1976).
Alford, B. W. E. and Barker, T. C., *A History of the Carpenters' Company* (1968).
Appleby, A. B., 'Nutrition and disease: the case of London, 1550–1750', *Journal of Interdisciplinary History*, 6 (1975).
Armstrong, W. A., 'The use of information about occupation', in E. A. Wrigley (ed.), *Nineteenth-Century Society* (Cambridge, 1972).
Ashton, T. S., *An Economic History of England: The Eighteenth Century* (1955).
　Economic Fluctuations in England 1700–1800 (Oxford, 1959).
Aspinall, A., *The Early English Trade Unions* (1949).
Atkins, S. E. and Overall, W. H., *Some Account of the Worshipful Company of Clockmakers of the City of London* (1881).

Bailey, F. A. and Barker, T. C., 'The seventeenth-century origins of watchmaking in south-west Lancashire', in J. R. Harris (ed.), *Liverpool and Merseyside. Essays in the Economic and Social History of the Port and its Hinterland* (1969).

Barker, T. C., 'Business as usual? London and the industrial revolution', *History Today*, 39 (1989).

Barnes, D. G., *A History of the English Corn Laws from 1660 to 1846* (1930).

Baugh, D. A., *British Naval Administration in the Age of Walpole* (Princeton, 1965).

Beattie, J. M., *Crime and the Courts in England 1660–1800* (Oxford, 1986).

Bédarida, F., 'Londres au milieu du 19e siècle: une analyse de structure sociale', *Annales, Economies, Sociétés, Civilisations*, 23 (1968).

Beier, A. L., 'Engine of manufacture: the trades of London', in A. L. Beier and R. A. P. Finlay (eds.), *London 1500–1700: The Making of the Metropolis* (1986).

Besant, W., *London in the Eighteenth Century* (1902).

Beveridge, W., *Unemployment: a Problem of Industry* (1909).

Booth, W., *Life and Labour of the People in London* (1902).

Borsay, P., *The English Urban Renaissance: Culture and Society in the Provincial Town, 1660–1770* (Oxford, 1989).

Boulton, J., *Neighbourhood and Society: a London Suburb in the Seventeenth Century* (Cambridge, 1987).

Bovill, E. W., *English Country Life, 1780–1830* (Oxford, 1962).

Bowden, W., *Industrial Society in England towards the End of the Eighteenth Century* (New York, 1925).

Bowley, A. L., 'The statistics of wages in the United Kingdom during the last hundred years', *Journal of the Royal Statistical Society*, 61 (1898).

Wages in the United Kingdom in the Nineteenth Century (Cambridge, 1900).

Boyd, P. (ed.), *Roll of the Drapers' Company of London* (1934).

Braudel, F., *Capitalism and Material Life, 1400–1800* (1974).

Brazzel, J. H., *The London Weather* (1968).

Breuilly, J., 'Artisan economy, artisan politics, artisan ideology: the artisan contribution to the nineteenth-century European labour movement', in C. Emsley and J. Walvin (eds.), *Artisans, Peasants and Proletarians 1760–1860* (1985).

Brimblecombe, P., *'The Big Smoke.' A History of Air Pollution in London since Medieval Times* (1987).

Broodbank, Sir J. G., *History of the Port of London* (2 vols., 1921).

Brooks, C. E. P. and Hunt, T. H., 'Variation of wind direction since 1341', *Quarterly Journal of the Royal Meteorological Society*, 59 (1933).

Brown, E. H. Phelps and Hopkins, S. V., 'Seven centuries of building wages', in E. M. Carus-Wilson (ed.), in *Essays in Economic History*, II (1962).

'Seven centuries of the price of consumables compared with builders' wage rates', reprinted in E. M. Carus-Wilson (ed.), *Essays in Economic History*, II (1962).

Brownlee, J., 'The health of London in the eighteenth century', *Proceedings of the Royal Society of Medicine*, 18 (1924–5), epidemiology section.

Buer, M. C., *Health, Wealth and Population in the Early Days of the Industrial Revolution* (1926).

Burgess, K., 'Technological change and the 1852 lock out in the British engineering industry', *International Review of Social History*, 14 (1969).

Burley, K. H., 'An Essex clothier of the eighteenth century', *Econ. Hist. Rev.*, 2nd ser., 11 (1958–9).

Burnett, M. D., *Plenty and Want: a Social History of Diet* (Harmondsworth, 1968).

Bythell, D., *The Sweated Trades. Outwork in Nineteenth-Century Britain* (1978).

Cairncross, A. K. and Weber, B., 'Fluctuations in building in Great Britain, 1785–1849', in E. M. Carus-Wilson (ed.), *Essays in Economic History*, III (1962).

Carlin, N., 'Levelling the liveries: some aspects of the outlook of craftsmen in the London livery companies of the mid-seventeenth century', *Middlesex Polytechnic History Journal*, 1 (4).

Carmichael, Ann C., 'Infection, hidden hunger and history', in R. I. Rotberg and T. K. Rabb (eds.), *Hunger and History* (Cambridge, 1985).

Chalklin, C. W., *The Provincial Towns of Georgian England* (1974).

Chambers, J. D., *Nottinghamshire in the Eighteenth Century* (1932).

Church, R. A., 'Labour supply and innovation 1800–1860: the boot and shoe industry', *Business History*, 12 (1970).

Clapham, J. H., 'The Spitalfields Acts, 1773–1824', *Economic Journal*, 6 (1916).
An Economic History of Modern Britain (3 vols., 1930–8).

Clark, P., 'Migration in England during the late seventeenth and early eighteenth centuries', *Past and Present*, 83 (1979).
The English Alehouse, 1200–1800 (1983).

Clark, P. and Slack, P. (eds.), *English Towns in Transition, 1500–1700* (Oxford, 1976).

Clout, H., 'London in transition', in H. Clout and P. Wood (eds.), *London: Problems of Change* (1986).

Clout, H. and Wood, P. (eds.), *London: Problems of Change* (1986).

Coase, R. H., 'The nature of the firm', *Economica* (1937).

Cole, W. A., 'Factors in demand, 1700–80', in R. Floud and D. N. McCloskey (eds.), *The Economic History of Britain since 1700* (2 vols., Cambridge, 1981).

Coleman, D. C., *The British Paper Industry 1495–1860: a Study in Industrial Growth* (Oxford, 1958).
'Labour in the English economy of the seventeenth century', in E. M. Carus-Wilson (ed.), *Essays in Economic History*, II (1962).

Cooney, E. W., 'The origins of the Victorian master builders', *Econ. Hist. Rev.*, 2nd ser., 13 (1960–1).

Coppock, J. T. and Prince, H. C. (eds.), *Greater London* (1964).

Corfield, P. J., *The Impact of English Towns, 1700–1800* (Oxford, 1982).

Corfield, P. J. and Keene, D. (eds.), *Work in Towns, 850–1850* (Leicester, 1990).

Crafts, N. F. R., *British Economic Growth during the Industrial Revolution* (Oxford, 1985).
'Real wages, inequality and economic growth in Britain: a review of recent research', in P. Scholliers (ed.), *Real Wages in Nineteenth- and Twentieth-Century Europe: Historical and Comparative Perspectives* (Berg, Oxford, 1989).

Creighton, C., *A History of Epidemics in Britain* (2 vols., 1894).

Crossick, G., *An Artisan Elite in Victorian Society: Kentish London, 1840–1880* (1978).

Darby, H. C. (ed.), *An Historical Geography of England* (Cambridge, 1936).

Davies, E. Jeffries, 'The Great Fire of London', *History*, 8 (1923).

Davis, D., *A History of Shopping* (1966).

Davis, R., *The Rise of the English Shipping Industry in the Seventeenth and Eighteenth Centuries* (1962).

The Industrial Revolution and Foreign Trade (Leicester, 1979).

Deane, P. and Cole, W. A., *British Economic Growth, 1688–1959* (Cambridge, 1961).

Derry, T. K., 'The repeal of the apprenticeship clauses of the Statute of Apprentices', *Econ. Hist. Rev.*, 1st ser., 3 (1931–2).

de Vries, Jan, *European Urbanization, 1500–1800* (1984).

Dickson, P. G. M., *The Sun Insurance Office 1710–1960* (1960).

Dobson, C. R., *Masters and Journeymen: A Prehistory of Industrial Relations, 1717–1800* (1980).

Dobson, Mary J., 'The last hiccup of the old demographic regime: population stagnation and decline in late seventeenth- and early eighteenth-century south-east England', *Continuity and Change*, 4 (3), December 1989.

Dowell, S., *A History of Taxation and Taxes in England* (3 vols., 1884).

Drummond, A. J., 'Cold winters in Kew observatory', *Quarterly Journal of the Royal Meteorological Society*, 69 (1943).

Dunlop, O. J. and Denman, R. D., *English Apprenticeship and Child Labour: A History* (1912).

Dyer, A., 'Epidemics of measles in a seventeenth-century English town', *Local Population Studies*, 34 (1985).

Dyos, H. J., *Victorian Suburb. A Study of the Growth of Camberwell* (Leicester, 1961).

Earle, P., *The Making of the English Middle Class. Business, Society and Family Life in London, 1660–1730* (1989).

*The female labour market in London in the late seventeenth and early eighteenth centuries', *Econ. Hist. Rev.*, 2nd ser., 42 (1989).

Ehrman, J., *The British Government and Commercial Negotiations with Europe, 1783–1793* (Cambridge, 1962).

The Younger Pitt. The Years of Acclaim (1969).

Ellmers, C., 'The impact of the 1797 tax on clocks and watches on the London trade', in J. Bird, H. Chapman and J. Clark (eds.), *Collectanea Londiniensia. Studies in London Archaeology and History presented to Ralph Merrifield* (London and Middlesex Archaeological Society, special paper no. 2, 1978).

Farr, W., *Vital Statistics* (1885).

Fildes, V., *Breasts, Bottles and Babies: A History of Infant Feeding* (Edinburgh, 1986).

Finlay, R. A. P., *Population and Metropolis. The Demography of London, 1580–1650* (Cambridge, 1981).

Finlay, R. A. P. and Shearer, B., 'Population growth and suburban expansion', in A. L. Beier and R. A. P. Finlay (eds.), *London 1500–1700: The Making of the Metropolis* (1986).

Fisher, F. J., 'The development of London as a centre of conspicuous consumption in the sixteenth and seventeenth centuries', *Transactions of the Royal Historical Society*, 4th ser., 30 (1948).

Flinn, M. W., 'Trends in real wages, 1750–1850', *Econ. Hist. Rev.*, 2nd ser., 27 (1974).

'Real wage trends in Britain, 1750–1850: a reply', *Econ. Hist. Rev.*, 2nd ser., 29 (1976).

Floud, R. and McCloskey, D. N. (eds.), *The Economic History of Britain since 1700* (2 vols., Cambridge, 1981).

Floud, R., Wachter, K. and Gregory, A., *Height, Health and History. Nutritional Status in the United Kingdom, 1750–1980* (Cambridge, 1990).

Fogel, R. W., Engerman, S. and Floud, R., 'Secular changes in American and British stature and nutrition', in R. I. Rotberg and T. K. Rabb (eds.), *Hunger and History* (Cambridge, 1985).

Forbes, T. R., 'Mortality books for 1774–93 and 1833–35 from the parish of St Giles, Cripplegate, London', *Bulletin of the New York Academy of Medicine*, 47 (1961).

'Burial records for the parish of St Ann Soho, London, in 1814–1828', *Yale Journal of Biology and Medicine*, 47 (1974).

'By what disease or casualty: the changing face of death in London', *Journal of History of Medicine*, 31 (1976).

'Weaver and cordwainer: occupations in the parish of St Giles without Cripplegate, London, in 1654–1693 and 1729–1743', *Guildhall Studies in London History*, 4 (1980).

Fortescue, J. W., *A History of the British Army* (13 vols., 1899–1930).

The County Lieutenancies and the Army, 1803–1814 (1909).

Galloway, P. R., 'Annual variations in deaths by age, deaths by cause, prices and weather in London 1670 to 1830', *Population Studies*, 39 (1985).

Galton, F. W. (ed.), *Select Documents Illustrating the History of Trades Unionism: The Tailoring Trade* (1896).

Gayer, A. D., Rostow, W. W. and Schwarz, A. J., *The Growth and Fluctuation of the British Economy, 1790–1850* (2 vols., Oxford, 1953).

George, M. D., 'The London coalheavers', *Economic History*, 1 (1927).

'The early history of registry offices', *Economic History*, 1 (1927).

England in Transition (1953).

London Life in the Eighteenth Century (1965 ed.).

Gilboy, E. W., *Wages in Eighteenth-Century England* (Cambridge, Mass., 1934).

'The cost of living and real wages in eighteenth-century England', *Review of Economic Statistics*, 18 (1936), subsequently republished in A. J. Taylor (ed.), *The Standard of Living in Britain in the Industrial Revolution* (1975).

Gittings, C., *Death, Burial and the Individual in Early Modern England* (1984).

Glass, D. V., 'London inhabitants within the walls, 1695', *London Record Society Publications*, 2 (1966).

'Notes on the demography of London at the end of the seventeenth century', *Daedalus*, Spring 1968.

'Socio-economic status and occupations in the City of London at the end of the seventeenth century', in A. E. J. Hollaender and W. Kellaway (eds.), *Studies in London History presented to Philip Edmund Jones* (1969).

Goodway, H., *London Chartism* (Cambridge, 1982).

Gourvish, T. R., 'Flinn and real wage trends in Britain, 1750–1850: a comment', *Econ. Hist. Rev.*, 2nd ser., 29 (1976).

Grassby, R., 'Social mobility and business enterprise in seventeenth-century England', in D. Pennington and K. Thomas (eds.), *Puritans and Revolutionaries. Essays in Seventeenth-Century History presented to Christopher Hill* (Oxford, 1978).

Halévy, E., *A History of the English People in the Nineteenth Century: II The Liberal Awakening* (1961).

Hall, P. G., 'The East London footwear industry: an industrial quarter in decline', *East London Papers*, 5, no. 1 (1962).

The Industries of London since 1861 (1962).

'Industrial London: a general view', in J. T. Coppock and H. C. Prince (eds.), *Greater London* (1964).

Hammond, J. L., 'The industrial revolution and discontent' (review of *London Life*), *New Statesman*, 21 March 1925.

Hardy, Anne, 'Diagnosis, death and diet: the case of London, 1750–1909', *Journal of Interdisciplinary History*, 18 (1988).

Harrison, B., *Drink and the Victorians* (1971).

Hattendorf, J., *England in the War of the Spanish Succession* (1987).

Hay, D., 'War, dearth and theft in the eighteenth century: the records of the English courts', *Past and Present*, 95 (1982).

Heal, Sir A., *The London Goldsmiths, 1200–1800* (Cambridge, 1935).

Hecht, J. J., *The Domestic Servant Class in Eighteenth-Century England* (1956).

Hilton, G. W., *The Truck System* (Cambridge, 1960).

Hobcraft, J. and Rees, P. (eds.), *Regional Demographic Development* (1977).

Hobsbawm, E. J., 'The nineteenth-century London labour market', in E. J. Hobsbawm, *Worlds of Labour* (1984).

'Artisan or labour aristocrat?', *Econ. Hist. Rev.*, 2nd ser., 37 (1984).

Hollaender, A. E. J. and Kellaway, W. (eds.), *Studies in London History* (1969).

Holmes, G., *Augustan England: Professions, State and Society, 1680–1730* (1982).

Hope-Jones, A., *Income Tax in the Napoleonic Wars* (Cambridge, 1939).

Hoppit, J., 'Financial crises in eighteenth-century England', *Econ. Hist. Rev.*, 2nd ser., 39 (1986).

Risk and Failure in English Business, 1700–1800 (Cambridge, 1987).

Howe, E. and Waite, H. E., *The London Society of Compositors. A Centenary History* (1948).

Imlah, A. H., *Economic Elements in the Pax Britannica* (Cambridge, Mass., 1958).

Johnson, C. H., 'Economic change and artisan discontent: the tailors' history, 1800–1848', in R. Price (ed.), *Revolution and Reaction* (1975).

Jones, E., 'London in the early seventeenth century: an ecological approach', *London Journal*, 6 (1980).

Jones, E. L., *Seasons and Prices* (1964).

Jones, P. E. and Judges, A. V., 'London's population in the late seventeenth century', *Econ. Hist. Rev.*, 1st ser., 6 (1935–6).

Jones, S. R. H., 'Technology, transaction costs and the transition to factory production in the British silk industry, 1700–1870', *J. Econ. Hist.*, 47 (1987).

Kahl, W. F., 'Apprenticeship and the freedom of the London livery companies, 1690–1750', *Guildhall Miscellany*, 7 (1956).

The Development of the London Livery Companies: An Historical Essay and Select Bibliography (Boston, 1960).

Kanefsky, J. and Robey, J., 'Steam engines in eighteenth-century Britain: a quantitative assessment', *Technology and Culture*, 21 (1980).

Kellett, J. R., 'The breakdown of gild and corporation control over the handicraft and retail trade in London', *Econ. Hist. Rev.*, 2nd ser., 10 (1957–8).

Kirkham, P. and Hayward, H., *William and John Linnell: Eighteenth-Century London Furniture Makers* (2 vols., 1980).

Kitch, M. J., 'Capital and kingdom: migration to later Stuart London', in A. L.

Beier and R. A. P. Finlay (eds.), *London 1500–1700: The Making of the Metropolis* (1986).

Klein, B., Crawford, R. G. and Alchian, A. A., 'Vertical integration, appropriable rents and the competitive contracting process', *Journal of Law and Economics* (1978).

Lamb, H. H., *Climate: Present, Past and Future* (2 vols., 1972 and 1977).

Landers, J. 'Mortality, weather and prices in London, 1675–1825: a study of short-term fluctuations', *Journal of Historical Geography*, 12 (1986).

'Mortality and metropolis: the case of London, 1675–1825', *Population Studies*, 41 (1987).

Landers, J. and Mouzas, A., 'Burial seasonality and causes of death in London 1670–1819', *Population Studies*, 42 (1988).

Landes, D. S., *Revolution in Time* (1983).

Lee, C. H., *British Regional Employment Structures, 1841–1971* (Cambridge, 1979).

Leeson, R. A., *Travelling Brothers* (1979).

Lemire, B., 'Consumerism in pre-industrial and early industrial England: the trade in secondhand clothes', *Journal of British Studies*, 27 (1988).

Lenger, H., 'Polarisierung und Verlag: Schuhmacher, Schneider und Schreiner in Düsseldorf, 1816–1861', in U. Engelhardt (ed.), *Handwerker in der Industrialisierung* (Stuttgart, 1984).

Lewis, J. Parry, *Building Cycles and Britain's Growth* (1965).

Lewis, W. S., *Three Tours through London in the Years 1748, 1776, 1797* (New Haven, 1941).

Lindert, P. H. and Williamson, J. G., 'Revising England's social tables 1688–1812', *Explorations in Economic History*, 19 (1982).

'English workers' living standards during the industrial revolution: a new look', *Econ. Hist. Rev.*, 2nd ser., 36 (1983).

'Reply to Michael Flinn', *Econ. Hist. Rev.*, 2nd ser., 37 (1984).

Linebaugh, P., in *Bulletin of the Society for the Study of Labour History*, 25 (1972).

'Labour history without the labour process: a note on John Gast and his time', *Social History*, 7 (1982).

Little, A. J., *Deceleration in the Eighteenth-Century British Economy* (1976).

Livi-Bacci, M., 'The nutrition–mortality link in past times: a comment', in R. I. Rotberg and T. K. Rabb (eds.), *Hunger and History* (Cambridge, 1985).

Lloyd, C., *The British Seaman* (1968).

Lovell, J., *Stevedores and Dockers* (1969).

Luckin, Bill, *Pollution and Control. A Social History of the Thames in the Nineteenth Century* (Bristol, 1986).

McBride, T. M., *The Domestic Revolution. The Modernisation of Household Service in England and France, 1820–1920* (1976).

McKeown, T., *The Modern Rise of Population* (1976).

'Food, infection and population', in R. I. Rotberg and T. K. Rabb (eds.), *Hunger and History* (Cambridge, 1985).

McKeown, T. and Brown, R. G., 'Medical evidence relating to English population change in the eighteenth century', *Population Studies*, 9 (1955).

Mackesy, P., *The War for America, 1775–1783* (1964).

Mander, C. H. W., *A Descriptive and Historical Account of the Guild of Cordwainers of the City of London* (1931).

Manley, G., 'The great winter of 1740', *Weather*, 13 (1958).

'Central England temperatures: monthly means 1659–1973', *Journal of the Royal Meteorological Society*, 100 (1974).

Mansfield, N., 'John Brown: a shoemaker in Place's London', *History Workshop*, 8 (1970).

Marshall, D., *The English Poor in the Eighteenth Century* (1926).

Dr Johnson's London (New York, 1968).

Mathias, P., *The Brewing Industry in England, 1700–1830* (Cambridge, 1959).

'The lawyer as businessman in eighteenth-century England', in D. C. Coleman and P. Mathias (eds.), *Enterprise and History. Essays in Honour of Charles Wilson* (Cambridge, 1984).

Matthews, R. C. O., *A Study in Trade-Cycle History* (Cambridge, 1954).

Matossian, M. K., 'Mold poisoning: an unrecognized English health problem, 1500–1800', *Medical History*, 25 (1981).

'Mold poisoning and population growth in England and France 1750–1850', *J. Econ. Hist.*, 44 (1984).

'Death in London, 1750–1909', *Journal of Interdisciplinary History*, 16 (1985).

Mercer, A. J., 'Smallpox and epidemiological change in Europe: the role of vaccination', *Population Studies*, 39 (1985).

Mirowski, P. E., 'The rise (and retreat) of a market: English joint stock shares in the eighteenth century', *J. Econ. Hist.*, 41 (1981).

'Adam Smith, empiricism, and the rate of profit in eighteenth-century England', *History of Political Economy*, 14 (1982).

Mitchell, B. R., *British Historical Statistics* (Cambridge, 1988).

More, C., *Skill and the English Working Class, 1890–1914* (1980).

Morriss, R. A., *The Royal Dockyards during the Revolution and Napoleonic Wars* (Leicester, 1983).

Moss, B. H., 'Parisian producers' associations (1800–1851): the socialism of skilled workers', in R. Price (ed.), *Revolution and Reaction* (1975).

Musson, A. E., 'Industrial motive power in the United Kingdom, 1800–1870', *Econ. Hist. Rev.*, 2nd ser., 29 (1976).

Nef, J. U., *The Rise of the British Coal Industry* (2 vols., 1932).

Newman, P. K., 'The early English clothing trade', *Oxford Economic Papers* (1952).

O'Brien, P. K., 'British incomes and property in the early nineteenth century', *Econ. Hist. Rev.*, 2nd ser., 12 (1959–60).

'The analysis and measurement of the service economy in European economic history', in P. K. O'Brien and R. Fremdling (eds.), *Productivity in the Economies of Europe* (Stuttgart, 1983).

Oliver, W. H., 'The Consolidated Trades Union of 1834', *Econ. Hist. Rev.*, 2nd ser., 17 (1964–5).

Olsen, D. J., *Town Planning in London. The Eighteenth and Nineteenth Centuries* (Yale, 1964).

Oppenheim, M., 'The royal dockyards', *Victoria County History*, Kent, II (1926).

Owen, J. B., *The Rise of the Pelhams* (1957).

Palliser, D. M., 'The trade guilds of Tudor York', in P. Clark and P. Slack (eds.), *Crisis and Order in English Towns, 1500–1700* (1972).

Parkinson, C. N. (ed.), *The Trade Winds. A Study of British Overseas Trade during the French Wars, 1793–1815* (1948).

Parsinnen, T. M. and Prothero, I. J., 'The London tailors' strike of 1834 and the collapse of the Grand National Consolidated Trades' Union: a police spy's report', *International Review of Social History*, 22 (1977).

Pearce, A., *The History of the Butchers' Company* (1929).

Pinchbeck, I., *Women Workers and the Industrial Revolution, 1750–1850* (1930).

Pinchbeck, I. and Hewitt, M., *Children in English Society* (2 vols., 1969, 1973).

The Autobiography of Francis Place (1771–1854), ed. M. Thale (Cambridge, 1972).

Plummer, A., *The London Weavers' Company, 1600–1970* (1972).

Pollard, S., 'The decline of shipbuilding on the Thames', *Econ. Hist. Rev.*, 2nd ser., 3 (1950–1).

'The insurance policies', in C. H. Feinstein and S. Pollard (eds.), *Studies in Capital Formation in the United Kingdom, 1750–1920* (Oxford, 1988).

Pool, B., *Navy Board Contracts 1660–1832* (1966).

Post, J. D., *Food Shortage, Climatic Variability and Epidemic Disease in Pre-Industrial Europe. The Mortality Peak in the Early 1740s* (Ithaca, N.Y., 1985).

Power, M. J., 'The East London working community in the seventeenth century', in P. J. Corfield and D. Keene (eds.), *Work in Towns, 850–1850* (Leicester, 1990).

Prest, J., *The Industrial Revolution in Coventry* (Oxford, 1960).

Prothero, I. J., *Artisans and Politics in Early Nineteenth-Century London. John Gast and his Times* (1979).

Radzinowicz, L., *A History of English Criminal Law and its Administration from 1750* (1948–).

Rappaport, S., 'Social structure and mobility in sixteenth-century London', *London Journal*, 10 (1984).

Razzell, P., *The Conquest of Smallpox* (1977).

Reader, W. J., *Professional Men* (1966).

Reddaway, T. F., *The Rebuilding of London after the Great Fire* (1940).

Redford, A., *Labour Migration in England, 1800–1850* (Manchester, 1926).

Rediker, M., *Between the Devil and the Deep Blue Sea* (Cambridge, 1987).

Rendell, Jane, *The Origins of Modern Feminism* (1985).

Richards, E., 'Women in the British economy since about 1700: an interpretation', *History*, 59 (1974).

Richardson, H. E., 'Wages of shipwrights in H.M. dockyards, 1496–1788', *Mariners' Mirror*, 33 (1947).

Rose, R. B., 'Eighteenth-century price riots and public policy in England', *International Review of Social History*, 6 (1961).

Rotberg, R. I. and Rabb, T. K. (eds.), *Hunger and History*, report of the conferees: 'The relationship of nutrition, disease and social conditions: a graphical presentation' (Cambridge, 1985).

Rothstein, N. K. A., 'The calico campaign of 1719–1721', *East London Papers*, 1964.

'The introduction of the Jacquard loom to Great Britain', in V. Gervers (ed.), *Studies in Textile History in Memory of Harold B. Burnham* (Toronto, 1977).

Rowe, D. J., 'Chartism and the Spitalfields silk weavers', *Econ. Hist. Rev.*, 2nd ser., 20 (1967).

Rudé, G., *Wilkes and Liberty* (Oxford, 1962).

'"Mother Gin" and the London riots of 1736', in G. Rudé, *Paris and London in the Eighteenth Century* (1970).

Paris and London in the Eighteenth Century (1970).

Hanoverian London, 1714–1808 (1971).

Rule, J., *The Experience of Labour in Eighteenth-Century Industry* (1981).

Samuel, R., 'Workshop of the world: steam power and hand technology in mid-Victorian Britain', *History Workshop*, 3 (1977).

Schmiechen, J. A., *Sweated Industries and Sweated Labour: the London Clothing Trades, 1860–1914* (Illinois, 1984).

Schwarz, L. D., 'Occupations and incomes in late eighteenth-century East London', *East London Papers*, 14 (1972).

'Income distribution and social structure in London in the late eighteenth century', *Econ. Hist. Rev.*, 2nd ser., 32 (1979).

'Social class and social geography: the middle classes in London at the end of the eighteenth century', *Social History*, 7 (1982).

'The standard of living in the long run: London 1800–1860', *Econ. Hist. Rev.*, 2nd ser., 38 (1985).

'London apprentices in the seventeenth century: some problems', *Local Population Studies*, 38 (1987).

'The formation of the wage: some problems', in P. Scholliers (ed.), *Real Wages in Nineteenth- and Twentieth-Century Europe* (Berg, Oxford, 1989).

'Trends in real wage rates, 1750–1790: a reply to Hunt and Botham', *Econ. Hist. Rev.* 2nd ser., 43 (1990).

Schwarz, L. D. and Jones, L. J., 'Wealth, occupations and insurance in the late eighteenth century: the policy registers of the Sun Fire Office', *Econ. Hist. Rev.*, 2nd ser., 36 (1983).

Scott, J. W., 'Men and women in the Parisian garment trades: discussions of family and work in the 1830s and 1840s', in P. Thane, R. Floud and G. Crossick (eds.), *The Power of the Past* (1984).

Scouller, R. E., *The Armies of Queen Anne* (Oxford, 1966).

Searby, P., '"Lists of prices" in the Coventry silk industry, 1800–1860', *Bulletin of the Society for the Study of Labour History*, 27 (1973).

Sen, A., 'Starvation and exchange entitlements: a general appraisal and its application to the great Bengal famine', *Cambridge Journal of Economics*, 1 (1977).

Sharpe, J. A., *Crime in Early Modern England, 1500–1750* (1984).

Shelton, W. J., *English Hunger and Industrial Disorders: A Study of Social Conflict During the First Decade of George III's Reign* (1973).

Sheppard, F. H. W., *Local Government in St. Marylebone, 1688–1835* (1958).

London 1808–1870. The Infernal Wen (1971).

Sheppard, F. H. W., Belcher, V. and Cottrell, P., 'The Middlesex and Yorkshire deeds registries and the study of building fluctuations', *London Journal*, 5 (2) (1979).

Snell, K. D. M., *Annals of the Labouring Poor. Social Change and Agrarian England, 1600–1900* (Cambridge, 1985).

Souden, D., 'Migrants and the population structure of later seventeenth century provincial cities and market towns', in P. Clarke (ed.), *The Transformation of English Provincial Towns 1600–1800* (1984).

Spate, O. H. K., 'The growth of London, A.D. 1600–1800', in H. C. Darby (ed.), *An Historical Geography of England before 1800* (Cambridge, 1936).

Stedman Jones, G., *Outcast London* (Oxford, 1971).

Stern, W. M., *The Porters of London* (1960).

'The bread crisis in Britain, 1795–96', *Economica*, new series, 19 (1964).

Stigler, G. J., 'The division of labour is limited by the size of the market', *Journal of Political Economy*, 59 (1951).

Styles, J., 'Embezzlement, industry and the law', in M. Berg, P. Hudson and M. Sonenscher (eds.), *Manufacture in Town and Country before the Factory* (Cambridge, 1983).

Summerson, J., *Georgian London* (Harmondsworth, 1962).

Supple, Barry, *The Royal Exchange Assurance. A History of British Insurance 1720–1970* (1970).

Sutherland, I., 'When was the Great Plague? Mortality in London 1563 to 1665', in D. V. Glass and R. Revelle (eds.), *Population and Social Change* (1972).

Taylor, B., *Eve and the New Jerusalem* (1983).

Taylor, J. S., *Jonas Hanway, Founder of the Marine Society. Charity and Policy in Eighteenth-Century Britain* (1985).

Thompson, E. P., *The Making of the English Working Class* (1968 ed.).

Thompson, E. P. and Yeo, E. (eds.), *The Unknown Mayhew. Selections from the Morning Chronicle 1849–1850* (1971).

Tucker, R. S., 'Real wages of artisans in London, 1729–1935', *Journal of the American Statistical Society*, 31 (1936).

Tunzelmann, G. N. von, 'Trends in real wages, 1750–1850, revisited', *Econ. Hist. Rev.*, 2nd ser., 22 (1979).

Unwin, G., *Industrial Organisation in the Sixteenth and Seventeenth Centuries* (1904, 2nd ed. 1957).

The Gilds and Companies of London (1908).

Ville, S., 'Total factor productivity in the English shipping industry: the north-east coal trade, 1700–1850', *Econ. Hist. Rev.*, 2nd ser., 39 (1986).

Wadsworth, A. P. and Mann, J. de L., *The Cotton Trade and Industrial Lancashire* (Manchester, 1931).

Wales-Smith, B. G., 'Monthly and annual totals of rainfall representative of Kew, Surrey, from 1697–1970', *Meteorological Magazine*, 100 (1971).

Wall, R., 'Mean household size in England from the printed sources', in P. Laslett and R. Wall (eds.), *Household and Family in Past Time* (1972).

'Regional and temporal variations in English household structure from 1650', in J. Hobcraft and P. Rees (eds.), *Regional Demographic Development* (1977).

Wallas, G., *The Life of Francis Place, 1771–1854* (1898).

Walter, J. and Schofield, R., 'Famine, disease and crisis mortality in early modern society', in J. Walter and R. Schofield (eds.), *Famine, Disease and the Social Order in Early Modern Society* (Cambridge, 1989).

Warner, Sir F., *The Silk Industry of the United Kingdom. Its Origins and Development* (1921).

Watkins, S. C. and van de Walle, E., 'Nutrition, mortality, and population size: Malthus' court of last resort', in R. I. Rotberg and T. K. Rabb (eds.), *Hunger and History* (Cambridge, 1985).

Weatherill, L., *Consumer Behaviour and Material Culture in Britain, 1660–1760* (1988).

Webb, S. and B., *Industrial Democracy* (1902).

The History of Liquor Licensing (1903).

English Poor Law History (1929).
History of Local Government:
  The Parish and County (1906).
  The Manor and Borough (1912).
  Statutory Authorities for Special Purposes (1923).
The History of Trade Unionism (1920).
Weinreb, B. and Hibbert, C. (eds.), *The London Encyclopedia* (1983).
Wells, R., *Wretched Faces, Famine in England, 1793–1801* (Gloucester, 1989).
Western, J. R., *The English Militia in the Eighteenth Century* (1965).
Wood, L. B., *The Restoration of the Tidal Thames* (Bristol, 1982).
Woodward, D., 'Wage rates and living standards in pre-industrial England', *Past and Present*, 91 (1981).
Wrigley, E. A., 'A simple model of London's importance in changing English society and economy, 1650–1750', *Past and Present*, 37 (1967).
Wrigley, E. A. and Schofield, R. S., *The Population History of England, 1541–1871. A Reconstruction* (1981).
  'English population history from family reconstitution: summary results, 1600–1799', *Population Studies*, 37 (1983).

Unpublished Theses

Alexander, J. M. B., 'The economic and social structure of the City of London, c.1700', London University, Ph.D. thesis, 1989.
Bondois-Morris, M., 'Spitalfields: unité economique et diversité sociale dans "l'East End" londonien, 1760–1830', Universite de Paris, I, thèse pour doctorat du Troisième Cycle, 1980.
D'Sena, P., 'Perquisites and pilfering in the London docks, 1700–1795', Open University, M.Phil. thesis, 1986.
Elliott, Vivien Brodsky, 'Mobility and marriage in pre-industrial England', Cambridge University, Ph.D thesis, 1978.
French, C. J., 'The trade and shipping of the Port of London, 1700–1776', Exeter University, Ph.D. thesis, 1980.
Hartridge, R. J., 'The development of industries in London south of the Thames', London University, M.Sc. (Econ.) thesis, 1955.
Jordan, W. M., 'The silk industry in London 1760–1830, with special reference to the condition of the wage earners and the policy of the Spitalfields Acts', London University, M.A. thesis, 1931.
King, P. J. R., 'Crime, law and society in Essex, 1740–1820', Cambridge University, Ph.D. thesis, 1984.
Kirkham, P., 'Furniture making in London, c.1700–1870: craft, design, business and labour', London University, Ph.D. thesis, 1982.
Landers, J., 'Some problems in the historical demography of London, 1675–1825', Cambridge University, Ph.D. thesis, 1984.
Macfarlane, S. M., 'Studies in poverty and poor relief in London at the end of the seventeenth century', Oxford University, D.Phil. thesis, 1982.
Martindale, L., 'Demography and land use in the late seventeenth and eighteenth centuries in Middlesex', London University, Ph.D. thesis, 1968.
Rothstein, N. K. A., 'The silk industry in London, 1702–66', London University, M.A. thesis, 1961.

Schwarz, L. D., 'Conditions of life and work in London, c.1770–1820, with special reference to East London', Oxford University, D.Phil. thesis, 1976.

Walker, M. J., 'The extent of the guild control of trades in England, c.1660–1820: a study based on a sample of provincial towns and London Companies', Cambridge University, Ph.D. thesis, 1985.

Index

Cambridge Studies in Population, Economy and Society in Past Time

Titles available in paperback are marked with an asterisk